THE PSYCHOLOGY

OF THE

METHODIST REVIVAL

An Empirical & Descriptive Study

BY

SYDNEY G. DIMOND, M.A.

OXFORD UNIVERSITY PRESS

LONDON: HUMPHREY MILFORD

1926

PREFACE

THE aim and scope of this work are indicated in the first chapter. It is only necessary to say here that it is based upon a study of original authorities, and includes material from hitherto unpublished manuscripts. Since an earlier draft of the book was submitted as a dissertation for the degree of Master of Arts in the Leeds University I have re-written the greater part of it, omitting certain technical discussions, and expanding the treatment of some topics in view of their general interest.

My method of giving references may need a word of explanation. At many points in the argument issues are opened up which it is impossible to discuss adequately within the limits I have laid down. Readers who desire to pursue the subject will, perhaps, find the footnotes and bibliography of service. At some points also I cannot expect all readers to accept my interpretation of the facts, and, as far as possible, I have indicated where treatment from an opposite or different point of view may be found.

I wish to acknowledge my indebtedness to my tutors in Philosophy, Professor Alfred Caldecott, D.D., D.Litt., of King's College, London, and Professor C. M. Gillespie, M.A., of Leeds University, for critical guidance on the subject matter. My thanks are also due to the Rev. John Naylor and the Rev. G. G. Hornby, M.A., B.D., and to the publishers, for helpful criticisms and suggestions ; and to the Rev. Vincent Taylor, Ph.D., D.D., Principal A. C. Underwood, M.A., D.D., of Rawdon College, and to my wife, for assistance in the reading of the proof-sheets.

S. G. DIMOND.

KEIGHLEY, *July*, 1926.

CONTENTS

CONTENTS

CONTENTS

CHAPTER PAGE

IV. WESLEY'S RELIGIOUS SENTIMENT - - 74
    1. Sentiment and organized unity of character 74
    2. Three stages in Wesley's development : 75
       Mr. Shand's analysis of character - - 78
        (i) Prior to 1725 - - - - - 78
        (ii) 1725-1738 - - - - - 80
    3. Wesley's mysticism - - - - - 83
    4. Psychological factors in his conversion :
       (i) Unconscious : - - - - - 88
        (a) Re-direction or sublimation - 89
        (b) Suggestion : - - - - 91
          Modified by faith, prayer and
           effort - - - - - 93
        (c) Repression and complex - - 95
      (ii) Conscious : - - - - - 100
        (a) Volition or purpose - - - 101
        (b) Emotion - - - - - 101
        (c) Cognition - - - - - 102

V. THE GENESIS OF THE REVIVAL - - - 104
    1. Wesley's new mental autonomy - - 105
    2. Crowd psychology and the Fetter Lane
      love-feast - - - - - - 106
    3. Whitefield's preaching - - - - 107
    4. The development of Wesley's task : - - 109
      (i) Organization - - - - - 110
      (ii) Preaching - - - - - 114
    5. Suggestibility of the crowd - - - 116
    6. Novelty of field-preaching and of the
      message - - - - - - 117
    7. Laws of rhythm in nature and in human
      nature : - - - - - - 118
      (i) Relation of the hymns to :
        (a) Traditional festivals - - - 119
        (b) Suggestion - - - - - 121
        (c) Education - - - - - 122
      (ii) Emotional effect of the music - - 123
b

CONTENTS

ABBREVIATIONS

E.R.E.	Hastings' *Encyclopaedia of Religion and Ethics.*
F.C.	Shand, A. F. *The Foundations of Character* (2nd ed. 1920).
G.M.	McDougall, W. *The Group Mind* (1921).
H.N.C.	Dewey, John. *Human Nature and Conduct* (1922).
I.L.P.	Freud, S. *Introductory Lectures on Psychoanalysis* (1923).
I.M.	Drever, James. *Instinct in Man* (2nd ed. 1921).
I.P.R.	Thouless, R. H. *Introduction to the Psychology of Religion* (1923).
J.W.J.	*John Wesley's Journal.* 8 vols. ed Curnock (1909-1916).
L.T.W.	Tyerman, L. *Life and Times of John Wesley.* 6th ed. (1890).
M.M.C.	de Fursac, J. R. *Une mouvement mystique contemporain* (1907).
N.H.M.	*A New History of Methodism.* Workman, Townsend and Eayrs. 2 vols. (1909).
N.P.	Tansley, A. G. *The New Psychology* (5th ed. 1922).
O.P.	McDougall, W. *Outline of Psychology* (1923).
P.F.	Le Bon, G. *Psychologie des Foules.* 28th ed. (1921).
P.P.	James. W. *Principles of Psychology* (1890).
P.S.B.	Watson, J. B. *Psychology from the Standpoint of a Behaviourist* (1922).
R.C.	Pratt, J. B. *The Religious Consciousness* (1921).
R.S.	Caldecott, Alfred. *The Religious Sentiment.* (1909).
S.A.	Baudouin, C. *Suggestion and Autosuggestion* (tr. Paul, 1921).
S.P.	McDougall, W. *Social Psychology* (13th ed. 1922).
V.R.E.	James, W. *Varieties of Religious Experience* (1903).
W.H.S.	*Proceedings of the Wesley Historical Society.*
W.W.	*Wesley's Works.* 4th ed. (1840-2).

I

INTRODUCTION

THE science of psychology aims at making human nature intelligible to us, and one of the most important subjects included within its range is the study of religious experience. While the philosopher and the theologian find in religion a revelation of Divinity, the psychologist finds a revelation of humanity. In the individual and social evolution of the great forms of religion, all the characteristic forces and capacities of human nature are called into activity, and a psychological treatment of the various aspects of religious experience throws new light upon the problems of mental life.

A specially fruitful field for psychological research is offered by the records of Methodism, not only because the rise and development of the movement constitute the most important fact in the history of religion since the Reformation, but because within the system from the beginning, the social communication of individual experience has been systematically cultivated. The scope of the present work is limited to an empirical and descriptive study of the mental processes exhibited in the beginnings of the Revival under John Wesley in the eighteenth century. It is hoped that the exploration of a limited field of well-documented religious experience from the point of view of scientific psychology will provide an opportunity for testing the application of recent psychological theories to religious phenomena, and it may, in so far as our data justify certain inferences, make a definite contribution to the psychology of religion.

A quarter of a century ago, in his famous Gifford Lectures,[1] William James applied himself to this great theme. His work was that of a pioneer, and all who follow this path are heavily indebted to him. Two criticisms, however, at once occur to his readers to-day. The exceptional, explosive and spectacular experiences with which he is so largely concerned do not occur in normal religious life. Moreover, he treats of religious experience in the lives of individuals, selected at random from all periods and types, without any reference to their social or religious environment. He deals only with immediate personal experiences, and expressly limits his work by defining religion as ' feelings, acts and experiences of individual men in their solitude.'[2] Perhaps the greatness of James will stand out more clearly when we have considered the present tendency to go to the opposite extreme and to explain religion entirely in terms of social psychology. In the last resort, religion is an essentially individual experience. We shall also find grounds for holding that the primitive elemental processes of religious life are exhibited with extraordinary clearness in experiences which are violent and convulsive. There is, however, need for patient and careful study of the psychology of religion in its social and historical aspects, and for an examination of the mental activity which is characteristic of great and comparatively normal religious movements.

[1] *The Varieties of Religious Experience*, 1901-2.
[2] *Ibid.* p. 31.

In his second lecture on Conversion, James remarked, ' I cannot but think that the most important step forward that has occurred in psychology since I have been a student of that science is the discovery, first made in 1886, that, in certain subjects at least, there is not only the conscious- ness of the ordinary field, with its usual centre and margin, but an addition thereto in the shape of a set of memories, thoughts, and feelings which are extra-marginal and outside the primary consciousness altogether, but yet must be classed as conscious facts of some sort, able to reveal their presence by unmistakeable signs. I call this the most important step forward, because, unlike the other advances which psychology has made, this discovery has revealed to us an entirely unsuspected peculiarity in the constitution of human nature. No other step forward which psychology has made can proffer any such claim as this.' [1] Although James used the terms ' sub-conscious ' and ' subliminal consciousness ' with great care and dis- crimination, regarding them with a scientific reserve, he looked to the future of psychology for a verification of the hypothesis of unconscious or non-conscious regions of mental life. For the purpose of this proof, he foresaw a vast programme of work, including the examination of hypnotic, hysteric and other pathological phenomena, with special reference to the study of religious experience. The tentative suggestions of James, based upon the earlier work of Binet, Janet, Freud and Prince, have been amply justified, and it is now possible to supplement his work, in the light of research which has been even more fruitful than he anticipated.

Recent tendencies in psychological theory are so radically divergent that it would seem almost impossible

[1] James, *V.R.E.*, Lec. x. p. 233.

to make an empirical examination of the records of Methodism without first defining and adopting the point of view of one of the modern schools. By way of reaction from the narrow individualist psychology of consciousness, we are to-day presented with a group of theories which are collectively described as ' the new psychology.' The main ground common to all the members of this group is a growing appreciation of the significance for psychology of non-conscious or semi-conscious factors in human life and conduct, together with an indebtedness to the excellent results of recent studies of animal behaviour. In the work of these schools there is a marked tendency to resist both criticism and compromise, and their teachings appear to be mutually exclusive and contradictory. But the student of religious psychology is entitled to a certain freedom of criticism, because his interest is focussed at a point where many paths meet. No attempt is made here to select the doctrines of any one school, nor on the other hand to minimize the difference between them. They all represent research which throws light upon the facts of the Methodist Revival, and as they find illustration in the documents they are to that extent provisionally justified.

A brief indication may be given here of certain critical judgments which are confirmed in the testing of these theories by their application to the facts of the Methodist experience. The grounds upon which these judgments rest are set forth in the succeeding chapters.

Behaviourism, which began in America with a denial of the value of introspection and an emphasis upon observation as the only source of data for psychology, has developed into an uncompromising mechanical interpretation of mind. The idea of the self or soul is dismissed as a superstition, and thought is resolved into the action of language-mechanisms. There is a healthy objectivity about the behaviourist method, and many of the physiological explanations offered are obviously true, so far as they go. But as an account of human nature and of religious experience they are also obviously trivial. When John Nelson cried, ' Lord, Thy will be done, damn or save,' and found himself immediately set free from self-despising and filled with boundless delight in life and love and God, his behaviour was no doubt conditioned by habits, memory beliefs and language-mechanisms, but though the psychology which has nothing more to say may be scientifically accurate, it brings us no nearer to the meaning of his experience, and throws no light on the essential nature of the mental processes involved. It may be that religion can supply a terminology and perhaps ultimate entities for psychology which shall be more consonant with the facts.

The study of *animal behaviour*, in which Aristotle was the pioneer, has made quite remarkable advances in recent years. We have learned that the gap between the human and the animal mind is not so wide as it seemed half a century ago. Immense though the difference really is, we have abundant evidence that some rudiment of every type of mental function may be discovered in animal behaviour. Three important results accrue for psychology : it is clear that purposive activity is characteristic of the whole of the animal world ; the bases of human nature are exhibited in relative simplicity in animal modes of activity ; and mental evolution is shown to have led the way in the development of the organism, being followed as a consequence by the evolution of the bodily structure.[1] The place of instinct in religious experience is

[1] See McDougall, W., *Psychology the Study of Behaviour.*

established by these comparative studies of men and animals. But it is none the less true that man differs from other organisms in three main ways : he has the power of thinking in concepts—of reaching the general from the particular ; by means of speech, writing and printing, he has developed a mode of inheritance which adds in an immeasurable degree to physical heredity ; and the human type of mind is more elastic and flexible than any mental equipment in other organisms, substituting general susceptibility to education for specific response to instincts. The mode of life, even in the highest type of animals, is one of comparative fixity ; whereas a man can change his nation or city, belong to a dozen organizations, follow one profession in the morning, another in the evening, and play golf in between. When we are discussing instinctive activity in human behaviour, we must guard against an unscientific identification of animal and human mentality.

The term *psychoanalysis* has been adopted to describe a method and theory derived from the study of nervous pathology. As expounded by Dr. Freud, it results in a thoroughgoing determinism. From this conclusion Dr. Jung is saved by his philosophy of vitalism. Both the Vienna and the Zurich schools, however, would agree that conscious deliberation is mainly a symptom and not a cause of our actions, and that it is our unconscious wishes under the pressure of primal instincts and propensities that really make up our minds for us. A mass of evidence has been accumulated in support of this doctrine, but it has not yet been scientifically arranged, so that its value for psychology has still to be determined. If the theory were worked out to its logical issues, the denial of consciousness by the behaviourist would be less serious for psychology than the impotence of consciousness as taught by the psychoanalyst. Happily for our well-being in the business of living, when the psychoanalyst applies his theory in therapeutic practice, he is radically inconsistent. He turns to conscious catharsis for his cure. He endeavours to bring his patient to a knowledge of the real nature of the instincts and impulses which give rise to mental and moral conflict, and to induce him consciously to re-direct his energies along lines of harmonious and fruitful activity. But if consciousness is impotent except to find excuses for what we are bent upon doing, then the whole of the practical application of psychoanalysis is futile. This confusion in the Freudian theory is due to unscientific overstatement. And the accounts of ' libido,' ' basic forces ' and ' insatiable urges ' reveal a poverty of reflection akin to that of the old faculty-psychology which mistakes a name for an explanation.

A further criticism of these psychoanalytic doctrines is directed against their frequent confusion of psychology with metaphysics. Determinism and an empirical view of the ego are assumptions which the psychological student is bound to make for the purposes of his inquiry. But he goes beyond the limits of his subject when he pronounces on these problems of philosophy, and with still less legitimacy can he discuss the idea of God as an objectification of the ethical ideal. On the other hand, the usefulness of the pioneer work that is being done by the psychoanalysts lies in the serious attempt that they have made to estimate the relative dynamic and potency in the various native impulses and propensities of human nature, and to determine the point at which wise inhibition becomes dangerous repression. The resultant emphasis upon congenital endowment, early training in infancy, and

upon physical and mental environment, is of vital value
for psychology.   And it remains for the student to gather
up the material which is provided by the study of neuro-
paths, and to establish its true relation to the psychology
of character as a whole ; including, of course, the functions
of reflective and deliberate control.   It will then be seen
that the complexity of experience demands a more
comprehensive explanation than that offered by the
psychoanalysts, and the scientific value of their contribution to psychology may be set in its proper perspective.

The New Nancy School, M. Coué and Prof. Baudouin,
manifest the same tendency to discredit volition and
purposive action.   Responsible conscious control must
be eliminated, they say, in favour of sleepy rhythmic
suggestion, by means of which all the ills that flesh is
heir to may, presumably, be banished.   But when it is
propounded that one of the worst things we can do in
facing the work-a-day problems of life, is to think or to
resolve, then the fundamental nature of human character
is in question, and the wisdom of experience expressed
alike in mother-wit and in philosophy is at stake.   But
here again the difficulties and inconsistencies which arise
are due to undisciplined thinking.   To mention two only
of the contradictions which are inherent in the theory as
expounded by Baudouin :   concentrated attention in
which the will must not intervene is a psychological
impossibility ;   and subconscious teleology is a contradiction in terms, because end and purpose have no meaning
if they are not conscious.   No one would deny the significance and usefulness of suggestion and self-suggestion,
but a serious estimate of their place and value would not
exalt them to the position of a master-key to the problems
of human conduct and its psychology.   The elaborate

doctrines based upon the psychotherapy of M. Coué and his colleagues are more dependent upon the personality of the practitioner than upon any laws of the mind. The laws of suggestion, to the extent to which they can be definitely formulated, have an important bearing upon religious experience, and contribute to its psychological interpretation. But more than thirty years ago Wundt described suggestion as the ' modern hypnotism-psychology,' [1] and his judgment still stands.

The study of human behaviour under crowd conditions has not yet reached the point at which it can be satisfactorily described. M. Le Bon has popularized a doubtful distinction between *the psychology of the crowd* and that of the individual. But it can be shown that they are not entirely antithetic, and that a low estimate of crowd mentality is based upon imperfect acquaintance with the facts. In Le Bon's discussion [2] of the ' soul of the crowd,' and of impulsivity, suggestibility, irritability and the like, we are beset by the Idols of the Market-place, words being used without empirical definition, and names being given which exalt abstractions to the position of agents and forces. The pervasive influence of social contagion is a manifest factor in all mass-movements, including religious revivals ; but the words crowd-suggestion, contagion, or domination do not explain this influence. Again, the plausibility of Dr. Trotter's book [3] proves nothing with reference even to the existence of the ' herd instinct ' as a factor in human conduct. Before these aspects of our behaviour can be scientifically described, a prolegomena

---

[1] Wundt, Wilhelm, *Human and Animal Psychology*, tr. Creighton and Titchener, London, 1894, p. 336.

[2] Le Bon, Gustave, *Psychologie des Foules.*

[3] Trotter, W., *Instincts of the Herd in Peace and War.*

to crowd-psychology must be written, dealing with those deep-seated rhythms in human nature which depend upon even deeper rhythms in our bodies, in the seasons, and in the material and spiritual constitution of the universe.

Apart from the work of these newer schools, the widening of the scope of scientific research to include such subjects as psychology, anthropology and ethics, has revolutionized the study of the mind. In accordance with the natural tendency of the human mind to assume greater simplicity and uniformity among phenomena than actually exist, psychology had been treated as a branch of epistemology, and its problems had been narrowed down to the question, ' What are the laws by which the mind thinks or knows ? ' The resultant theory of knowledge was accepted as the frame into which the various investigations of science must be fitted. Bacon [1] accused Aristotle of fashioning the world out of categories : placing arbitrary restrictions on the nature of things, and aiming at the conquest of the mind by argument, instead of at the conquest of nature by searching for the inner truth of things. This indictment has been applicable to many phases of science, including psychology. And in recent years, psychoanalysis, experimental psychology, and the psychology of religion have not been free from the perils which Bacon pointed out in his criticism of the Sophistical, Empirical, and Superstitious schools of philosophy. But it may be conceded that, to a greater extent than in the past, the scientific student of psychology to-day has adopted the rule which Bacon made for himself three hundred years ago, that of resolutely entering on the true road, and submitting his mind to Things.

[1] Bacon, Francis (1561-1626), *Novum Organum*, Bk. I. lxiii.

Psychology is a descriptive science, but a number of converging influences have compelled the traditional psychology of the static type to give way before a study of mind which makes use of dynamic categories.   According to the mental science which dominated the philosophy of the eighteenth century, the mind was a ' sheet of white paper ' or a wax tablet, or a cabinet to be furnished, and experience provided the writing or the furniture, of which the mind was little else but the passive recipient.   Sensations were received by the mind and merely transformed into a mosaic of perceptions, images and conceptions. Cognition came first.   Will, determination and effort, feelings and desires, all followed in the wake of sensations and images.[1]   Emotion and will were regarded as merely a compound of ideas mingled with sensations of pleasure and pain.   Reaction came in the latter half of the nineteenth century through the increasing sway of the scientific spirit, and in particular through the influence of biology. The new movement expressed itself first in the psychology of Voluntarism, with its emphasis upon attention and will. Man was seen to be more than a spectator receiving ideas from the game of life ; he was a player in the field. Activity was seen to be fundamental.   But the later developments of biology even more completely reversed the picture presented by the Associationist school.   Far from being almost passively receptive, the mind was seen to be continuously at work transforming and making use of the surrounding medium.   From the point of view of developing life, mind was revealed as an active dynamic unity : the instrument by which the organism interacts with its environment and keeps itself alive.

This functional and organic viewpoint in psychology

[1] See Dewey, John, *Reconstruction in Philosophy*, p. 84.

has been in part responsible for a new evaluation of instinct and emotion. Thus Mr. Shand writes, ' If we are to have a complete science of mind, this will include a science of character as the most important part of it ; and if we are to make any approach to such a science, it would seem that we must begin by a study of the fundamental emotions and of the instincts connected with them. But we have to conceive of the problem as essentially dynamical. The emotions are forces, and we have to study them as such. . . If these primary emotions belong to our mental constitution, they would presumably not belong to it unless they had some biological value.' [1] Aristotle inaugurated the method thus set forth by Mr. Shand. His ἐνέργεια σώματος [2] anticipates the tendency of modern scientific psychology to recognize the complex psycho-physical organism as a unitary object of investigation. He called attention to the semi-physiological character of some mental phenomena,[3] and thus showed a sound grasp of the human essentials of psychology which has been sadly lacking in some of its later exponents. Aristotle's discussion of the emotions not only suggests a famous modern theory,[4] but when he points out that ' where the requisite bodily conditions are present, emotions such as anger and fear are produced by the slightest mental cause or in the absence of any,'[5] he anticipates certain features in the twentieth-century psychology of character and religion.

Quite naturally, Aristotle, as the son of a medical man,

[1] Shand, Alexander F., *F.C.* pp. 1, 4.

[2] Aristotle, *Metaphysics*, H. 3, 1043a 35.

[3] See Wallace, Ed., ed. of Aristotle, *De Anima*, Introd. pp. xli-xlii.

[4] The James-Lange theory of emotion. *Vide infra*, 156 n.

[5] Ross, W. D., *Aristotle* (1923), p. 131.

was interested in biology, and the greatest of modern biologists said of him, ' Linnaeus and Cuvier have been my two gods, though in very different ways, but they were mere schoolboys to old Aristotle.'[1] But from his amazingly interesting study of animals, he turned to the study of the mind, as though his recorded facts were a preliminary work in preparation for his psychology. From his point of view, biology and psychology are not two separate sciences. It is this definite recognition of the mind as in very close connection with the body which marks Aristotle as the true forerunner of modern scientific psychology. He also regarded the soul as constituting the real significance of the body, and thus held that a valid functional psychology is bound to reject any interpretation of mind that is based upon purely physiological or even upon purely biological conceptions. Dr. Haldane, discussing the scientific view of personality, writes, ' The higher organisms display characters which do not belong to the conception of them as mere organisms : for they are conscious—in conscious relations of perception and active response with their environment.'[2] This conscious activity in pursuit of an end we regard as fundamental in the study of mind : only where there is consciousness do we find initiative, enterprise and the capacity for experiment in construction and invention, and creative originality in the quest of truth, goodness and beauty.[3]

From a point of view thus broadly indicated, the writer has attempted an interpretation of the Methodist Revival as representing a specific type of religious experience. The

[1] Darwin, *Life and Letters*, iii. 252. Quoted Ross, *op. cit.* p. 112.

[2] Haldane, J. S., *Mechanism, Life and Personality* (1914), chap. iv. p. 106.

[3] See Hoernlé, *Matter, Life, Mind, and God*, pp. 162-3.

social psychology of Dr. McDougall has, in spite of certain limitations, proved of great value in the explanation of the social aspects of the movement. But in the interpretation of individual experience, the greatest help has been derived from the psychology of the sentiments as it has been developed by Mr. Shand. If a synthesis of psychological theories is possible, the study of the sentiments seems to be a point at which many lines of research will converge. Instead of an exclusive treatment of ' behaviour ' or the instincts, or of the emotions or the ' unconscious,' or any one of the special fields of research, the whole of human nature thus comes under review. The co-ordination of emotions, thoughts, volitions, instincts and propensities under a dominant disposition or sentiment, is a psychological conception that is much more in harmony with the wealth and variety of human character as we know it.

The relation of descriptive psychology to philosophy creates a difficulty for the student of religious experience. Dispassionate observation and criticism of religious phenomena frequently become subordinate to a practical interest in the truth or falsehood of religious presuppositions. It is as easy as it is dangerous to attempt to base a belief in the existence of God on a subjective sense of His presence. This is what is known as ' the objective validity of religious experience,' a phrase which is perilous alike for philosophy and psychology. The religious inference is based upon data from the whole field of history and human life,[1] and all the great world-religions have very definite systems of metaphysics : they stand for a

[1] See Waterhouse, E. S., *The Philosophy of Religious Experience* (1923), Part II., for a very thorough treatment of the philosophical issues.

particular interpretation of the universe and of ultimate reality ; and anyone who undertakes to discuss these metaphysical conceptions must explore the entire range of facts upon which they are based. The notion of a religion which is founded upon psychology and involves nothing else is a delusion. Psychology is concerned only with the processes of the mind in all its complex relations, and cannot either assume or deny the existence of God. Consequently when Professor Leuba asserts that ' in religious lives accessible to psychological investigation, nothing requiring the admission of superhuman influences has been found,' [1] he is applying his researches in an illegitimate way, by pronouncing a judgment of validity, when, as a psychologist, he should only have pronounced a judgment of fact.[2]

Although an impartial and scientific study of the facts is not concerned with the admission or denial of an objective reality, it may provide grounds of presumption in favour of the interpretation put upon their experience by those whose records are under discussion. In this sense, ' the psychology of religion may be said to take the concept of revelation more seriously than does orthodox theology.' [3] A practical interest in a religious explanation of the facts is not incompatible with a purely scientific method of approaching the data. ' The most useful investigator, because the most sensitive observer, is always

[1] Leuba, J. H., *A Psychological Study of Religion*, p. 272. See also his latest work. Mystical ' experiences reveal not the Christian God, but the lawful workings of our psycho-physiological organisms ' (*Psych. of Rel. Mysticism* (1925), p. 316.

[2] For a careful discussion of the whole question, see Galloway, George, *The Philosophy of Religion* (1920 ed.). Part II. Religious Knowledge and Validity (Epistemological). See also Rashdall, H., *Philosophy and Religion*, p. 116.

[3] Höffding, Harald, *Philosophy of Religion*, p. 198. Cf. Edward, Kenneth, *Religious Experience : its Nature and Truth* (1926).

he whose eager interest in one side of the question is balanced by an equally keen nervousness lest he become deceived.' [1]   But the refusal to resort to metaphysics in order to solve the problems of science is as necessary in psychology as it is in physics.[2]   Even from the point of view of the philosophy of religion, ' Since God is the final cause of all things, He is not the scientific explanation of any one thing.' [3]

The material for an inductive study of the Methodist Revival is found in the autobiographies, journals and other records of the movement.   Where the records are accounts of the writer's experiences based upon intro-spection, valuable supplementary material is available in contemporary histories, letters and memoirs.

Throughout the present study of the subject, the facts examined are in the main limited to the period covered by John Wesley's life.[4]   In Curnock's Standard Edition of John Wesley's *Journal*,[5] a considerable quantity of new material has been published.   The private diaries of Wesley were not intended for publication, and were written in a secret code, composed of a peculiarly abbre-viated long-hand, two systems of short-hand, and a system of code figures and symbols especially invented for the purpose by Wesley himself.   By a painstaking study of the script, involving hypotheses, comparison, and repeated tests, covering many years of work, Curnock succeeded in deciphering it and codifying the system.   The resulting

[1] James, William, *The Will to Believe*, p. 21.

[2] See also Höffding, *op. cit.* p. 192 (Eng. trans. 1906).

[3] Sabatier, Auguste, *Esquisse d'une philosophe de la religion d'après la psychologie et l'histoire*, p. 268.

[4] 1703-1791.

[5] *The Journal of the Rev. John Wesley, A.M., enlarged from the original MSS., &c.*   Edited by Nehemiah Curnock.

intimate chronicles were made available in his edition of the *Journal*, the eight volumes of which were published at intervals during the years 1909-1916. These volumes constitute our most valuable documentary evidence. Private and hitherto unpublished manuscript letters, and other sources of information, are used only as they serve to supplement or correct the account of the movement given by Wesley himself.

Basing our study on a somewhat arbitrary selection of contemporary literature, chiefly memoirs and letters, it is intended first to sketch in a summary manner the characteristics of English society in Wesley's time. Wider political and social events are briefly indicated, in so far as these gave Methodism its opportunity or influenced the course of the Revival. An attempt is made to describe the character and personality of John Wesley from the point of view of a Behaviourist, and in relation to the psychology of the sentiments. The beginnings of the Revival are sketched, with special reference to the mental conditions created by the preaching and the hymns ; and with explanations of the physical phenomena based upon their connection with crowd psychology and the primary instincts. Three chapters are devoted to the study of conversion, with typical illustrations, and a discussion of the psychological factors involved. The development of the Methodist Societies is analysed as an example of the activity of the group spirit. An examination of the empirical bases of Methodist doctrine is followed by a final chapter surveying the psychological characteristics of Methodism as they are manifested in the intellectual and social life of the time, and in their influence on modern history.

II

THE HISTORICAL BACKGROUND OF
THE REVIVAL

A STUDY of the mental conditions which influenced the work of John Wesley, and gave Methodism its opportunity, must include political and social as well as philosophical and religious factors. This method involves the danger of taking the whole choir of heaven and furniture of earth [1] as our data. But Wesley was psychologically the child of his time, and the mental processes characteristic of the Revival and its leader were conditioned by the whole of the historical setting in which they occurred. ' Isolé du milieu où il se développe, un mouvement religieux n'est plus qu'une froide abstraction et une énigme impénétrable. Cela est si vrai que, quand on veut étudier les mouvements religieux du passé, le premier soin de l'auteur doit être d'en reconstituer le cadre et d'en évoquer les acteurs.' [2] It is necessary for our purpose here to indicate without describing the main features of eighteenth-century history, and consequently certain events will be referred to as typical of the environment of Methodism, and relevant material will be quoted from contemporary documents.

[1] Cf. Ward, James, ' Psychology,' *Encyclopaedia Britannica*, 9th ed. vol. xx. p. 38.

[2] De Fursac, *M.M.C.* p. 5.

While it 'must be recognised that religion in all its actual historical forms is always to a great extent a social product,'[1] some confusion has been introduced into the psychology of religion by the attempt to reduce it to sociological terms. Thus Durkheim writes in *L'Année Sociologique*, 'ce n'est pas dans la nature humaine en général qu'il faut aller chercher la cause déterminante des phénomènes religieux ; c'est dans la nature des sociétés auxquelles ils se rapportent, et s'ils ont évolué au cours de l'histoire, c'est que l'organization sociale elle-même s'est transformée.'[2] Similarly an American psychologist, as the result of researches in anthropology and social science, reaches the conclusion that ' the social consciousness, in its most intimate and vital phases, is identical with religion.'[3] There is in these group theories a false simplification of the problem, and they ignore the empirical and rational bases of religion, with which psychology is at least equally concerned. A truer estimate of the social and historical factors will be arrived at by a more purely functional and biological line of approach. The organism cannot be understood apart from its environment. But there is reciprocal action between the two. This is true psychologically both of the individual and of the group. If the terms are carried over from psychology into sociology with the care used by Dr. McDougall in *The Group Mind*, in order to avoid the assumption of any mythical ' collective consciousness,' a sound biological and social psychology becomes possible,

[1] Pratt, J. Bissett, *R.C.* p. 12.

[2] Durkheim, Emile, ' De la definition des phénomènes religieux,' in *L'Année Sociologique*, vol. ii. p. 24, quoted by Dr. Thouless, *I.P.R.* p. 144. For a critical examination, see Prof. C. C. J. Webb's *Group Theories of Religion and the Individual* (1916), especially pp. 191-2 note.

[3] Ames, Edward Scribner, *Psych. of Rel. Experience*, p. 377.

which will have a very real value in the discussion of religious phenomena.

There are certain outstanding facts in the wider environment of Methodism which must not be overlooked if we are to understand a movement which before the end of its second century numbers forty million adherents.[1] ' The expansion of England in the New World and in Asia,' wrote Seeley, ' is the formula which sums up for England the history of the eighteenth century.' [2] The world-parish of John Wesley is very closely related to the remarkable enterprise of England in exploration and colonization in the period between the Spanish War of the sixteenth century and the Seven Years' War of the eighteenth century. From the days of the Merchant Adventurers (1554) [3] to the days of Captain Cook (1728-1779) the consciousness of the meaning and value of sea power had steadily developed in England. The period of Wesley's lifetime witnessed that peculiar combination of fortune and management which gave to Britain the beginnings of her Empire and her colonies.[4] By the Peace of Utrecht (1713), ten years after Wesley's birth, England had gained Gibraltar from Spain and Newfoundland and Hudson's Bay from France. The death of Louis XIV two years later marked the end of the ascendancy which France had maintained in Europe for a century and a half. At the end of the Seven Years' War (1763), France abandoned her claims to Canada and

[1] *Report of Methodist Oecumenical Conference*, London, 1921. See also *U.M.C. Minutes*, 1925, p. 366, for actual members.

[2] Sir John Seeley, *The Expansion of England*, 1883.

[3] See Doyle, J. A., *The English in America*, vol. i. p. 50.

[4] See Mahan, A. T., *The Influence of Sea Power upon History*, 1660-1783, chaps. v-xiv. Cf. Workman, H. B., *Methodism*, pp. 4-5.

India, and the destinies of both countries were from that time bound up with that of Great Britain. One important result of these events was the decision that North America should belong to the Protestant Anglo-Saxon, and not to the Roman Catholic Latin race. Meanwhile, Spain was achieving that spiritual conquest of the new democracies of South America, the result of which has been a new variety of the Latin spirit, in which all the Mediterranean peoples find elements of their national character. Spaniards, French, Portuguese, Italians and Greeks, in the various South American States, have not proved a fruitful field for the later Methodist Missions,[1] because they were ruled by Roman Catholicism with an imperial force which is a legacy of the Latin genius.[2]

Even before Wesley's day, North America was already to a great extent an English-speaking country. The history of many of the States is written in their names : Virginia recalls the adventurers of Elizabeth's reign ; Maryland was named after his Queen by Charles I. To these original colonies the Puritan emigrations of the early seventeenth century added the four New England States : Massachusetts, New Hampshire, Connecticut, and Rhode Island. The war with Holland transferred to British rule the district which stretches from the Hudson to the inner lakes, and the name of New Amsterdam was changed to New York in honour of the Duke of York. North and South Carolina received their names and their charter from Charles II ; and the well-ordered government of South Carolina, the constitution of which was drawn

[1] For an account of the Methodist Mission work in South America, see *N.H.M.* vol. ii. pp. 172, 382-9.

[2] See Calderon, F. Garcia, *Latin America : its Rise and Progress*, tr. Miall (1913).

up by John Locke,[1] attracted Puritans from New York, Huguenots from France, and Presbyterians from Scotland. The first Quaker colony was established in New Jersey in 1674.[2] Across the Delaware, in 1681, the Quakers followed William Penn into the forest lands, and there established a colony which recalled its founder and the woodlands among which he planted it in its name, Pennsylvania. After a long interval, Penn's example was followed by General Oglethorpe, who established a settlement on the Savannah, in 1732, as a refuge for English debtors and for persecuted Protestants from Germany, the title of Georgia being conferred by the reigning monarch, George II. A glance at the map will show that before Wesley's campaign began in 1738, the whole of the Atlantic sea-board from Maine to Florida was in English hands.[3]

By their conspicuous diversity, religious conditions in the New World contrasted strongly with those in England. In the four Southern colonies the Church of England enjoyed a definite and specified supremacy, granted to it in Virginia by the original constitution, in the other colonies by legal enactment ; but although the majority of the settlers clung to the Episcopal Church, there were a considerable number of Roman Catholics in Maryland. Pennsylvania was composed mainly of Quakers. Presbyterians and Baptists had fled from tests and persecutions to colonize parts of New Jersey. Lutherans and Moravians from Germany abounded among the settlers of Carolina

---

[1] Note criticism of this in Doyle, *The English in America*, vol. i., ' Virginia, Maryland and the Carolinas,' pp. 446-452.

[2] *Ibid.* vol. iv., ' The Middle Colonies,' chap. vii.

[3] For a summary account on which these paragraphs are based, see J. R. Green, *Short History of the English People*, p. 759. See also Caldecott, A., *English Colonization and Empire*, chaps. iii.-iv.

OF THE REVIVAL 23

and Georgia. The early intolerance of a bigoted Puritanism [1] became impossible amid such a chaos of creeds, and by the middle of the eighteenth century religious persecution gave way to a healthy and necessary tolerance. Doyle estimates the population of the American colonies in 1720 as amounting to 339,000 whites, and 96,000 negroes, and he says that the population in most of the colonies doubled itself every twenty years; [2] which justifies Green's estimate of 1,200,000 whites and a quarter of a million negroes as the total for the middle of the eighteenth century.[3] Distinguished service was rendered in limited areas by individual ministers, Congregational, Presbyterian and Anglican, and others, and by agents of the Society for the Propagation of the Gospel. But a very dark picture is drawn by Doyle of the clergy in the Southern States,[4] and in 1711 there was only one clergyman in the whole of North Carolina.[5] Vast populations in these great and growing English settlements were uncared for, and their religious needs constituted an important factor in the development of Wesley's task.

When we turn to the religious and social conditions in the home country, the opportunity afforded to Methodism is seen to have depended upon even more complex circumstances. The materials are not available for a description of the collective mental life of England in the eighteenth century. It may be doubted whether such a study in social psychology would be possible except upon the basis

[1] See Doyle, *op. cit.* vol. v., *The Colonies under the House of Hanover*, p. 217, on the execution of Quakers at Boston.
[2] *Ibid.* pp. 615-616.   [3] *Op. cit.* p. 759.
[4] *Op. cit.* vol. v. pp. 257-263.
[5] *Ibid.* p. 263. For a useful single volume on the colonies, see Lodge, H. Cabot, *A Short History of the English Colonies in America* (N.Y. 1881).

of a preliminary survey of the history, literature and folk-lore of the period. Discussing the psychology of instinctive activities, Professor John Dewey writes, ' when it tries to explain complicated events in personal and social life by direct reference to these native powers, the explanation becomes hazy and forced. . . . We need to know about the social conditions which have educated original activities into definite and significant dispositions before we can discuss the psychological element in society. This is the true meaning of social psychology.' [1] If we adopt the functional and biological point of view already defined, this statement may be accepted as applying to our study of social England in its relation to the revival of religion in the eighteenth century.

In any attempt to sketch the social life and conditions upon which Wesley's work impinges, difficulties arise from the fact that John Wesley himself lived and worked in two worlds. He started his campaign in the England of Walpole and George II. He was prosecuting it at the age of eighty-six, in the time of George III, under the ministry of the younger Pitt ; he died in 1791, the year after the publication of Burke's *Reflections on the French Revolution.* Pope was writing his *Pastorals* in the year of Wesley's birth ; and Coleridge was a student at Cambridge in the year of his death. Wesley's lifetime covers the ' Augustan ' and the earlier part of the Romantic Age in English literature. And his later activities synchronised with the beginnings of those political, social and economic changes which completed the transition from feudal to modern England. The year 1760 may be regarded as the term of the earlier period, and the thirty years immediately following that date witnessed the great change in the

[1] Dewey, John, *H.N.C.* pp. 90-91.

thought, literature and society of Western Europe, three
phases of which are seen in the Industrial Revolution in
England, the Revolution in France, and the Romantic
Revolt in European literature. The characteristic
eighteenth-century conditions are those of the earlier
period, ending with the year 1760 ; but it is necessary
to examine both in so far as they created the need and
the opportunity for the development of the Methodist
movement.

The typical mental attitude in the early eighteenth
century was that of acceptance, as distinct from that of
wonder, curiosity or challenge. Apart from the dominant
English habit of thinking politically, the chief psychological characteristic which can be attributed to all classes
of the people would be described by a behaviourist as an
' average low level of adjustment,' or a ' habitual mode
of response,' [1] which has become ' stereotyped in a social
dead level.' The pedestrian philosophy of Locke was still
supreme ; reason and common sense were the watchwords
of theology ; *tranquilla non movere* [2] the motto of statesmanship and politics ; and *vos exemplaria Graeca nocturna
versate manu, versate diurna* [3] the golden rule for men of
letters. Among the peasants and the working classes
this attitude was manifest in a certain docility and
submissiveness under the crass injustice of their political
and economic disabilities. ' Neither in philosophy, theology, nor political and social strata, was there any belief in
the necessity of radical changes, or prescience of a coming

[1] Watson, J. B., *Psychology from the Standpoint of a Behaviourist*
(1922), pp. 225-226.

[2] Walpole's motto ; see Hervey, *Memoirs of George II*, ii. p. 66.

[3] Horace, *Ars Poetica*, lines 268-9.

alteration of the intellectual atmosphere.'[1]   The national mind was expressed in a certain unity of acquiescence, a kind of tacit conspiracy to maintain the *status quo*.

A class consciousness is discoverable in the early eighteenth century, based on the economic distinction of two social strata.   In a significant and ironical passage in *Tom Jones*, which was published in 1749, Fielding writes, ' By the poor here I mean that large and venerable body which in English we call the mob.   Now whoever hath had the honour to be admitted to any degree of intimacy with this mob must well know, that it is one of their established maxims to plunder and pillage their rich neighbours without any reluctance : and that this is held to be neither sin nor shame among them : and so constantly do they abide and act by this maxim, that in every parish almost in the kingdom there is a kind of confederacy ever carrying on against a certain person of opulence, called the squire, whose property is considered as free booty by all his poor neighbours ; who, as they conclude that there is no manner of guilt in such depre-dations, look upon it as a point of honour and moral obligation to conceal and to preserve each other from punishment on all such occasions.   In like manner are the ancients, such as Homer, Virgil, Horace, Cicero and the rest, to be esteemed among us writers, as so many wealthy squires, from whom we, the poor of Parnassus, claim an immemorial custom of taking whatever we can come at.   This liberty I demand, and this I am ready to allow again to my poor neighbours in their turn.'[2]   This

---

[1] Stephen, Leslie, *English Literature and Society in the Eighteenth Century* (1910), p. 199.

[2] Fielding, Henry, *Tom Jones*, bk. xii. chap. i.   See also Hammond, J. L. and B., *The Village Labourer*, pp. 213-15, for another inference from this passage.

paragraph from a contemporary novel, especially in its context, where Fielding is replying to a charge of plagiarism, is very instructive.   It contains a hint of the unwritten history of the eighteenth century.   Here is the background of Gray's *Elegy*, published two years later. The mental attitude of the time is symbolised by the fact that

> ' Some village Hampden that with dauntless breast
>   The little tyrant of his fields withstood '

should be regarded by Gray as a figure in

> ' The short and simple annals of the poor.'

But Fielding's novel reveals more than a reminder that the annals of the poor are neither short nor simple.   His implicit assumption of a public to which the classics were an open book gives us a picture of the cultivated and leisured class, the gentlemen-scholars of the time.   Thus Fielding portrays two groups, each with its own memories, traditions and interests, and each with its own standard of morality.   ' For segregated classes develop their own customs, which is to say their own working morals.   As long as society is mainly immobile these diverse principles and ruling aims do not clash.   They exist side by side in different strata. Power, glory, honor, magnificence, mutual faith here ; industry, obedience, abstinence, humility, and reverence there : noble and plebeian virtues.' [1]

The eighteenth century historians and writers of memoirs give us gossipy and amusing accounts of the doings of court and political society, and of the aristocracy generally.   But questions of social welfare and the life of the rank and file of the population only emerge when

[1] Dewey, John, *H.N.C.* p. 82.

they are forced to the front by riots.[1]   Lord John Hervey, after making an elaborate apology for the egotism of his *Memoirs*, concludes, ' To whom, then, can a history of such times be agreeable or entertaining, unless it be to such as look into courts and courtiers, princes and ministers, with such curious eyes as virtuosos in microscopes examine flies and emmets and are pleased with the dissected minute parts of animals, which in the gross herd they either do not regard, or observe only with indifference or contempt ? ' [2]   The psychological value of this passage lies in the unconscious presuppositions of the writer, who may be regarded as typical of the mental attitude of those who were the hereditary rulers of the country.   Several assumptions strike the reader at once.   The history of the times is the history of courts and courtiers, princes and ministers. The purpose of historical records is to be agreeable and entertaining. Scientific research is a pursuit the object of which is to satisfy curiosity or to please virtuosos.

Horace Walpole, in his letters, and even more in his Memoirs, reveals the same aristocratic aloofness and affectation. ' Serious business was a trifle to him, and trifles were his serious business. . . .   While he was fetching and carrying the gossip of Kensington Palace and Carlton House, he fancied that he was engaged in politics, and when he recorded that gossip, he fancied that he was writing history.' [3]   Bishop Burnet was a good representative of the dominant Churchmanship of his time, but his

---

[1] Note, on the Corn Riots, Hervey, Lord John, *Memoirs of George the Second*, vol. ii. p. 308.

[2] Hervey, Lord John, *Memoirs of the Reign of George the Second*, vol. ii. p. 67.

[3] Macaulay, *Horace Walpole*, Crit. and Mis. Essays, i. p. 332.

History of His Own Time reflects a mind that is dominated by the prevailing standards of the court. His pages are filled, like those of Hervey and Walpole, with stories of royal and ducal immorality. He does not seem to have any notion of the existence of the vast public to which Wesley's work appealed ; or he does not think their affairs worth recording, when he has so much court scandal to fill his diverting volumes. This age was the Augustan Age in more senses than one. It is hard to find in the Roman writers any records of the poor. So it is with the records of eighteenth-century England. There are bright and ample chronicles of fashionable scenes in high politics and high play, but dim and meagre records of the dis-inherited peasants, and of the deserted villages,[1] and of the women and children working in coal mines,[2] or, in general, of ' that large and venerable body which in English we call the mob.'

The unconscious mentality of the masses of the people is best revealed, according to Freud, in the symbolism which ' is to be found in greater perfection in the folk-lore, in the myths, legends, and manners of speech, in the proverbial sayings, and in the current witticisms of a nation.'[3] It is not possible here to make a psycho-analytic investigation into the mother-wit of the period. But there are two examples of popular irony which have a very plain significance. During the absence of George II,

---

[1] J. L. and B. Hammond, *op. cit.* p. 308.   Note also the literal truth of Goldsmith's *Deserted Village*, published 1770.

[2] Galloway (*Annals of Coal Mining*, 1st series, p. 305) says employ-ment of women and girls underground in Tyne and Wear district ceased about 1780.   See Hammond, J. L. and B., *Town Labourer*, p. 27. See also Prof. Wilt Bowden's *Industrial Society in England towards the End of the Eighteenth Century* (1925).

[3] Freud, S., *The Interpretation of Dreams*, ch. v. pp. 245-6.

with Madame Walboden in Germany, the following advertisement was pasted on St. James's Gate : ' Lost or strayed out of this house, a man who has left a wife and six children on the parish ; whoever will give any tidings of him to the churchwardens of St. James's Parish, so as he may be got again, shall receive four shillings and sixpence reward. N.B. This reward will not be increased, nobody judging him to deserve a Crown.' [1] The only comment Hervey makes on this, with reference to the king, is that, ' as the two characters he most affected were the brave warrior and the tender lover, so he looked on all these satires and lampoons as so many proofs of his eminence in the last of these callings.' An oft repeated pun relating to the juridical evils of the day is related by Walpole. ' Crowle was a noted punster. Once on a circuit with Page, a person asked him if the Judge was not just behind ? He replied, " I don't know ; but I am sure he was never *just* before." ' [2] Behind the popularity of this story, must be remembered the ferocious nature of the laws to be administered. As late as 1818, a boy of fifteen was sentenced to death for stealing £3 3s. 6d. ; for housebreaking with intent to commit robbery a lad of seventeen received the same sentence, as also did a labourer aged thirty for stealing one pair of shoes, one half boot and one half top boot.[3] ' The haphazard list of two hundred crimes punishable by death had not even consistent severity to recommend it. . . . Although only a small proportion of the death sentences pronounced were carried out, the number of men and women hanged in

---

[1] Hervey, *Memoirs of George II*, vol. ii. pp. 364-5.

[2] Walpole, Horace, *Memoirs of the Reign of George II*, vol. i. p. 21 note.

[3] Crown Calendar for Lincolnshire Lent Assizes, 7th March, 1818. See Appendix to *Reminiscences of Sir Henry Hawkins*.

England every year was greater in proportion to the population than on the Continent.' [1]

Associate with these typical stories the ' pluralities, non-residence, the neglect of their cures and the irregularities in the lives of the clergy which were too visible,' [2] and the inference becomes irresistible as to the bearing of all this on the religious ideas of those for whom concrete images take the place of discursive thought. However obscure and unexplicit, there are links of association connecting an absentee king and absentee clerics with the absentee god of deism, just as there is more than a fantastical relation between the figure of Queen Victoria and the maternal and family Deity of nineteenth century popular theology. And similarly, the notorious injustice both of legislation and of administration is reflected in current sceptical questioning as to the justice of Providence. Divine justice is always conceived in terms of human justice, and it was certainly felt that the actual condition of affairs was not easily reconciled with a Providential order. In the schools this scepticism in matters religious may have been due to the rise of the inductive spirit,[3] but in a dumb way the same questions were being asked and the same challenges were being made by a few burdened spirits among the unlettered masses.

---

[1] Trevelyan, G. M., *British History in the Nineteenth Century* (1782-1901), 1922. Preface on ' Eighteenth Century,' p. 31.

[2] Burnet, Bishop, *History of His Own Time*, ed. 1857, p. 751. See also Richardson, Samuel, *Pamela* (pub. 1740) for a contemporary criticism of pluralities and dispensations, 4 vols. ed. Chapman and Hall, 1902, vol. iii. 189-204 ; vol. iv. pp. 183 ff. Compare John Wesley's comment, ' O what a curse in this poor land are pluralities and non-residence ' (*J.W.J.* vii. 173).

[3] It appears in the sceptical writings of Bayle, and it was the subject of the *Theodicy* of Leibniz, the *Essay on Man* by Pope, and the *Analogy* of Butler. See Lecky, *History of England in the Eighteenth Century*, vol. iii. p. 4.

Into such a society came John Wesley, making the world his parish. He toured the whole country, visiting almost every town and village in England and Wales, and not a few in Scotland and Ireland, on the merely human side carrying personal interest and sympathy into the lives of the unshepherded populations, and appointing preachers who, in the majority of cases, lived with and shared the toil of their followers. It is not surprising that one of the best understood of the cardinal doctrines of Methodism was the great catholic doctrine of universal grace.[1] The psychoanalyst would use the magic word *projection*[2] as a complete explanation of this change from a fear and distrust of remote and unjust spiritual powers, to a trust in a God who was realised as in living contact with His children. It is quite reasonable to suppose that the ubiquity and accessibility of the great revival leader created an unconscious predisposition among the masses to recognize in the phenomena of the revival the immediate action of God upon human nature.

Between the two extremes of the social scale, at which we have identified two distinct groups, each with its own interests, traditions and morals, there was steadily emerging into consciousness the collective spirit of the middle classes. While in the higher circles of society there was a combination of aristocratic affectation with grossness and immorality, and in the lower circles ignorance and brutality, the old Puritan spirit lived on in the middle classes. The community of interest which arose in the first place from religious group consciousness, was further

---

[1] I have used the term universal grace as being less ambiguous than universal redemption.

[2] See Tansley, A. G., *N.P.* pp. 156 ff., on Idealization. Cf. Hart, Bernard, *The Psychology of Insanity*, chap. ix. on Projection.

strengthened in the early eighteenth century by the fact that the middle class was rapidly constituting a new reading public. Literary work was being more and more distinctly addressed to the middle class. Johnson's incomparable letter rejecting Chesterfield's attempt to impose his patronage is the familiar indication of the change.[1] The success of *Robinson Crusoe* [2] was due to the fact that it captured a new circle of readers, not only because it embodies the type of the middle-class Briton, and is the very incarnation of eighteenth-century individualism, but because of its journalistic use of realism and homely diction. Both Richardson and Defoe belonged to the lower middle classes, and wrote the English of common speech ; and in *Pamela* [3] Richardson challenged the prevalent idea that dukes and princesses were the only suitable heroes and heroines. Richardson had also the distinction of evoking the genius of Fielding,[4] whose first novel was commenced as a parody upon *Pamela*. Fielding claimed to be the founder of a new province in literature, and he saw with perfect clearness what was to be its nature. He crowded the stage with men and women of all sorts and conditions, mainly of the middle and lower classes, because, he explains, he considered that ' the highest life presents very little Humour or Entertainment.' [5] Fielding admired his friend Hogarth [6] for painting ' The Rake's Progress ' ' without bothering about old masters or the

[1] 1755. See Boswell's *Life of Johnson*, Oxford edition, vol. i. p. 173 ; see also Leslie Stephen, *English Literature and Society in the Eighteenth Century*, p. 147.

[2] 1719. Defoe was John Wesley's uncle by marriage. See Stephen, *op. cit.* p. 135.

[3] 1740.   [4] 1707-1754.

[5] Dobson, Austin, ' The Eighteenth Century,' in *Chambers's Encyclopaedia of English Literature*, vol. ii. p. 7.

[6] 1697-1764.

grand style.' Defoe, Richardson and Fielding, each of them in his own way, felt the need of appealing to the new class of readers by direct portraiture of the readers themselves.[1] The new fiction reflects the life, as it also appealed to the taste, of the new public : a class not very highly cultivated, but which had reached the point of reading its newspaper and magazine regularly, and which bought books enough to make it worth while to supply a growing demand.[2] The existence of this new class of readers, before the days of cheap journalism in the modern sense, provided Wesley to some extent with a public for his cheap editions of devotional classics, his abridgments, translations and works, over four hundred of which are catalogued in Green's *Bibliography*.[3] And it must be remembered that Wesley himself and his own immediate circle of Oxford Methodists belonged to this middle class, with its strong Puritan tradition, its domestic sentiment, its sturdy morality, and its conservative tendencies.

The difference between the England of George the Second (1727-1760) and the England of George the Third (1760-1820), is comparable with the difference between mental stability and mental instability. 'A row of eighteenth century houses, or a room of normal eighteenth century furniture, or a characteristic piece of eighteenth century literature, conveys at once a sense of satisfaction and completeness.'[4] But the end of the clearly defined first period did not come with the chronological ending of

[1] Stephen, *op. cit.* p. 166.

[2] *Ibid.* p. 149. The first daily newspaper was published in 1702 : *The Daily Courant.* See Dobson, *op. cit.* p. 2.

[3] Green, R., *Works of John and Charles Wesley : A Bibliography.* Wesley made £30,000 by his publications, every penny of which he distributed in charity in his lifetime.

[4] Hammond, J. L. and B., *Village Labourer*, p. 301.

the century. From the year 1760 onwards, the forces, philosophical, religious, literary, social and economic, which had been maturing beneath the conscious satisfaction and immobility, became manifest in changes that were rapid and revolutionary. In comparison with the dishevelled century which followed, the eighteenth century was an ordered and complete whole.

As it is impossible to understand the function of Methodism among the English-speaking peoples of the world without taking into account the expansion of England and the rise of the Empire and the Colonies, so it is impossible rightly to estimate the place of Methodism in the religious experience of the populations in the home country, unless we first examine the totally new conditions created by the *Industrial Revolution*. As the colonies constituted the opportunity and the need for Methodism across the seas, so the age of iron and steam with its newly developed manufacturing areas provided Wesley's field in England. It is an essential and not an accidental element in the situation, that the birth of the Methodist movement synchronises with the birth of modern England.

A comparison of two maps showing the distribution of the *population* in England at Wesley's birth and at the time of his death, would reveal the effects of the Industrial Revolution, and the later map would also be a map of Methodist strongholds. It is difficult to obtain materials for an accurate determination of the population. There are no official returns before 1801. A proposal for a census in 1753 was rejected as ' subversive of the last remains of English liberty.' [1] Computations based upon

---

[1] Mr. Thornton, member for the City of York ; see Preface to *Preliminary Census Returns*, 1881, p. 1. Quoted by Toynbee, *Industrial Revolution*, p. 7.

an examination of the registers of baptisms and burials of the eighteenth century were made by Mr. Finlaison (Actuary to the National Debt Office) and published in the Preface to the *Census Returns* of 1831. These are generally accepted. He gives the population of England and Wales in 1700 as 5,134,516, and in 1750 as 6,039,684, an increase of not quite a million, or between 17 and 18 per cent. in the first half of the century. In 1801 the population of England and Wales was 9,187,176, showing an increase of three millions, or more than 52 per cent. in the second half of the century.[1] The latter is the period of the transition to the modern industrial system, and to improved methods of *agriculture*. ' At the time of the great Whig Revolution, England was in the main a country of commons and of common fields ; at the time of the Reform Bill, England was in the main a country of individualist agriculture and of large enclosed farms.'[2] The histories of the time tell us very little of this agricultural revolution. The injustice of the Enclosures Acts must not be discussed here. But it is very significant for our understanding of the mental qualities of the new era that, writing in 1770, Arthur Young ascribes to the last ten years, ' more experiments, more discoveries, and more general good sense displayed in the walk of agriculture than in a hundred preceding ones.'[3]

Together with the growth of the population, and the progress in agriculture, must be considered the concentration of the population in the north of England and in the large towns. Macaulay's famous description of the

[1] For an analysis of these figures, and a comparison with Price, Howlett, and Arthur Young, see Toynbee, *Industrial Revolution*, chap. ii.

[2] Hammond, J. L. and B., *Village Labourer*, p. 2.

[3] Quoted by Toynbee, *Industrial Revolution*, p. 21.

northern counties in 1685 is borne out by Defoe, who
writes in 1725, ' The country south of the Trent is by far
the largest, as well as the richest and most populous.' [1]
In 1700 the five most populous counties are believed to
have been Middlesex, Somerset, Gloucester, Wiltshire,
and Northampton.   In 1800 they were Middlesex, Lanca-
shire, the West Riding of Yorkshire, Staffordshire,
and Warwickshire.[2]   The growth of the towns may be
seen by comparing various estimates of the population
of six provincial towns in the years 1685 and 1760 :
Liverpool grew from 4,000 [3] to 40,000 ; [4] Manchester
from 6,000 [3] to 40,000 ; [5] Birmingham from 4,000 [3] to
30,000 ; [5] Sheffield from 4,000 [3] to 30,000 ; [4] Leeds from
7,000 [3] to 150,000 [3] (in 1841) ; and Bristol from 29,000 [3]
to 100,000.[5]   These increases, together with the redis-
tribution of the population, are only of importance for
our purpose in that they indicate the emergence of a new
social order, and reveal the changes in the social structure
which created a new spiritual need.

It has been remarked that the difference between the
first half and the second half of the eighteenth century is
comparable with the difference between mental stability
and mental instability.[6]   But it must be remembered that
mental instability, like organic instability, means capacity
for fresh evolution.[7]   The French Revolution is the
obvious symbol of this truth.   It is traceable, however, in

[1] Defoe, Daniel, *Tour through the Whole Island* (1725), iii. 57 (7th
edition, 1769). See Toynbee, *op. cit.* p. 9.

[2] Hammond, J. L. and B., *The Town Labourer*, p. 4. For the figures
and references as to population and its distribution, the writer is
indebted entirely to the Hammonds and to Toynbee's researches.

[3] Macaulay's *History of England*, chap. iii.

[4] Arthur Young, *Tour* (1769).

[5] Macpherson's *Annals of Commerce*.

[6] *Vide supra*, p. 34.   [7] Tansley, A. G., *N.P.* p. 256.

the social and economic changes in England, of which a brief account has been given.   The figures set out in the preceding paragraph reveal large concentrated groups of industrial workers, engaged in specialised tasks, and developing mental characteristics which definitely distinguish them from the slow-moving inhabitants of the conservative village areas.   The change has been described from the literary side as one from the age of reason to the age of passion.   This description may apply to the new industrialist, if we substitute the word routine for the word reason and limit our reference to those who were influenced by Methodism.   But there were marked transformations in the instinctive activities and in the intellectual powers, as well as in the emotional dispositions of the new social organism.

The stimulus of a new environment for the industrial worker combined with the rise of the inductive spirit in evoking an intellectual curiosity and delight in wonder, which manifested itself in scientific discoveries and in mechanical inventions.   The literary revolt which followed a little later [1] presents the same psychological features, in that it is a transition from the spirit of criticism to that of creation.   With a qualification to be made later, the change in social life and conditions brought also a change in mental attitude, from dependence and self-distrust to independence and self-confidence, or to what might be described as positive self-feeling.[2]   Evidence of the increasing power of the social sentiment, and of organizing capacity, is found in the birth of the Trade Unions, Friendly Societies, Co-operative Societies, and Mechanics'

[1] See Vaughan, C. E., *The Romantic Revolt* (1788-1805).

[2] Ribot, Theodule Arnaud, *Psychology of the Emotions*, p. 240.   See also McDougall, *S.P.* p. 62.

Institutes,[1] as well as in the Sunday Schools and Methodist Chapels. Other and deeper forces were at work, culminating in the social evolution of the modern nations, but these forces were not consciously realized and directed. The men who were first influenced by them were least aware of their trend and significance. In England, at least, eighteenth-century individualism broke down through the pressure of economic forces, and it was largely due to these that a new public spirit and social consciousness was manifest in the industrial populations.

The significant fact for the interpretation of Methodism, from the point of view of social psychology, is the incapacity of either Church or State to discern or comprehend the forces which were remoulding society, or to provide in any way for the intellectual or spiritual needs of the new populations. No effort was made in the direction of religious or educational improvement. Schools there were none, save the grammar schools of Edward and Elizabeth, and some newly established ' circulating schools ' for religious education in Wales. The pathetic picture of Bartle Massey's night school, in George Eliot's *Adam Bede*,[2] is typical of the only education available for thousands both in town and country. The national Church failed both in spiritual vision and in administrative wisdom, through a poverty due in part to the secession of the Non-jurors,[3] and in part to the Hanoverian preference of the ' safe ' man in the political appointment of ecclesiastical leaders.[4] Among the vast populations of the mining areas and in the rapidly growing textile towns,

---

[1] See Hammond, J. L. and B., *op. cit.*   [2] Book ii. chap. xxi.
[3] See Abbey and Overton, *The English Church in the Eighteenth Century* (1878), vol. i. p. 384 ff. ; vol. ii. p. 170.
[4] Wakeman, H. F., *Introd. to Hist. of C. of E.* pp. 425-33.

the Established Church scarcely existed for the poor,
except as one of the forces of law and order. Not a new
parish had been created.[1] It is not surprising that, when
it was too late, in 1792, the Mayor of Liverpool wrote to
the Home Office, urging the Government to build churches
in the numerous villages which had sprung up with the
growth of manufactures, giving as his reason, not the
advantage of spiritual exercises, but the danger of leaving
these places to the Methodists. ' For, Sir,' he writes, ' in
all these places are nothing but Methodist and other
Meeting Houses, and as the people in the country are in
general disposed to go to some place of Worship on the
Sunday, they go to these because there is no other ; and
thus the youth of the Country are trained up under the
instruction of a set of men not only ignorant, but whom
I think we have of late too much reason to imagine are
inimical to our happy Constitution.' [2] It is interesting
to note that the grant of a million pounds for the
building of churches in 1818 was justified on this very
ground.[3]

The concrete historical setting of Methodism, thus
briefly described, makes it clear that the work of John
Wesley was one element in an extremely complex period
of renascence. Beginning his campaign with the object
of spreading scriptural holiness throughout the land, amid
the comparatively static society of 1738, preaching to the
neglected masses an individualist gospel of personal salvation, he found himself involved in the organization and
administration of a great religious community, amid the

---

[1] Green, John Richard, *Short History of the English People*, p. 736.

[2] Home Office Papers in Public Record Office, 42.29, quoted by
Hammond, J. L. and B., *Town Labourer*, p. 270.

[3] Hammond, J. L. and B., *op. cit.* p. 270.

chaotic conditions of modern English life.[1] The nature of the forces which were at work, and which reacted on the Revival, has not yet been fully explored. But it is sufficiently evident that the religious awakening was part of a wider movement, involving not only the English-speaking peoples of England and America, but the whole of Western Europe.

[1] See Wesley's observations on the growth of the population, and the increase of trade in twelve counties in 1776, *J.W.J.* vol. vi. p. 104 ; and in London, in 1778, vol. vi. p. 180 ; and on unemployment in Birmingham, in 1789, vol. viii. p. 479.

III

THE MIND OF JOHN WESLEY

THE Methodist Revival, as to its matter, was determined by the various historical factors which have been considered. But its form was the contribution of one man. After due attention has been given to all the conditions which constituted the environment of the movement, and to the work of his colleagues, it still remains true that the primary element in Methodism was the religious experience and activity of John Wesley. No social psychology, concerned with the systems of interacting mental forces discernible in the eighteenth century, can account for the creation of Methodism. Wesley was the means of making articulate the dumb or unconscious desires of vast masses of the people of England. He built up a great organization on lines determined largely by the social needs of the time. But the distinctive features of Methodism, as a type of religious life, bear the unmistakable impress of the personality of its founder. If the generic function of mind is to organize life by correlating its parts, then John Wesley was the mind of Methodism.

Professor J. B. Watson, in his *Psychology from the Standpoint of a Behaviourist*, outlines a scheme for the study of personality which will form a basis for our study of the mind of John Wesley. But it must be understood that for our purpose behaviour includes the language in which Wesley describes his own experiences and intro-spections, and also that it includes those unconscious tendencies which are discoverable by inference from his conduct and confessions. A behaviourist psychology includes the study of a man as ' working or playing, reading, writing or talking, making money or spending it, constructing or destroying, curing disease, alleviating poverty, comforting the oppressed, and promoting one or another sort of orderliness.' [1]   It will be seen that this is a return to Aristotle's position.   The soul is the body in action, and personality is behaviour, in the sense that it includes and is revealed in all the activities which are specifically human.

(1) *General Level of Behaviour*.[2]   Wesley's *range of information and interests* indicates very wide reading and an alert mind.   The list of books read in the interval between his ordination (September 1725) and his election to the Fellowship of Lincoln College (March 17, 1726) [3] is typical of the general reading in classics, science, philosophy and divinity, which he kept up in later life mainly by reading on horseback on his long journeys.   After the advent of the turnpike roads,[4] Wesley nailed up one side of the coach which he used, and fitted it with book-shelves and a writing desk.   Curnock comments on the remarkable admixture of plays which Wesley read as an undergraduate.   The inclusion of one novel, abridged and

[1] E. B. Holt, quoted by Hoernlé, *op. cit.* p. 150.   Cf. also Ross, W. D., *Aristotle* (1923), p. 134.

[2] Watson, *P.S.B.* p. 399.   The arrangement of Professor Watson's suggestions has been revised, and certain repetitions are thus avoided.

[3] *J.W.J.* vol. i. pp. 65-6.

[4] See Trevelyan, G. M., *British History in the Nineteenth Century*, Introduction, p. xiii.

edited,[1] among his publications, is notable, as is also his reason for regarding it as excellent, because ' it perpetually aims at inspiring and increasing every right affection, at the instilling gratitude to God, and benevolence to man.' [2] Wesley's learning was general rather than special, and his interests were largely vocational. In his written sermons and in his letters and the *Journal*, he reveals a command of clear nervous English ; his vocabulary is singularly pure, and his literary style terse and dignified. There is no evidence of any marked mathematical ability. He had a ' peculiar constitution of soul,' according to one of his sermons, and he was convinced, ' by many experiments, that he could not study, to any degree of perfection, either mathematics, arithmetic, or algebra, without being a deist, if not an atheist ; though others may study them all their lives without sustaining any inconvenience.' [3]

Wesley had a natural and highly trained logical acuteness. He published, in 1750, a translation of Aldrich's *Artis Logicae Compendium*.[4] For several years he was Moderator in the disputations which were held six times a week at Lincoln College.[5] ' I could not,' he writes, ' avoid acquiring hereby some degree of expertness in arguing ; and especially in discerning and pointing out well covered and plausible fallacies. I have since found abundant reason to praise God for giving me this honest art. By this, when men have hedged me in by what they called demonstrations, I have been many times able to dash them in pieces ; in spite of all its covers, to touch

---

[1] Brooke, Henry, *The Fool of Quality*. See Green's *Bibliography*, p. 209.

[2] Preface, dated Bristol, March 4, 1780.

[3] *W.W.* vol. vi. p. 120.   [4] Oxon. 1691.

[5] Tyerman, *op. cit.* vol. ii. p. 90.

the very point where the fallacy lay ; and it flew open in a moment.' [1] This logical faculty was evident in other ways as part of Wesley's special vocational equipment. It dominated his dramatic and rhetorical gifts as a preacher, and gave definition and distinctness to his theological teaching. To his general scholarship, Frederic Loofs, of Hallé, paid tribute : ' In the many-sidedness of his education, and in his unwearied interest in all branches of knowledge, he is without peer amongst revival preachers in any age.' [2]

In mastering *languages*,[3] at any rate to the point of usefulness in preaching and in translation, Wesley showed facility. Greek, Latin, Hebrew, Arabic, and French he learned as an undergraduate. To these he added German in order to converse with the Moravians on the voyage to Georgia, and Spanish and Italian in order to read the Scriptures and preach to the Spanish and Italian colonists in Savannah and Frederica.[4]

Of Wesley's *manual activity*,[5] there is evidence in the entry in his private diary for May 16, 1726 : ' Cut stakes, made two benches in the arbour.' With this may be noted two entries in the private diary, made eleven years later. On the 14th May, 1737, he records, ' felling trees,' and on the 20th May, ' tree-felling.' Another interest attaches to the entry for the 7th Feb. 1736, in view of the fact that he regarded ' strong drink as the curse of the colony ' of Georgia. He notes as apparently his own action, ' staved rum.' [6] In the private diary two days earlier, with a whole page to itself, appears the

---

[1] *W.W.* vol. x. p. 340.
[2] Loofs, Dr. Frederic, quoted Brigden, *N.H.M.* i. 162.
[3] Watson, *P.S.B.* p. 399.   [4] *J.W.J.* vol. i. p. 435.
[5] Watson, *op. cit.* p. 399.   [6] *J.W.J.* vol. i. p. 149.

record, 'Nos tres proponimus, Deo juvante, neq carnem neq vinum gustare, ante Diem Dominicum.'[1]

Wesley was a shrewd and careful observer,[2] and his *Journal* provides many examples of his capacity for seeing things clearly and recording them faithfully. But in the estimation of numbers, when recording the size of his congregations, he habitually exaggerated to the point of absurdity. For example, he writes, 'I preached at Basingshaw church (Wed. 27, Dec. 1738); Sunday the 31st to many thousands in St. George's, Spitalfields. And to a yet more crowded congregation at Whitechapel in the afternoon.'[3] Many thousands could not have been accommodated in St. George's, Spitalfields; and a yet more crowded congregation at Whitechapel is unthinkable. Curnock points out that if we wish to arrive at approximately accurate estimates of the congregations, indoors and out-of-doors, we shall probably find it necessary to substitute hundreds for thousands. Whitefield and Cennick shared this idiosyncrasy, in which there is probably an element of megalomania. But against this must be set Wesley's habit of writing names, and the rigidly exact record of the members of societies upon which he always insisted.[4]

(2) *General Habits of Work.*[5] Wesley was not an erratic or irregular worker. He was prompt, neat and punctual. He laid down a scheme of studies for 1722, a time-table for each day of the week, a list of subjects which he hoped to study, and an order of correspondence with his father, mother, sisters and brother.[6] The systematic planning of

---

[1] *J.W.J.* vol. i. p. 146, probably referring to the two Wesleys and Delamotte.
[2] Watson, *P.S.B.* p. 399.   [3] *J.W.J.* vol. ii. p. 119, and note.
[4] *J.W.J.* vol. i. p. 116; vi. p. 223.
[5] Watson, *P.S.B.* p. 400.   [6] *J.W.J.* vol. i. p. 46.

his work for every hour of the day, which he learned from Jeremy Taylor's *Holy Living and Dying*, he maintained from 1725 to the year of his death. The private diary which runs parallel with the fourth Savannah Journal (1736) reveals a slavishly methodical life. As a rule, wherever he was, or however occupied, one hour is divided from another by five, six or seven minutes spent in prayer, singing, or some other form of devotion. Interruptions caused by urgent duties, or by sickness, he accepted as inevitable, but if thrown out of gear for an hour, a day, or a week, he returned unerringly to his normal routine.[1] His plan of study for 1727 included Greek and Roman classics for Mondays and Tuesdays ; logic and ethics for Wednesdays ; Hebrew and Arabic for Thursdays ; metaphysics and natural philosophy for Fridays. Saturday he devoted to oratory and poetry, chiefly composing ; and Sundays to divinity. ' In intermediate hours, he perfected himself in the French language,' amused himself with optics and mathematics, and studied Euclid, Keil, and Sir Isaac Newton.[2] Wesley's private diary gives details of his doings every hour of the day, from four o'clock in the morning,[3] his usual hour of rising, till eight, nine or ten in the evening, when he retired to bed. If he rose later, he retired later, and there is one day recorded of twenty-one hours of continuous strain.[4]

There is little evidence that he ever, as boy or man, planned a new production, or wrote anything original I discovered an interesting manuscript, in Wesley's writing, in the Colman Collection of Wesley relics, entitled ' The Procedure, Extent and Limits of the Human

---

[1] *J.W.J.*, vol. i. pp. 280-282 note.
[2] Tyerman, *L.T.W.* vol. i. p. 55.
[3] *W.W.* vol. vii. p. 65.   [4] *J.W.J.* vol. i. p. 138.

Understanding,' comprising 103 pages, divided into two books, and dated Christmas Eve, 1730. Book I deals with ' The Ideas of Sensation,' and Book II with ' Pure Intellect,' ' Knowledge and Evidence,' and the last two chapters reveal the purpose of the essay ; they deal with ' Ye Improvement of Knowledge by Revelation ' and ' Ye Improvement of Morality by Revelation.[1] But the source of this little treatise is found in a work published two years earlier by the Bishop of Cork ; a work with the same title, which Wesley frequently read and explained to his preachers, and which he regarded as ' in most points far clearer and more judicious than Mr. Locke's, as well as designed to advance a better cause.' [2] Wesley's earliest attempt at versification was a translation of a Latin poem,[3] and his hymns, with few exceptions, were translations, mainly from the German. His ' method ' he acquired from Jeremy Taylor, in field preaching he followed Whitefield, and his most characteristic doctrines he learned from the Moravians. The essential features also of the Methodist organization were suggested to Wesley by other men.

The vocational achievements of John Wesley are symbolized by the fact that in the last ten years of his life the number of members of the Methodist Societies increased from 43,380 to 71,568 in the United Kingdom ; and during the same period, nineteen missionaries were appointed to Antigua, Barbadoes, St. Vincent's, Nova

[1] Bound MSS. volumes, Colman Collection, vol. v.

[2] *J.W.J.* vol. iv. p. 192, and note. Dr. Peter Browne (Bishop of Cork, 1710-1735) published *The Procedure (or Progress), Extent and Limits of Human Understanding*, London, 1728. See *Proceedings of Wesley Historical Society*, vol. iv. p. 109. Note also that Wesley read and prepared extracts from Locke's *Essay*, and published his *Remarks* on Locke in 1781. See *W.W.* vol. xiii. pp. 429-37.

[3] Tyerman, *L.T.W.* vol. i. p. 25.

Scotia, Newfoundland and other stations ; and in 1790 there were 114 circuits, 228 itinerant preachers, and 57,631 members of the Societies in America.[1] Wesley exemplifies the truth of Dr. Johnson's dictum, ' It is prodigious the quantity of good that may be done by one man if he will but make a business of it.'

(3) *Activity Level*.[2] Wesley was, constitutionally and through physical infirmity, a lazy man.[3] But he trained himself into the habit of ceaseless diligence. In his private confessions of sin, in the diaries, ' intemperance in sleep,' and ' immoderate sleep ' occur frequently. And one of his Saturday night reviews consists only of two words, written in cipher,[4] ' Idleness slays.' The advice he gave to his preachers he exemplified himself : ' Never be unemployed a moment. Never be triflingly employed. Never while away time.'[5] To another he wrote, ' Lie down before ten ; rise before six. Every day use as much exercise as you can bear ; or—Murder yourself by inches.'[6] But though always diligent, he never seemed in a hurry. ' He mostly wrote standing ; and, to look at, he was a very slow writer.'[7]

In Wesley's deportment there was an ' easy simplicity . . . his gestures were graceful and harmonious.'[8] Bradburn writes, ' He had an almost inexhaustible fund of stories and anecdotes, adapted to all kinds of people, and to every occurrence in life. . . . When speaking of any who imagined religion would make people morose or gloomy, I have heard him say in the pulpit, " that sour

[1] Tyerman, *L.T.W.* vol. iii. p. 620.　　[2] Watson, *P.S.B.* p. 400.
[3] *J.W.J.* vol. i. p. 54.　　[4] *J.W.J.* vol. i. pp. 54-5.
[5] Bradburn, *Select Letters*, p. xxiii.
[6] Eayrs, G., *Letters of J. W.* (1915), p. 454.
[7] and [8] Bradburn, *op. cit.* pp. 23, and xv.

godliness is the devil's religion." ' [1]   The *Journal* reveals
many examples of his fine sense of humour.   Against this
must be set Dr. Johnson's remark, that ' John Wesley's
conversation is good, but he is never at leisure.   He is
always obliged to go at a certain hour.   This is very
disagreeable to a man who loves to fold his legs and have
his talk out as I do.' [2]

(4) *Recreation and Sports*.[3]   Wesley was too frail to be
an athlete, but as an Oxford undergraduate, he was able
to hold his own on the tennis-court, to pull an oar on the
river, to swim, ride, hunt, and to walk long distances.[4]
Customary outdoor and indoor recreations he shared with
his friends.   Tea-drinking and gossip, light literature and
plays, books like *Gulliver* and *Hudibras*, found their
place in Wesley's life at Oxford and Wroot.   At one period
his mind inclined towards drama.   His sister Martha, in
a well-known letter, thanks him for good plays, and craves
more.   On the first page of his diary, a mediaeval writer
of plays is named twice as a subject of study, and three
times on the same page he says that he ' acted an hour.' [5]
In later years he came to regard nearly all these diversions
as a sinful waste of time ; he found his recreation in
incessant work, and his journeys on horseback or walking
provided him with an unceasing outlet for his physical
energies.

(5) *Social Adaptability*.[6]   John Wesley, like the other
members of his family, was critical in temper, independent
in opinion, and self-willed.   The Wesleys differed, not
only from friends and foes outside the family circle, but

---

[1] Bradburn, S., *Select Letters*, Introd. p. xvii.
[2] Boswell, *Life of Johnson*, Oxford edition, vol. ii. p. 176.
[3] Watson, *P.S.B.* p. 401.   [4] *J.W.J.* vol. i. p. 20.
[5] *J.W.J.* vol. i. p. 47.   [6] Watson, *P.S.B.* p. 401.

among themselves. Heated controversy fills the letters
of John and his brother Samuel. John and Charles
frequently differed seriously. Yet as a family they were
clannish, and whenever emergency arose, with need for
practical service, their differences vanished. ' John is
absolutely loyal to Samuel, as head of the family, even
when he is in the act of quarrelling with him ; and Samuel,
desiring that a scholar should read the proofs of his latest
book, sends them to John in Savannah, and, probably by
the same mail, posts a letter which sparkles with satire.
Charles in trouble, sick, slandered, deserted, and left to
die in misery by his chief, turns to the brother with whom
he is at variance. John flies to his help, and not only
clears his character, but does his work both as pastor and
secretary.' [1] Both in relation to his parents, and to his
brothers and sisters, Wesley maintained an attitude of
independence combined with complete loyalty.

Tactfulness and capacity for co-operation were acquired
through painful experiences. Wesley's method of select-
ing his friends at Oxford is significant. ' I narrowly
observed the temper and behaviour of all that visited me.
I saw no reason to think that the greater part of these
truly loved or feared God : therefore, when any of them
came to see me, I behaved as courteously as I could ; but
to the question, " When will you come and see me ? " I
returned no answer. When they had come a few times,
and found I still declined to return their visit, I saw them
no more. And, I bless God, this has been my invariable
rule for about three score years.' [2] One of his ' Rules of a
Helper ' is, ' Tell everyone what you think wrong in him.' [3]

[1] *J.W.J.* vol. i. p. 197, Curnock's note.
[2] Sermon, ' On Leaving the World,' *W. Works*, vol. vi. p. 447.
[3] Rule 7. *W.W.* vol. viii. p. 298.

During the voyages across the Atlantic, and while in
Georgia, Wesley had to deal with undisciplined types,
and the clash with his over-disciplined rule created the
situation, which, while it injured the Georgia mission,
gave Wesley a special knowledge of the human problems
which arise in all administration.

(6) *Reactions to Conventional Standards.*[1] John Wesley
was habitually truthful, faithful, loyal, frank and honest.
The scriptural holiness which he wished to spread throughout the land was of a homely and conventional type.
In a sermon written as late as the year 1787, he thanks
God for the advice given to him half a century before by
Bishop Potter, namely, ' That if he wished to be exten-
sively useful, he must not spend his time in contending
for or against things of a disputable nature, but in testify-
ing against notorious vice, and in promoting real, essential
holiness.' [2]

(7) *Instinctive and Emotional Equipment.*[3] On the
basis of Dr. Drever's analysis of six specific ' instinct '
tendencies,[4] no great variety of ' drives to activity ' is
discoverable in Wesley's life. Naturally irritable though
he was,[5] there is no evidence that anger was a characteristic impulse. Pugnacity rarely emerges in his dealing
with difficult situations. The chief manifestation of this
tendency is in controversy on points of administration or
theology.[6] Apparently without fear in the face of angry
and hostile crowds, he was the victim of superstitious
fears,[7] and he had a landsman's fear of the sea.[8] Wesley's
most dominant impulse of the ' fear ' type in later life

[1] Watson, *P.S.B.* p. 402.
[2] *W.W.* vol. vii. p. 176.
[3] Watson, *P.S.B.* p. 399.
[4] Drever, J., *I.M.* p. 173.
[5] Tyerman, *op. cit.* vol. iii. p. 659.
[6] See *J.W.J.* vol. i. p. 435.
[7] *J.W.J.* vol. i. p. 435.
[8] *Ibid.*

was his fear of sin as an offence against the moral law of God. Self-abasement seems in the case of Wesley to have been entirely limited to his attitude in self-examination as in the presence of God. He made little of his aristocratic ancestry, and never used the Wellesley coat of arms, but he was at his ease in any society. His preference for the company of the boys of the lower forms at the Charterhouse when challenged by the master one day, was explained by young Wesley, then sixteen years of age, in Milton's phrase (misquoted), ' Better to rule in hell than to serve in heaven.' [1]   ' Self-display ' [2] or personal ambition, thus indicated, may have been a subsidiary impulse traceable in his later activity.

The sense of vocation which possessed Wesley would seem to be the chief driving power in all his actions, and this must have found its source in a powerful self-sentiment. The destruction of the Epworth parsonage by fire, when John was five years old, the boy being forgotten and snatched from a bedroom window just before the roof fell in, left a family tradition that John was ' plucked as a brand from the burning.' And his mother gave him special teaching and care, with the idea that this incident marked him out as in some way a dedicated spirit. Wesley never lost the consciousness that he was the child of destiny. If it be true that ' the little human being is frequently a finished product in his fourth or fifth year, and only gradually reveals in later years what lies buried in him,' [3] the direction given to Wesley's native tendencies by his mother's training is of decisive importance in estimating his instinctive and emotional equipment.

Susannah Wesley, assisted by her husband, was the

[1] See Tyerman, *op. cit.* vol. i. p. 20.   [2] Drever, *op. cit.* p. 191.
[3] Freud, *I.L.P.* p. 298.

'sole instructor of her daughters,' and of her sons until they went to school in London. She taught them, at the age of one year, to fear the rod, and to 'cry softly.' She limited them to three meals a day, and forbade all drinking and eating between meals. All the children (there were nineteen, but nine died in infancy) were washed and put to bed by eight o'clock, and on no account was a servant allowed to sit by a child until it fell asleep. They were all taught the Lord's prayer as soon as they could talk, and repeated it every morning and night. Psalms were sung every morning when school opened, and every night when the duties of the day were ended.[1] John was peculiarly sober and studious from early childhood. To argue about a thing seemed natural to him, but curiosity rather than pugnacity is suggested. ' I profess, sweetheart,' said the rector, ' I think our Jack would not attend to the most pressing necessities of nature, unless he could give a reason for it.' [2] Such was the boy's devotion, that his father admitted him to the Communion Table when he was only eight years old.

Wesley's childhood, thus generally described in Tyerman's *Life*, was dominated by two ideas concerning his future. He was taught to regard himself as set apart for a divinely appointed task; and the strong Puritan and Anglican tradition of his ancestors was ingrained into his thought and life by a system as rigid and regular as the hours of his meat and drink. The element of suggestion in all this is apparent, as is also the repression of the play-impulse and of the buoyant joy of childhood. Wesley inevitably developed along the normal lines of psycho-

[1] Tyerman, *L.T.W.* i. 17. See also Mrs. Wesley's letter, *J.W.J.* iii. 34-9.

[2] Clarke's *Wesley Family*, vol. ii. p. 321, quoted by Tyerman, *L.T.W.* vol. i. p. 18.

logical growth. Instinctive behaviour was modified by
incidental pains and pleasures. The rewards and punishments of the social environment were administered by his
mother, behind whom was the collective moral judgment
of a religious society of indefinable vastness. The unusual
feature in Wesley's childhood is the quickness with which
he passed these stages, and the further stage in which
conduct is controlled by the anticipation of social praise
and blame, and decided his conduct by his own ideal of
right, regardless of the praise or blame of his immediate
social environment.[1] While it is true that no individual
can make a conscience for himself, and always needs a
society to make it for him,[2] still, in the case of Wesley,
society, represented by Susannah Wesley, enabled him
to absorb the moral tradition, and to give evidence of
independent ethical judgment at a very early age. ' If
asked, out of the common way of meals, to have, for
instance, a piece of bread or fruit, he would answer with
the coolest unconcern, " I thank you ; I will think of
it." ' [3] Thus at the age of six, John Wesley had attained
a high degree of self-control, and a self-sentiment [4] which
was already identified with his family, home and Church.
This self-sentiment, expanded to include the judgments,
emotions and social sentiment of the Church, and later, of
his own Societies, was the driving power dominating
Wesley's character, and the organizing influence in his
instinctive and emotional life.

Susannah Wesley died in 1742, when John Wesley was
thirty-nine years of age. He was very strongly attached

[1] See McDougall, W., *S.P.* p. 181.
[2] See Green, T. H., *Prolegomena to Ethics*, chap. iii.
[3] Tyerman, *op. cit.* vol. i. p. 18.
[4] Drever, James, *I.M.* p. 217, and chapter ix *passim*.

to her.   Soon after leaving home, he wrote to her in terms
of pathetic endearment, expressing the hope that he
might die before her, in order to escape the anguish of
witnessing her death.[1]   He wrote to her for advice on all
critical matters concerning his own life.   A full account
of his evangelical conversion was written and read to her·
And the detailed record of his relations with Sophia
Hopkey in Georgia was probably written for his mother·
All John Wesley's attempts at courtship seem to have
been influenced by Susannah Wesley as his ideal of
womanhood.   One pathetic feature of the Georgia episode
is his effort to dragoon ' Miss Sophy ' into his mother's
image.   It is not yet proved that there is ' no clear-cut
difference between the nature of early filio-parental
affection and that of the later loves of adolescent and
adult life.' [2]   But the probability must be recognized
that the personality of Susannah Wesley combined with
her son's self-sentiment in preventing his achieving a
successful marriage, and thus, indirectly, in diverting all
the complex sources of energy grouped under the sex
and parental instincts into the channels of his main
life work.

   (8) *Personal Bias and Peculiarities.*[3]   On several occasions Wesley found himself in conflict with the modes of
reacting which had become habitual through his early
religious training.   His refusal to accept the living at
Epworth, which would have secured the old home for
his mother and three unmarried sisters when his father's
health was failing, reveals the consciousness of a new
sentiment of value gathering around the little group of

[1] Brigden, T. E., ' John Wesley ' in *N.H.M.* vol. i. p. 169.
[2] Flügel, J. C., *The Psychoanalytic Study of the Family*, p. 9.
[3] Watson, *P.S.B.* pp. 402-3.

friends at Oxford.[1]   This decision was reached in spite
of the opposition of the whole of his family, and his
action was in conflict with his own traditional reverence
for the vocation of a parish priest.   But the result was
seen in the more energetic organization of the Oxford
Methodists, which led later to the Georgia mission, and
thus to Wesley's meeting with the Moravians, and his
evangelical conversion.

A similar directness of action, in cases of conflict
between the demands of his chosen task and the traditions
of the church of his fathers, is seen in his overcoming his
distaste for field-preaching in 1738, and for lay-preaching
in 1739, and in his consecration of bishops for America,
in 1784.   Charles Wesley was shocked that his brother
should ' assume the episcopal character, ordain elders,
consecrate a bishop, and send him to ordain lay preachers.'
John replied, ' I firmly believe that I am a Scriptural
episcopos as much as any man in England or Europe.
For the uninterrupted succession I know to be a fable,
which no man ever did or can prove.' [2]   Overton's comment on this, with reference to the urgent need of America,
is that ' the true explanation of Wesley's conduct in this
matter is the intensely practical character of his mind. . .
Everything must be sacrificed for the sake of his work.' [3]

In physical appearance Wesley was not unlike his
relative, the Duke of Wellington.[4] At manhood his
height was only five feet five inches ; ' his habit of body
in every period of life the reverse of corpulent, and

---

[1] See correspondence with Wesley's father, and his brother Samuel,
throughout the year 1734.   Tyerman, *L.T.W.* i. pp. 95-8.

[2] Letter, Aug. 19, 1785.   See *W.W.* xiii. p. 240.

[3] Abbey and Overton, *The English Church in the Eighteenth Century,*
vol. ii. p. 83.

[4] Wesley's pedigree is in the Bodleian Library, MS. EL. d. 20.

expressive of strict temperance and continual exercise ; and notwithstanding his small size, his step was firm and his appearance, till within a few years of his death, vigorous and muscular.' [1] His voice had a peculiar effect in stilling riotous crowds, and he notes twice on one page of his diary that he soothed a crying child to sleep.[2] He suffered from chronic bilious catarrh, and only preserved his health by strict abstemiousness, and by constant physical exercise.[3] In person, Wesley was scrupulously neat and clean ; and his counsel to his followers is a reflection of his own habits, . . . ' Be cleanly. In this let the Methodists take pattern by the Quakers. Avoid all nastiness, dirt, slovenliness, both in your person, clothes, house and all about you. Do not stink above ground. This is a bad fruit of laziness. . . . Whatever clothes you have, let them be whole ; no rags, no tatters, no rents. These are a scandal to either man or woman, being another fruit of vile laziness. Mend your clothes, or I shall never expect you to mend your lives. Let none ever see a ragged Methodist.' [4] Wesley was equally punctilious in money matters ; insisting upon strict account keeping, and recording every penny of his own expenditure. This habit of carefulness is not unrelated to his early acquaintance with the domestic problem of his father's large household and small income. Before John was three years old his father had been thrust into gaol for debt.[5]

[1] Contemporary pen portrait, by John Hampson, Jr., Eayrs, p. 6.
[2] Extract from diary, *J.W.J.* vol. i. p. 124.
[3] *J.W.J.* vol. i. pp. 66, 413 ; *W.W.* vol. iii. p. 382 ; Tyerman, *L.T.W.* i. 28.
[4] Bradburn, *Select Letters*, pp. 80-1. Cf. *J.W.J.* vol. v. p. 118, ' avoid sloth, prodigality, and sluttishness . . . be patterns of diligence, frugality and cleanliness.'
[5] Tyerman, *L.T.W.* vol. i. p. 17.

In curious contrast with the balanced and practical
judgment which is characteristic of Wesley, is the element
of sheer superstition which he reveals throughout his
life.   At the age of sixteen, he accepted quite uncritically
the accounts of the poltergeist noises which were heard
in his father's house.   He was away from home, at the
Charterhouse School at the time, but he took the trouble
to obtain minute and detailed accounts of the incidents
from his mother, from his four sisters, and from Robin
Brown.[1]   And he transcribed his father's diary, con-
taining a record of the disturbances.[2]   He wrote to his
mother, when he was twenty years old, asking her opinion
of several ghost stories, in which he showed very deep
interest.[3]   The Epworth noises, he suggested, were
occasioned by a messenger of Satan, sent to buffet his
father for a rash vow alleged to have been made fifteen
years before.[4]   The lad's attitude indicates an adolescent
absorption in problems of the supernatural and their
relation to moral conduct.   Dr. Johnson criticised Wesley
for believing in the Newcastle ghost story on insufficient
evidence.   He added, ' Charles Wesley, who is a more
stationary man, does not believe the story.'[5]   Wesley
habitually decided important issues by the Moravian
method of casting lots.   And he used the Bible in the
manner of the Vergilian dip, sometimes with singular
success, at other times with ridiculous results.[6]   He
regarded natural phenomena as arbitrary rewards and

[1] *W.W.* xiii. 472-7.   Knocking and violent noises were heard all over
the house, and the disturbances lasted several months.

[2] Tyerman, *L.T.W.* i. p. 22.

[3] Original Letters, published in *Wesleyan Times*, 1886.   See *Life and
Times of Rev. S. Wesley*, p. 251.

[4] See *Methodist Magazine*, 1784, p. 606.

[5] Boswell, *Life of Johnson*, Oxford edition, vol. ii. p. 224.

[6] *J.W.J.* vol. ii. pp. 97 and 157-9, and *passim*.

punishments,[1] and paid great respect to physical and mental abnormality, often explaining it as the work of God or of the devil.[2] These peculiarities in mental attitude contributed to Wesley's power of making the supernatural very real to those who heard him preach. In his personal bias and habits Wesley certainly exemplifies the statement that 'an individual's outlook and point of view in dealing with many of the most important questions of human existence can be expressed in terms of the position he has taken up with regard to the problems and difficulties arising within the relatively narrow world of the family.'[3]

(9) *Love Affairs and Marriage.*[4] Wesley has been described as singularly guileless in his relations with women. He consistently advised his preachers against freedom in such friendships. The dangers of what the psycho-analysts call *positive transference*[5] were well known to Wesley. ' On this and every other occasion ' (he writes), ' avoid all familiarity with women. This is deadly poison both to them and to you. You cannot be too wary in this respect ; therefore begin from this hour.'[6] In his first diary, after spending the Christmas of 1725 at Buckland and Stanton, he added to the entries made on the Saturday night, the following queries and resolves :

> ' *Enquire* :
> Have I loved women or company more than God ?
> *Resolve* : Never to let sleep or company hinder me
> from going to prayers.
> Have I taken God's name in vain ?

[1] *J.W.J.* vol. i. p. 444 ; v. 39-40, and *passim.*
[2] *Vide infra*, chap. vi.   [3] Flügel, J. C., *op. cit.* p. 4.
[4] Watson, *P.S.B.* pp. 401-2.
[5] See Thouless, *I.P.R.* pp. 22, 27 and 246.
[6] Bradburn, *Select Letters*, p. 80. Letter dated 1769.

Resolve : Never to mention it but in religion.
Irreverent behaviour at Church ?
  Resolve : Never to laugh or talk idly there. . . .
Intemperate sleep ?
  At five.
Unclean thoughts ?
  God's omnipresence.

                        Jan. 29, 1726.[1]

These hitherto secret and unknown meditations of a
young graduate were published by Curnock with diffidence
and misgiving. But the publication of all the private
records, and the examination of the vast mass of material
printed by friends and enemies, leaves the character of
Wesley singularly clear.

The importance of this self-examination lies in the fact
that among the company were Miss Betty Kirkham and
Mrs. Pendarves, a niece of Lord Lansdowne.[2] Wesley
made no attempt to disguise his regard for Miss Betty.
And her brother, in a letter dated Feb. 1727, tells him,
' You have been often in the thoughts of M. B., which
I have curiously observed, when with her alone, by inward
smiles and sighs, and abrupt expressions concerning you.
Shall this suffice ? I caught her this morning, in a
humble and devout posture on her knees.' [3] Curnock
has discovered from the cipher diary that Wesley was in
frequent correspondence with Miss Betty under the
pseudonym of ' Varanese,' and there is an entry in the
diary for April 1732 recording a meeting with V.,
followed by a cipher ejaculation of devout gratitude.[4]
Tyerman says that she married a Mr. Wilson, and died

---

[1] Private diary No. I.   See *J.W.J.* vol. i. p. 52.
[2] *J.W.J.* vol. i. p. 52.   Tyerman, *L.T.W.* vol. i. pp. 76, 79.
[3] Letter from Robert Kirkham, *Wesleyan Times*, Feb. 26, 1866.
[4] Private diary, see *J.W.J.* vol. i. p. 16, note.

in 1731. But John Wesley saw her and was writing to her in 1732, she was on his list of correspondents in 1735-7.[1] Tyerman says, ' Nothing more is known of this incipient courtship . . . and . . . Wesley soon became too much immersed in more serious things to have time to think of wooing.'[2] This is untrue to the facts and to Wesley's mental constitution. Dr. Rigg thinks that a stern parental decree intervened.[3] Certainly, on the evidence of the diary, it was not Wesley's fault that his friendship with Miss Betty Kirkham did not lead to a life-long union. He found consolation in the correspondence with Mrs. Pendarves, but she could not take the place in his life which had been taken by their mutual friend, and the intimacy waned, first on her side, and then on his. And in 1734, Wesley closed the correspondence.

While Wesley was in Georgia,[4] Sophia Christiana Hopkey, the niece of the chief magistrate's wife, was deliberately thrown into his company, and his attachment to her altered the course of his life. Wesley's own account of their relations reveals a curious piece of self-analysis. He definitely suggested marriage to her. But, he adds, in a private document, that this ' indeed was the expression of a sudden wish, not of any formed design.'[5] Three months later, he writes, ' I was now in a great strait. I still thought it was best for me to live

---

[1] *J.W.J.* vol. i. p. 16, note.   [2] Tyerman, *L.T.W.* vol. i. p. 50.

[3] Rigg, J. H., *The Living Wesley*, p. 47.

[4] The suggestion that John Wesley should undertake a mission to the infant colony of Georgia was first made in 1735, when the Oxford Methodists were scattered ; Whitefield, though not ordained, having departed on an evangelistic tour in Gloucester, Bristol, and other places. On Oct. 14, 1735, Wesley set sail for Georgia, and he remained there two years, landing in England again on Feb. 1, 1738. His brother Charles and Benjamin Ingham, one of the Oxford group, and Charles Delamotte accompanied him.

[5] Private Journal for 29th Oct. 1736. See *J.W.J.* vol. i. p. 290.

single. And this was still my design ; but I felt the
foundations of it shaken more and more every day.
Insomuch that I again hinted at a desire for marriage,
though I made no direct proposal.   For indeed it was only
a sudden thought, which had not the consent of my own
mind.   Yet I firmly believe, had she (Miss Sophy) closed
with me at that time, my judgment would have made
but a faint resistance.   But she said " she thought it was
best for clergymen not to be encumbered with worldly
cares, and that it was best for her, too, to live single,
and she was accordingly resolved never to marry."   I
used no argument to induce her to alter her resolution.
Upon reflection I thought this a very narrow escape ;
and after much consideration, I went to Mr. Toltschig,
the pastor of the Moravians, and desired his advice,
whether I had not best, while it was yet in my power,
break off so dangerous an acquaintance.'   When Toltschig
told Wesley that he saw no reason why he should not
marry, Wesley says, ' I went home amazed to the last
degree,' and it was ' now first that I had the least doubt
whether it was best for me to marry or not, which I never
before thought would bear a question.' [1]

A month later, Wesley records in the private journal,
that, while riding with Mr. Causton, the chief magistrate,
to visit his plantation, ' I was quite struck with the
pleasantness of the situation : the hill, the river, the
woods, were delightful, and shot a softness into my soul
which had not left me when at our return he asked me to
drink a dish of tea at his house.   Soon after I came in,
Miss Sophy went out, and walked to and fro between
the door and the garden.   I saw she wanted to speak to
me, but remembered my resolutions, especially that to

[1] Private Journal.   See *J.W.J.* vol. i. p. 315.

converse with her only in Mr. Delamotte's presence. Yet after a short struggle, the evil soul prevailed in me, and I went. Immediately she catched hold of both my hands, and with the most engaging gesture, look, and tone of voice, said, . . . " There is no trusting any but a Christian. And for my part, I am resolved never to trust any one again who is not so. . . ." I looked upon her, and should have said too much had we had a moment longer. But in the instant, Mr. Causton called us in. So I was once more " snatched as a brand out of the fire." ' [1]

Wesley here gives us a clue to the understanding of his own experiences of courtship.[2] A psychological analysis of Wesley's attitude reveals the fact that the complex self-sentiment, in which was included his sense of vocation, was stronger than the single sex-appetite ; and in every case of conflict the older habits of self-criticism and reasoned decision asserted themselves. There was a continual inhibition of instincts by habits,[3] and the habits which dominated Wesley's conduct in all these critical moments are symbolized by the phrase, ' snatched as a brand from the burning.' This prophetic phrase dates from his fifth year, and sums up all that was involved in his home training, and in his belief that he was schooled by a mysterious Providence, and destined for a special spiritual task. The difficulty of reconciling these factors in his self-sentiment with thoughts of marriage was rendered more complex by the fact that Wesley was living in the mental atmosphere of Locke's philosophy, with its distrust of native activities, and its tendency to emphasize the possibilities inherent in practice and habit-

---

[1] Private Journal. See *J.W.J.* vol. i. p. 328.
[2] Drever, James, *I.M.* p. 190.
[3] See James, Wm., *P.P.* vol. ii. p. 394.

acquisition. Hence it was that, after the curious submitting of the question to the Lord by casting lots, when the
lot came out, ' Think of it no more,'—at which Wesley was
able to say cheerfully, ' Thy will be done,'—he came to
regard the impulse to speak with Miss Sophy as ' the evil
soul,' and blamed the landscape which ' shot a softness into
my soul.' The ' sudden thought ' must have the ' consent
of his own mind.'

This piece of self-analysis illustrates the difference
between inhibition and repression of instincts. The evil
of repression arises from the fact that it is a refusal of
direct attention, which forces the impulse into disguise
and concealment, where it enacts its own uneasy private
life subject to no inspection and no control. There is a
wholesome directness and an open confrontation of
instinctive tendencies with all their implications, evident
in Wesley's behaviour, that differs entirely from the
damming up and ignoring of impulses which is the cause
of pathological conditions. ' The evil of checking impulses is not that they are checked. Without inhibition
there is no instigation of imagination, no redirection into
more discriminated and comprehensive activities.' [1]

The apparent inevitability of these inhibitions of instinct
by habit must not be allowed to disguise the fact that they
involved a marked affective element. Describing his
interview with Miss Sophy after she was betrothed to
Williamson, Wesley speaks of the ' complication of
passions and tumult of thought which I then felt : fear of
her approaching misery, and tender pity ; grief for my
own loss ; love shooting through all the recesses of my
soul, and sharpening every thought and passion . . . I came
home and went into my garden. I walked up and down,

[1] Dewey, J., *H.N.C.* pp. 165-6.

seeking rest and finding none. From the beginning of my life to this hour I had not known one such as this. God let loose my inordinate affection upon me, and the poison thereof drank up my spirit. I was as stupid as if half awake, and yet in the sharpest pain I ever felt. To see her no more : that thought was as the piercings of a sword ; it was not to be borne, nor shaken off. I was weary of the world, of light, of life. Yet one way remained, to seek after God—a very present help in time of trouble. And I did seek after God, but I found Him not. I forsook Him before : now He forsook me. I could not pray. Then indeed the snares of death were about me ; the pains of hell overtook me. Yet I struggled for life ; and though I had neither words nor thoughts, I lifted up my eyes to the Prince that is highly exalted, and supplied the place of them as I could : and about four o'clock He so far took the cup from me that I drank so deeply of it no more.' [1] Wesley always regarded this as one of the most sorrowful days of his life. His cipher diary for the day reads thus :

4 Private prayer, prayer, diary, $\frac{3}{4}$ private prayer.
5 Meditation, Prayers.
6 Coffee, conversed, $\frac{1}{2}$ Clement.
7 Within with Mrs. Ann, $\frac{3}{4}$ with Mrs. Bush.
8 Within, $\frac{1}{2}$ Clement.
9 Clement, $\frac{3}{4}$ Logic.
10 Mrs. Causton's, in talk with her. Miss Sophy to be married ; meditation.
12 At the Lot, within with her, quite distressed !
1 Within. Confounded !
2 Took leave of her, $\frac{1}{2}$ at home. Could not pray !
3 Tried to pray, lost, sunk.

[1] Private Diary. See *J.W.J.* vol. i. pp. 334-5.

4 Bread, conversed with Delamotte. Little better !
5 Mr. Causton came, in talk, tea.
6 Kempis ; Germans. Easier !
7 Prayers.
8 Miss Sophy et cetera, $\frac{1}{2}$ within with her, $\frac{3}{4}$ with Delamotte, prayer.
  No such day since I first saw the sun !
  O deal tenderly with Thy servant !
  Let me not see such another ! [1]

Forty-nine years after, Wesley wrote, referring to this event, ' I remember when I read these words in the Church at Savannah, " Son of man, behold I take from thee the desire of thine eyes with a stroke," I was pierced through as with a sword, and could not utter a word more.' [2]
The similarity of the reaction here, and indeed of the whole situation, to that thirteen years later in the case of Grace Murray, who has been described as John Wesley's last love,[3] is accentuated by his use of the same text of Scripture. Four days after Grace Murray's marriage to John Bennet, Wesley wrote, ' Then was the word fulfilled, " Son of man, behold I take from thee the desire of thine eyes at a stroke ; yet shalt thou not lament, neither shall thy tears run down." The fatal irrecoverable blow was struck on Tuesday last.' [4]   Dr. Leger, whose book is a special study of this last love affair, concludes, ' For God was, after all, the only absorbing passion of John Wesley. And it is not a little significant that this, the account of probably his most fervent attachment to a creature,

[1] Cipher Diary. See *J.W.J.* vol. i. p. 330.
[2] *W.W.* vol. xiii. p. 118. See also Tyerman, *L.T.W.* vol. i. p. 149.
[3] Leger, J. Augustin, D.Litt., *John Wesley's Last Love.*
[4] Oct. 7, 1749. See *W.W.* vol. xiii. p. 155, and Tyerman, *op. cit.* vol. ii. p. 54.

should, on the whole, enhance our idea of his all-sacrificing, self-sacrificing devotedness to his supernatural mission.'[1]

Immediately following this Grace Murray episode, Mrs. Vazeille appears in the London group of Methodists, and in Feb. 1751, John Wesley was married to her. His own reason for taking this step is given in his *Journal*, ' Having received a full answer from Mr. Perronet, I was clearly convinced that I ought to marry. For many years I remained single, because I believed I could be more useful in a single than in a married state. . . . I now as fully believed, that in my present circumstances I might be more useful in a married state ; into which, upon this clear conviction, and by the advice of my friends, I entered a few days after.'[2]

If Tansley's analysis of the three centres of interest in the sex ' complex '[3] is accepted, there is good ground for concluding that none of the three had any part in the marriage of John Wesley. The primitive biological basis was practically ruled out by the fact that Wesley married a middle-aged wealthy widow with four children. Intellectual intercourse between the scholar and the widowed servant girl who showed no interest in his pursuits was impossible. Further, the domestic ' complex ' was inconceivable on both sides, because her interests were with her own children, and his were with his societies all over the kingdom. Marriage was apparently a blundering attempt to avoid the recurrence of anguish caused by Wesley's love affairs, and, on the side of his work, to secure the Methodist movement against the scandal which such incidents inevitably aroused.

[1] Leger, J. Augustin, *op. cit.* p. 278.
[2] *J.W.J.* Feb. 2, 1751, vol. iii. pp. 513-6, and note.
[3] Tansley, A. G., *N.P.* pp. 249-250.

The consequences pathologically for Wesley were not nervous and emotional breakdown, but an inability to see the significance of his own marriage. Crippled by an accident, he was compelled to kneel whilst preaching, for the first fortnight of his married life, and then, ' tolerably able to ride, though not to walk,' [1] he set out for Bristol, leaving his newly married wife behind him. After his Conference at Bristol, he returned to London, and left again five days later, accompanied by his wife. At this time he wrote in his *Journal*, ' I cannot understand how a Methodist Preacher can answer it to God, to preach one sermon, or travel one day less, in a married, than in a single state. In this respect, surely, " it remaineth, that they who have wives be as though they had none." ' [2] Holding such views, and having married for reasons which have no relation to the marriage state, Wesley violated biological laws,[3] if not moral laws, and in consequence he suffered thirty years of varying degrees of mental strain and misery.

' Perversion' appears in the case of his wife, who was violently jealous. John Hampson, senior, is reported to have said to his son, ' Jack, I was once on the point of committing murder. Once, when I was in the north of Ireland, I went into a room, and found Mrs. Wesley foaming with fury. Her husband was on the floor, where she had been trailing him by the hair of his head ; and she herself was still holding in her hand venerable locks which she had plucked up by the roots. I felt as though

---

[1] *J.W.J.* Mar. 4, 1751, vol. iii. 516.
[2] *J.W.J.* Mar. 19, 1751, vol. iii. p. 517.
[3] Compare Whitefield, who said when proposing marriage, ' I bless God. . . . I am free from that foolish passion which the world calls love.' His marriage was a failure (Lecky, *op. cit.* p. 86). Cf. *N.H.M.* i. pp. 265-6.

I could have knocked the soul out of her.' [1] Wesley was absorbed in his work ; his wife was jealous of his friendships, and by libel and forgery she blackened his character, and attempted to ruin his career.[2] Their attempts at reconciliation were never successful,[3] and when, in 1771, she left him for a time, Wesley entered in his *Journal*, ' For what cause I know not, my wife set out for Newcastle, (to her married daughter) purposing " never to return." Non eam reliqui : non dimisi : non revocabo.' [4] Her death (October, 1781) is recorded thus in his *Journal*, ' I came to London and was informed that my wife died on Monday. This evening she was buried, though I was not informed of it till a day or two after.' [5]

The whole of this experience is best understood in the light of the Georgia story. As spiritual guide to Sophia Hopkey, Wesley had attempted to make a girl of nineteen years live by the discipline of Susannah Wesley and the rules of Jeremy Taylor. Meanwhile he drifted into the conflict between instinct and habit which has been described. But as in the later case of Grace Murray, he allowed the situation to develop in dissociation from his self-sentiment. He always regarded his love-affairs as an intrusion, and never flung his whole personality into the issue. Yet when another stepped in, he was overwhelmed with grief, the sources of which were in native capacities that he had not until then faced and measured. Then, confronting them with the clearest understanding, and while still torn by conflicting habit and tendency, his critical judgment and his intuitive judgment decide that he is

---

[1] Private MSS. See Hampson, vol. ii. p. 127 ; Tyerman, *L.T.W.* i. 110-111.

[2] See Eayrs, *Letters of John Wesley*, p. 445, and refs.

[3] See Eayrs, *op. cit.* pp. 353-8.

[4] *J.W.J.* vol. v. pp. 399-400.   [5] *J.W.J.* vol. vi. p. 337.

'snatched as a brand from the burning.' This is the dictum of the self-sentiment which ruined his marriage.

(10) *Balancing Factors*.[1] Renunciation never left Wesley unadjusted for more than a short time. He quickly recovered mental harmony by turning to intense activity, and thus avoided serious emotional or nervous breakdown. A furious study of Jeremy Taylor and William Law followed Wesley's visits to Stanton Rectory and his conversations with Miss Betty Kirkham. And when renunciation became inevitable, Wesley became a Methodist in great and small. His correspondence with Mrs. Pendarves aroused an emotion which, he says, resembled ' that with which my heart frequently overflowed in the beginning of my intercourse with our dear V.'[2] But the real balancing factor in his first great disappointment was the intense religious life of the Oxford Methodists.

The private diary for the days following Wesley's break with Sophia Hopkey gives details indicating the stages by which mental balance was restored. The black day was March 9, 1737. Ten days later he was busy working at hymns, and he writes,[3]

Sat. 19.   7 Hymns.
          8 Hymns.
          9 Made verse.
         10 Verse.
         11 Writ verse, $\frac{1}{2}$ Mrs. Woodruffe, within, Mrs. Burnside's, within.
         12 Dinner, in talk, $\frac{3}{4}$ Verse.
          1 Visited. They seemed affected.
          2 Catechised, $\frac{1}{2}$ Verse.
          3 Verse.

[1] Watson, J. B., *P.S.B.* pp. 403-5.
[2] Letter to Mrs. Pendarves. See Rigg, *Living Wesley*, p. 52.
[3] Private cipher diary. See *J.W.J.* vol. i. pp. 339-340.

> Tues. 22. 8 Walked, verse, sung.
>   9 Made verse, sung.
>   10 Verse, sung.

Obviously his verses were hymns, and were tested as he wrote them by singing. From this point in the diary, singing comes in regularly. On April 20, Wesley wrote his famous letter to Mrs. Chapman on ' Christian Cheerfulness.' [1] The significance of several varied entries which follow may be exaggerated, but they serve to illustrate Wesley's behaviour.[2]

> 1737, April 25th. Read Paradise Regained.
>   May   5th. Played upon the flute for an hour.
>   May   14th. Felling trees.
>   May   18th. Played flute 25 minutes.
>   May   26th. Felling trees.
>   June 13th. Verses, walking as he composed.
>   July   9th. Collected hymns.

The last entry points to the fact that he was preparing to publish a second collection of ' Psalms and Hymns.'

Beneath all these activities and the conscious direction of his energies, Wesley was subject to ' unaccountable apprehensions of I know not what danger.' He experienced a ' strange terror of death ' on the voyage home. And in surveying the lessons of his life in Georgia, he writes, ' What have I learned of myself in the meantime ? Why, what I least of all suspected, that I, who went to America to convert others, was never myself converted to God.' [3] Wesley's own comment on this entry, made at a later date, is ' I am not sure of this.' But at the time the doubt was genuine, and it was not

---

[1] *J.W.J.* vol. i. p. 343 ; *Works*, vol. xii. p. 44-5.
[2] *J.W.J.* vol. i. pp. 351-364.   [3] *J.W.J.* vol. i. p. 422.

resolved until, through his own spiritual development, he came to that conversion experience in the April of the following year when his heart was ' strangely warmed.' [1]

Various other elements entered into the mental processes by which Wesley found surcease from emotional strain in times of trouble. His voluminous correspondence on religious matters with his converts, especially among intelligent and educated women, provided some compensation for his lack of a wife who could be a mental and spiritual mate. As Wesley had no family, his parental emotion was diffused throughout his societies, and his converts were his children by spiritual adoption. Whenever there were difficulties which could not be overcome, he found relief in engrossing work. Every experience was estimated by its relation to his chosen task. When speaking of his marriage, ' He repeatedly told me,' writes Henry Moore, ' that he believed the Lord overruled this painful business for his good ; and that, if Mrs. Wesley had been a better wife, he might have been unfaithful in the great work to which God had called him, and might have too much sought to please her according to her own views.' [2] Thus his work and human intercourse were balancing factors in his instinctive and emotional life. But, in the last resort, Wesley's self sentiment was grounded in God. The immediate intuition of reality which he experienced after the Georgia tragedy, in his conversion, was the source of that certainty of himself and of his destiny which never thereafter left him.

[1] *J.W.J.* vol. i. p. 476.
[2] Moore, Henry, *Life of Wesley* (1824-5), vol. ii. p. 175.

IV

WESLEY'S RELIGIOUS SENTIMENT

THE specific type of religious experience which is characteristic of early Methodism was identical in its psychological factors with the experience of John Wesley. A study of his religious development and of his conversion will therefore indicate the essential nature of the spiritual crisis in the individual life which gave to the Methodist Revival its distinctive character. For this purpose we must turn to more comprehensive categories of psychology than are provided by Behaviourism.

If we accept Mr. Shand's special use of the word ' sentiment,' [1] Wesley's religious experience is best described for psychological purposes as the organization of his religious sentiment. In its simplest form, a sentiment may be defined as ' an organized system of emotional tendencies centred about some object.' [2] Such centres of interest have been described as complexes ; but it is preferable to reserve the term ' complex ' for abnormal or pathological tendencies. [3] A fairly simple fear-complex is that of the man who was kept under disciplinary dread of the police in his childhood, and who as he grew older unwittingly repressed this early fear, so that it was completely forgotten, yet the complex was manifest in

---

[1] Shand, *F.C.* Bk. I. ch. iv-v.

[2] McDougall, W., *S.P.* p. 122 ; *O.P.* p. 432.   [3] *Vide infra*, pp. 95-6.

the fact that he could never restrain an involuntary shudder when he came upon a policeman unawares. On the other hand, an interest in Beethoven or in growing roses may become a sentiment, gathering around it ' all the emotions, thoughts, volitional processes and qualities of character which are of advantage to it for the attainment of its ends.' [1] A sentiment is distinguished from instinctive tendencies in two ways. Instincts are innate : they are a part of our native endowment ; but the sentiment is a product of experience.[2] Moreover, instinct depends upon the perceptual consciousness for its stimulus, while a sentiment may become active apart from any perceptual situation.[3] In this way the popular notion of a ' religious instinct ' is disposed of. Instincts depend upon perceptions, while the object of the religious sentiment is conceptual or in the world of ideas. In the formation of character, a sentiment, if it is frequently active, tends to develop in strength and complexity, as in the case of Wesley, co-ordinating and organizing his emotions, thoughts and activities, and directing his natural impulses, so that all the wealth and variety of his energy are unified in its system.

There are three well-marked stages in the religious development of Wesley, which he has defined in his diaries and journals. The first is the period from his earliest childhood up to the year 1725 ; the second is from the year 1725 to 1738 ; and the third is from the time of his conversion in 1738 to the close of his life. This general description of the stages in his religious progress must be accepted as somewhat arbitrary. Important changes

[1] Shand, *op. cit.* p. 106.   [2] Drever, *I.M.* pp. 207-8.
[3] Drever, *I.M.* p. 210.

are included within each of these periods, and the characteristic features of one period are discoverable in the others with a difference only of degree. Epworth, Charterhouse, and Oxford, each with its own distinctive ' tone ' or group spirit, are included within the first. Oxford, Georgia, and London are the scenes in which the second act was unfolded. The whole history of developing Methodism up to the time of Wesley's death is included in the third act. Within this last period there were many critical moments in Wesley's experience, but these were largely changes consequent upon modifications of his doctrinal views, or of his administrative methods : they did not involve any radical alteration in his religious attitude. Wesley's introspections are, on the whole, supported by an examination of contemporary records, and the two landmarks in his religious history are his awakening in 1725, and his conversion in 1738.

The older theologians would distinguish the three stages in the ' way of salvation ' as Sin, Law, and Grace. Wesley's conventional schema of introspection would appear to justify the use of these terms as an approximately true description of his experience. Psychology, however, recognizes a variety and complexity in the facts which these simple categories do not cover.[1] ' Grace ' is a comprehensive term, and may be so defined as to include

[1] Cf. Von Hügel's triad in history, philosophy, and psychology : i. Historical-Institutional ; ii. Critical-Speculative ; iii. Mystical-Operative. See his *Mystical Element of Religion*, pt. i. chaps. i-ii. Pratt distinguishes between mystical and practical, and thus makes a four-fold scheme. See *R.C.* pp. 13-14. Dr. Caldecott holds that a six-fold discrimination is required : Traditional, Rational, Emotional, Volitional, Mystical, and Revelational. See *Modern Churchman*, Sept. 1925.
Contrast with these the parallel drawn by Spinoza between progress in religion and progress in knowledge. Sin is comparable with false opinion ; Law with reasoned opinion ; Grace with intuitive knowledge. (Short Treatise on God, Man and his well-being, ch. xix.)

Wesley's experience after conversion ; but his life before his awakening in 1725, and his conversion in 1738, cannot be adequately described by the terms ' sin ' and ' law.'

Dean Inge, in his study of Christian mysticism, points out that the mystics describe their progress in the spiritual life as marked by three familiar stages—Purgative, Illuminative, and Unitive.[1] Miss Underhill distinguishes five steps, which are described as (1) Awakening, ' the adolescent of the Infinite ' ; (2) Purgation, by Discipline ; (3) Illumination, or Vision ; (4) Mystic Death, or mortification ; (5) Union, or absorption in the Infinite. Of ' Illumination,' Miss Underhill says, ' Though this stage of growth is called by the old writers on Mysticism " the stage proper to those that be in progress," it seems *in the completeness of its adaptation to environment* to mark a ' terminal point ' of spiritual development—one of those halts in the upward march of the soul—and does, in fact, mark it for many an individual life, which never moved beyond this level of reality.'[2] Thus the first three stages only of the mystical life may be regarded as biologically normal, or as applicable to the average religious experience. The fourth and fifth stages she regards as limited to the ' great and strenuous seekers after God.'[3] Now Wesley has an undoubted place in this last category, and Miss Underhill is prepared to acknowledge his position among the pioneers of the spiritual world. But Wesley characteristically stopped short of the mystic ecstasy, and neither Mystic Death nor Union can be said to describe any experience in Wesley's life.[4] At the same time it must be admitted that

---

[1] Inge, W. R., *Christian Mysticism*, p. 10.
[2] Underhill, Evelyn (Mrs. Stuart Moore), *Mystic Way*, p. 54.
[3] Underhill, Evelyn, *Mysticism*, p. 206.
[4] The reasons for this are given later in the present chapter.

the first three stages correspond to the main lines of Wesley's religious development. Awakening, Purgation, and Illumination may be said to describe fairly accurately the crisis in 1725, the discipline during the intervening period, and the conversion in 1738.

Mr. Shand's analysis of the three principal stages in the development of character [1] is based upon a broader psychology, and enables us to relate Wesley's distinctively religious experience to the study of his behaviour contained in the previous chapter. The foundations of character are those primary emotional systems, ' in which the instincts play at first a more important part than the emotions.' [2] Some inter-organization of these systems provides, as the next step, the basis for higher and more complex systems, which we have described as sentiments. And the third and highest stage in the development of character is that in which the sentiments develop, ' for their own more perfect organization, systems of self-control, in which the intellect and will rise to a higher level than is possible at the emotional stage, and give rise to those great qualities of character that we name ' fortitude,' ' patience,' ' steadfastness,' ' loyalty,' and many others, and a relative ethics that is in constant interaction with the ethics of conscience.' Mr. Shand points out that this last stage is the most plastic, so that it is in constant state of flux in each of us. And in estimating the character of men, our judgment goes deeper than their outward success or failure, and rests upon what they have accomplished in this co-ordination of the sentiments.

In Wesley's first period, childhood and adolescence are included, and unfortunately prior to 1725 the records

---

[1] Shand, A. F., *op. cit.* p. 173.   [2] *Ibid.*

are scanty. But if the information is incomplete, it is
sufficient to form a basis for certain conclusions as to
Wesley's progress in character and religion. We have
seen that the discipline of his mother's régime was responsible in his infancy for a repression of the instinct
for play and of the expansive emotion of joy. The mirth
and buoyancy of childhood were cut out of his life.
Apparently the removal from the home circle to the
Charterhouse School led to various relaxations. ' Outward
restraints being removed, I was much more negligent
than before, even of outward duties, and almost continually guilty of outward sins, which I knew to be such,
though they were not scandalous in the eyes of the
world.' [1] Instincts were more compelling than emotions
and traditions. But, as evidence that the traditional
and moral elements were not forgotten, Wesley continues,
' However, I still read the Scriptures, and said my prayers
morning and evening. And what I now hoped to be
saved by was, (1) not being so bad as other people ; (2)
having still a kindness for religion ; and (3) reading the
Bible, going to church, and saying my prayers.' [2] Wesley's
' sins,' both at Charterhouse, and later at Oxford, were,
at the most, card-playing and the diversions of a youth
who was very much above the average level in moral
ideals and principles. Mr. A. D. Godley, who was a
genial critic, refers to the period 1714-1760 at Oxford
as ' the dark age for most colleges.' [3] Gibbon, writing
almost as a contemporary of Wesley, says, ' The schools
of Oxford and Cambridge were founded in a dark age of
false and barbarous science ; and they are still tainted

[1] *J.W.J.* vol. i. p. 466.   [2] *J.W.J.* vol. i. p. 466.
[3] Godley, A. D., *Oxford in the Eighteenth Century* (1908), p. 17.

with the vices of their origin.' [1]   The Methodists in the
University represent a revolt against the prevailing moral
and religious standards, and there is no evidence that
Wesley ever shared in any pursuits which flagrantly
violated the moral tradition in which he had been trained.

At the age of twenty-two, an event occurred which
changed the course of Wesley's life, leading him to a higher
and more complex spiritual experience, and eventually
through his character determining certain important
features in the constitution of Methodism.   Wesley writes,
' The providence of God directing me to Kempis's Christian
Pattern, I began to see that true religion was seated in the
heart.'   And, he continues, ' meeting likewise with a
religious friend, which I never had till now, I began to
alter the whole form of my conversation, and to enter
upon a new life.' [2]   This has been sometimes regarded as
Wesley's conversion,[3] but it is more correctly described
by Miss Underhill's term, ' awakening.'   Curnock has
proved that the Providence of God, in this case, operated
through the agency of the ' religious friend,' and that this
friend was Miss Betty Kirkham,[4] who also, a little later,
introduced Wesley to the works of Jeremy Taylor and
William Law.   Thus behind the intense and ascetic
discipline which Wesley from this time began to impose
upon himself, there was the instinctive and emotional
drive of a friendship with a highly gifted woman.

Wesley's own account of the beginning of this second
period indicates clearly what are its main characteristics.
He says, speaking of the influence of à Kempis, ' I began

[1] Gibbon, Edward, *Autobiography*, p. 37 (World's Classics).
[2] *J.W.J.* vol. i. pp. 466-7.
[3] Leger, J. Augustin, *La Jeunesse de Wesley*.   See also Eayrs, *op. cit.* p. 41.
[4] *J.W.J.* Introduction, vol. i. pp. 12-16.   *Vide supra*, pp. 61-2.

to see that true religion was seated in the heart, and that God's *law* extended to all our thoughts as well as words and actions.' [1]   And, referring to Law's *Christian Perfection* and *Serious Call to a Devout and Holy Life*, he says, ' Although I was much offended at many parts of both, yet they convinced me more than ever of the exceeding height and breadth and depth of the *law* of God.   The light flowed in so mightily upon my soul, that everything appeared in a new view.   I cried to God for help, and resolved not to prolong the time of obeying Him as I had never done before.   And by my continued endeavour to keep His whole *law*, inward and outward, to the utmost of my power, I was persuaded that I should be accepted of Him, and that I was even then in a state of salvation.' [2] The significance of this passage for the interpretation of the second period lies in the recurring emphasis on the word ' law.'

Allowing for the conventional and scriptural theology which forms the unconscious groundwork of this introspection, the facts of Wesley's life from 1725 to 1738 as revealed more in the private diary than in the *Journal,* are an almost wearisome corroboration of his own interpretation of the period.   In Wesley's religion at this time there was neither the natural joy and good spirits which occasionally emerged in his earlier days, nor the radiant cheerfulness of his later evangelical experience.   He was gifted with a genial temperament, but the repression of his childhood days made him a ready disciple of the austere and ascetic teachings which are to be found by those who seek in the pages of à Kempis and William Law. All the healthy and expansive tendencies of joy were severely checked, and the morbid symptoms which

---

[1] *J.W.J.* vol. i. p. 466.   [2] *J.W.J.* vol. i. p. 467.

result from early repression became apparent. Every
Saturday night he held inquisition on his own soul ; he
read his rules and resolutions,[1] examined his conversation,
studies and amusements, and brought all his most secret
motives and emotions to the bar of his conscience. He
had no mercy. No excuse or plea in extenuation was
ever entered. When the record was more humiliating
than usual, his only remedy was a pathetic strengthening
of the outward standard, or a new emphasis on an old
rule, and always the entry $\kappa.\beta.$ or $\kappa\acute{v}\rho\iota\epsilon$ $\beta o\acute{\eta}\theta\epsilon\iota.$[2] He
refers occasionally to brief moments of sensible comfort
or passing joy, and he regards these as anticipations of
future happiness. But it is sufficiently clear that this
stage, which has given us the first private diary, and of
which we have fuller introspective records than of any
later stage, was one in which the chief emotion was fear.
And on the intellectual side, the dominant conception of
the object of his religious sentiment was that of a law-giver
and judge. Justification in the sight of God was to be
achieved by bringing one's life into harmony with absolute
legislation. There was no hint of that gracious personal
relation between the human and the divine which is set
forth, for example, in the story of the Prodigal Son.
Miss Kirkham had directed Wesley to monastic and
Puritan ideals. His friend Clayton [3] had turned Wesley's
attention to the ancient ascetic practices of the Christian
Church. It remained for the Mystics and the Moravians
to re-discover for him the pages of the New Testament.

The nature of the fear which was characteristic of the

---

[1] Based on Jeremy Taylor's *Rules and Exercises of Holy Living* . . .
and . . . Holy Dying (1650-51).

[2] See Curnock's Introduction, *J.W.J.* vol. i. pp. 34-5.

[3] See *J.W.J.* vol. i. p. 100-101 ; vol. viii. pp. 275-281.

discipline period must be distinguished from primitive and instinctive fears. Wesley never manifests the elementary fear of suffering, or the fear of death and hell. On the voyage out to Georgia, having observed how soon the awe inspired by the storm disappeared, he writes, ' For the future, I will never believe them to obey from fear who are dead to the motives of love.' [1] In his preaching, Wesley was always sparing in the use of fear as a motive. The four volumes of his sermons, which form part of the doctrinal standard of the Methodist Church, [2] contain no sermon on hell, nor indeed on heaven. The only sermon of Wesley's on hell is an elaborate argument, illustrated by many quotations and classical allusions which stamp it as an early academic exercise. [3] The root of Wesley's fear was the danger of loss to his essential self through what he conceived as the just anger of the judge of all the earth. The moral law of the universe was represented in the person of God as the law-giver, and as the judge who administers eternal justice ; and Wesley's discipline period was haunted by fears which were inherent in his theological conceptions and in his moral character. [4]

The volitional and practical side of Wesley's nature was revealed, and, paradoxically, his growing social sentiment was strengthened by his excursion into mysticism. He writes, ' Soon after, a contemplative man convinced me more than I was convinced before, that outward works are nothing, being alone ; and in several conversations instructed me how to pursue inward

---

[1] *J.W.J.* vol. i. p. 139. [2] See *W.W.* vol. viii. p. 318.
[3] *W.W.* vol. vi. pp. 360-370.

[4] According to Wesley, ' The law of God is supreme, unchangeable reason ; it is unalterable rectitude ; it is the everlasting fitness of all things that are or ever were created.' *W.W.* v. p. 412.

holiness, or a union of the soul with God.' [1] Under the
influence of this ' contemplative man,' he began to make
a careful study of mysticism. In November 1736, he
wrote to his brother Samuel from Georgia, asking his
opinion upon a short scheme of the doctrines of the
mystic writers, which he had drawn up. He wrote also,
in the same letter, ' I think the rock on which I had the
nearest made shipwreck of the faith was the writings
of the mystics : under which term I comprehend all,
and only those, who slight any of the means of grace.'
After asking for his brother's ' thoughts upon it,' he
adds, ' Give me them as particularly, fully, and strongly
as your time will permit. They may be of consequence,
not only to this province, but to nations of Christians yet
unborn.' [2] In his meditations, written on the return
voyage from America, in Jan. 1738, he writes, ' All the
other enemies of Christianity are triflers ; the Mystics are
the most dangerous of its enemies. They stab it in the
vitals ; and its most serious professors are most likely
to fall by them.' [3]

James distinguishes four marks of the mystical experience : Ineffability, Noetic Quality, Transiency,[4] and
Passivity. The fourth of these seems to mark the point
at which Wesley rejected extreme mysticism. He believed,
rightly or wrongly, that mysticism taught a doctrine of
God, and of union with God, which destroyed the dignity
and minimized the value of human personality. In his

[1] *J.W.J.* vol. i. pp. 468-9. It is uncertain whether the ' contemplative man ' was Law, or Gambold, or Hoole.

[2] Priestley's Letters. Quoted Tyerman, *L.T.W.* vol. i. pp. 133-4.

[3] *J.W.J.* vol. i. p. 420. Cf. vol. vii. pp. 457-8.

[4] Transiency.—' Mystical states cannot be sustained for long. Except
in rare instances, half an hour, or at most an hour or two, seems to be
the limit beyond which they fade into the light of common day ' (James,
V.R.E. p. 381).

criticisms of the mystics, Wesley writes in the spirit
of Locke and of the age of reason. He distrusts
'enthusiasm,' the 'inner light,' and the 'fondling, amorous'
language and symbolism which characterized both the
poetry and the prose of the mystic writers. ' The doctrine
of " stillness," the negative Passivity, which makes
Eckhart [1] and Tauler [2] use language curiously similar
to that of Hegel, is not a doctrine of Methodism.' [3]
Quietism influenced Wesley through his reading of Molinos,[4]
Madame Guyon [5] and Fénelon,[6] but he rejected its
extreme interpretation by Molther [7] and the Moravians.
Molther taught that the way to attain faith was ' to sit
still, not to use (what we term) the means of grace ; not
to go to Church; not to communicate; not to fast; not to
use much private prayer; not to read the Scriptures; not
to do temporal good ; and not to attempt to do spiritual
good. These things I myself have heard him speak; as
I am ready to give upon oath whenever required.' [8]

The two principal factors in Wesley's rejection of this
extreme form of mysticism were his volitional and
practical predilections, and his social sentiment. He had
been taught from childhood that salvation was only
possible ' by universal obedience, by keeping all the
commandments of God ;' [9] and his strenuous efforts in
this direction are the distinguishing feature of this period

[1] 1260-1329. [2] 1290-1361.
[3] Workman, H. B., in *N.H.M.* vol. i. p. 59.
[4] Molinos, Miguel de (1640-97), *Guida Spirituale,* tr. and abridged
by Wesley, and pub. in his ' Christian Library,' 1754, vol. 38. See
J.W.J. i. p. 104, and 345, note.
[5] For Wesley's comments on her work and character, see his *J.W.J.*
vols. iii. 18, v. 382-3, vi. 130, vii. 319.
[6] Wesley's notes on Fénelon : *J.W.J.* iv. 363 ; v. 383 ; vi. 80.
[7] Molther, Philip Henry ; see *J.W.J.* vols. ii-iii *passim.*
[8] *J.W.J.* see vol. ii. pp. 328, 337, 492. [9] *J.W.J.* vol. i. p. 465.

of his life.   In his survey of his experience previous to
his conversion, given in the *Journal* for May 1738, the
important phrases are, ' set in earnest,' ' watched against,'
' began to aim at,' ' executed a resolution,' ' applied
myself,' ' continued endeavour,' and ' diligently strove.' [1]
These expressions indicate the strong volitional element ;
the higher use of the will in developing systems of self-
control, as his religious sentiment became more perfectly
organized ; and they explain the qualities of character
in Wesley's sentiment which were antagonistic to the
doctrine of quiescence or passivity.   The Oxford Methodist rule of common consultation every night,[2] the vow
made on board the ship at Cowes before sailing for
Georgia,[3] and the Society Meetings instituted in Savannah,[4]
reveal the development of an increasingly powerful
social factor, which provided Wesley with a constant
conservative criterion by which the aberrations of
mysticism were judged.

   While he rejected its extreme forms, Wesley owed a
debt to mysticism, and to its special doctrine of Quietism.
He laid stress on tranquil tarrying and spiritual quiet ;
the ' recollection ' urged by writers on prayer and on
psycho-therapy.[5]   Wesley brought into Methodism ' the
sane emphasis ' on quietness, ' which has been the great
contribution of the Friends, both the medieval Friends

---

[1] *J.W.J.* vol. i. pp. 467-8.   [2] Tyerman, *L.T.W.* vol. i. pp. 69-70.

[3] ' First : that none of us will undertake anything of importance
without first proposing it to the other three.   Second : that whenever
our judgments or inclinations differ, any one shall give up his single
judgment or inclination to the others.   Third : that in case of an
equality, after begging God's direction, the matter shall be decided by
lot.'   See *J.W.J.* vol. i. p. 127.

[4] Wesley's *Ecclesiastical History*, vol. iv. p. 175.   Quoted in *J.W.J.*
vol. i. pp. 197-205, note.

[5] Cf. Underhill, Evelyn, *The Life of the Spirit and the Life of To-day*,
pp. 95 *et seq.*

of God and the later Quakers, to the Catholic Church.'[1]
And it is notable that in the fifty volumes of his Christian
Library, Wesley included Fénelon's *Letters*, Brother
Lawrence's *Practice of the Presence of God*, Molinos'
Spiritual Guide, and the *Spiritual Letters of Juan d'Avila*.[2]
Methodism, as represented by the hymns of Charles
Wesley, even after they had been edited and pruned by
his brother's critical judgment, includes ineffability and
transiency in its songs of the religious life ; while the
noetic quality described by James is the empirical
basis of the Methodist doctrine of Assurance. 'Although
so similar to states of feeling, mystical states seem to
those who experience them to be also states of knowledge.
They are states of insight into depths of truth unplumbed
by the discursive intellect. They are illuminations,
revelations, full of significance and importance, all
inarticulate though they remain ; and as a rule they carry
with them a curious sense of authority for after-time.'[3]
This experience is common to mysticism and Methodism.

Wesley's experience throughout the whole of this
period between 1725 and 1738 is characterized by conflict,
strain, and mental discord. The necessity of that harmonizing of his inner life which he attained in conversion,
is evident in the vocabulary of his introspections : 'building on sand' ; 'I dragged on heavily' ; 'beating the
air' ; 'vile abject state of bondage' ; 'striving with,
not freed from sin.'[4] In an earlier review, written while
returning from America, he wrote, 'I had no heart, no
vigour, no zeal in obeying ; continually doubting whether

[1] Workman, H. B., *op. cit.* p. 59.

[2] Brigden, T. E., in *N.H.M.* vol. i. pp. 186-8.   See also Green's
Bibliography.

[3] James, Wm., *V.R.E.* pp. 380-1.   [4] *J.W.J.* vol. i. pp. 468-471.

I was right or wrong, and never out of perplexities and entanglements.'[1] Against these subjective estimates must be set the records of his ceaseless and strenuous activity, which fill the diaries and journals of the whole period. Traditional ordinances of the Church, the 'means of grace,' ascetic practices, fasting and rigid self-denial, unceasing charity and good works, the systematic pursuit of holiness by hourly prayer and ' pious ejaculations,' the mental prayer of the mystics, all these had been tried, and in none of them was satisfaction found. This condition of unresolved discord continued without appreciable relief until the time of Wesley's conversion.

A psychological examination of a sudden mental revolution such as Wesley's conversion usually reveals preparation for the experience by previous unconscious processes. The claims of Freud and Lipps may be exaggerated : ' The question of the unconscious in psychology is, according to the forceful words of Lipps,[2] not so much a psychological question as the question for psychology.'[3] But when he dismisses Freud's work as ' an appeal to the unknowable to explain the contradictory,'[4] Professor Pratt shows less than his usual catholicity of judgment. The morbid features and exaggerations in the theories of Freud are not discussed here, and have been dealt with by Dr. McDougall and others.[5] The effects of inhibition already considered in

[1] *J.W.J.* vol. i. p. 420.

[2] Lipps, *The Conception of the Unconscious in Psychology.* A lecture delivered at the Third International Congress on Psychology, at Munich, 1897. Quoted Pratt, *R.C.* p. 54.

[3] Freud, S., *Die Traumdeutung* (ed. 1909), p. 380.

[4] Pratt, *R.C.* p. 55.

[5] McDougall, W., *S.P.* Supplementary chapter ii, 17th ed. 1922. See also Wöhlegemuth, A., *A Critical Examination of Psycho-Analysis.*

Wesley's normal development,[1] are described by psycho-analysts as 'sublimation,' and are the healthy parallels of the pathological results of repression in nervous breakdown cases, with which Freud's clinical psychology is mainly concerned. In either case, experiences on the conscious level of activity leave their records, not in memory, but in the creation of unconscious tendencies to action, normal and abnormal. The bearing of this on the subject of conversion generally will be illustrated in a later chapter. But three factors in Wesley's experience prior to conversion involve mental processes which were not fully present to consciousness. These may be briefly described by the terms 'sublimation,' [2] suggestion, and repression.

Wesley's conversion must not be dissociated from the emotional stress of the break with Sophia Hopkey. After that frustrated love-affair, Wesley entered upon a period of uneasiness and unrest, which was never resolved until the moment of conversion. The psychoanalysts would explain John Wesley's first awakening as the result of his disappointment in the case of Betty Kirkham, and would regard his affair with Sophia Hopkey as the cause of his conversion.[3] Dr. Thouless has shown the psycho-logical weakness and absurdity of such a position.[4] And William James' note on the subject exposes some of its fallacies.[5] But on the other hand, the sex instinct is a part of the instinctive basis of religion, and as an integral part of human nature must be recognised in any study of religious experience which has a scientific purpose.

---

[1] *Vide supra*, pp. 64-5.

[2] For a definition of sublimation see Freud, *I.L.P.* p. 290.

[3] Cf. Schroeder, T., art. in *Amer. Journ. of Rel. Psych.* vol. vi.

[4] Thouless, R. H., ' Religion and the Sex Instinct,' *Psyche*, Oct. 1921.

[5] James, *V.R.E.* pp. 10-12.

Wesley's love affairs have been described in the previous chapter, with considerable fulness, because the passion of human love makes more insistent demands on mental and spiritual energy than any other instinctive impulse. As Dr. Thouless says of the mystic, ' it seems probable, indeed that the failure to find a satisfactory resting-place for his libido in a human love object is often the determining incident which turns his feet into the path which leads to mystical conversion. Pascal has left us a record of his own unsuccessful attempt to find happiness in human love in the work already quoted.[1] St. Catherine of Genoa and Madame Guyon were both extremely unhappy in their married lives before their mystical conversions.' [2] There is no empirical justification for the Freudian theory of specific mental energy ' primitively distributed among the mental complexes corresponding with the chief instincts.' [3] But among the elements which were organized in the formation of Wesley's religious sentiment, the passional side of his nature is clearly one of the initial psychological factors. The inhibition of his instinctive tendencies by his habits of reasoned decision and self-criticism,[4] diverted his capacity for intense devotion into religious channels. The facts revealed in his private diaries and journals, and already referred to,[5] show that the emotional disturbance following upon the Georgia tragedy was so deep and vital that it cannot be unrelated to the intense relief of his conversion experience, and to the remarkable forces of character which he manifested in the launching of his evangelistic campaign. And this view finds support from Wesley's own opinion, given

---

[1] Pascal, *Discourse on the Passions of Love* ; Thouless, *I.P.R.* 208.
[2] Thouless, *I.P.R.* pp. 212-13.   [3] Tansley, A. G., *N.P.* p. 88.
[4] *Vide supra*, pp. 64-5.   [5] *Vide supra*, pp. 65-7.

above, that the failure of his marriage contributed to the success of his life work.[1]

The psychology of suggestion is illustrated by the story of Wesley's relations with the Moravians. They first made it clear to him that his unhappiness and mental discord were due to a wrong attitude towards the object of his religious sentiment. This was first suggested to him by the behaviour of the Moravian missionaries and emigrants during the storm which occurred on the voyage to Georgia. Wesley and the English people were terrified, but the Germans continued the religious service in which they were engaged, and sang hymns 'without intermission.'[2] Wesley regarded this as revealing the 'difference between him that feareth God and him that feareth him not.' He sought the advice of their leader, and learned German in order to converse with them. Spangenberg asked him, 'Do you know yourself? Have you the witness within yourself? Does the spirit of God bear witness with your spirit that you are a child of God?' Wesley 'was surprised and knew not what to answer. Spangenberg observed it and asked, "Do you know Jesus Christ?" I paused and said, "I know that He is the Saviour of the world." "True," replied he, "but do you know He has saved you?" I answered, "I hope He has died to save me." He only added, 'Do you know yourself?" I said, "I do." But I fear they were vain words.'[3] From this time, the idea of 'the witness of the spirit,' or the definite consciousness of an intimate personal relationship with God through Christ, became an obsession.

[1] *Vide supra*, p. 73.   [2] Jan. 25, 1736, *J.W.J.* vol. i. p. 143.
[3] *J.W.J.* vol. i. p. 151.

These experiences explain the intimacy which Wesley cultivated, soon after arriving in England again, with a Moravian minister, named Peter Bohler, who was on his way to America as a missionary to Georgia and to Carolina. On Feb. 18, 1738, Wesley writes, ' All this time I conversed much with Peter Bohler ; but I understood him not, and least of all when he said, *Mi frater, mi frater, excoquenda est ista tua philosophia.*' [1] But on Sunday, March 5, he was at Oxford with his brother Charles, and was ' clearly convinced ' by Peter Bohler, ' in the hand of the great God,' ' of unbelief, of want of that faith whereby alone we are saved.' He immediately felt that he ought to give up preaching. ' How can you preach to others who have not faith yourself ? ' To this Bohler replied, ' Preach faith *till* you have it ; and then *because* you have it, you will preach faith.' [2] The similarity of this procedure to the practice of Coué, in prescribing the daily repetition of some formula,[3] is very apparent. By what Baudouin calls the ' law of concentrated attention,' [4] the idea suggested to Wesley in this way would tend to realize itself.

Bohler convinced Wesley, both from the pages of the New Testament and from the testimony of living witnesses that this ' faith should be given in a moment ' ; that ' a man could *at once* be thus turned from darkness to light, from sin and misery to righteousness and joy in the Holy Ghost.' When Bohler left London, Wesley entered in his *Journal*, ' O what a work hath God begun, since his coming into England ! Such an one as shall never come

---

[1] *J.W.J.* vol. i. p. 440.

[2] Coleridge remarked on this, ' Is not this *too* like, tell a lie long enough, and you will be sure to end in believing it.' See Oxford edition of Southey's *Life of Wesley* (1925), with S. T. C.'s notes.

[3] Baudouin, *S.A.* p. 227.   [4] Baudouin, *op. cit.* p. 114.

to an end till heaven and earth pass away.' [1] From
this time for several days Wesley was much depressed.
He writes, ' I was sorrowful and heavy ; being neither
able to read, nor meditate, nor sing, nor pray, nor do any
thing. Yet I was a little refreshed by Peter Bohler's
letter, which I insert in his own words.' The letter
prays, ' ut gustare et tunc videre possis, quam vehe-
menter te Filius Dei amaverit et hucusque amet, et ut
sic confidere possis in eo omni tempore, vitamque ejus in
te et in carne tua sentire. Cave tibi a peccato increduli-
tatis, et si nondum vicisti illud, fac ut proximo die illud
vincas, per sanguinem Jesu Christi. Ne differ, quaeso,
credere tuum in Jesum Christum.' [2] In his translation,
Wesley italicises ' *your* Jesus Christ.' The significant
phrases are, ' confidere' ; beware of ' incredulitas ' ;
' Ne differ, quaeso, credere ' ; nothing can offend God but
' incredulitas nostra ' ; ' crede igitur ' ; admonish one
another ' ad credendum ' ; ' permane in fidem.' Seven
times in the course of a letter of nine sentences is the
admonition to believe insisted upon. Affirmation and
repetition are part of the art of successful suggestion, and
the art of Peter Bohler is none the less perfect because it
was utterly unconscious.

At this time Wesley records a *resolve* to seek this ' true
living faith in Christ ' . . . ' (1) By absolutely renouncing
all dependence, in whole or in part, upon *my own* works
or righteousness ; on which I had really grounded my hope
of salvation, though I knew it not, from my youth up ;
(2) by adding to the *constant use* of all the other means
of grace, *continual prayer* for this very thing, justifying,
saving faith, a full reliance on the blood of Christ shed

---

[1] *J.W.J.* vol. i. pp. 459-460. See note.
[2] *J.W.J.* vol. i. p. 461.

for *me* ; a trust in Him, as *my* Christ, as *my* sole justification, sanctification, and redemption.'[1]   There is a very
apparent relation between this experience and what
Baudouin calls the ' law of subconscious teleology,'
whereby, when an end has been suggested, the ' subconscious ' finds means for its realization.   But in this,
as in the other laws of suggestion which Baudouin has
formulated, no attempt is made to express the causal
factors involved in the experience.[2]   The principle of
suggestion is not adequate to account for the facts of
Wesley's conversion.   Incidentally it may be noted that
the conflict of imagination and will which is a familiar
part of Coué's theory, does not appear to have occurred
in Wesley's case.   The *law of reversed effort*[3] is based
upon a very narrow and inadequate conception of the
will.   Resistance was offered by Wesley's mind, and he
was inclined to reject the new doctrine, but the resistance came, not from his will, but from his previous habits
of thought and belief.   He was definitely striving to
attain the new experience ; *resolving to seek it*, and
continually praying for this very thing.

The laws of suggestion depend more deeply than either
Baudouin or Coué is able or willing to acknowledge upon
hetero-suggestion, and upon causal conditions which are
only accessible to a more scientific psychology.   In the
case of Wesley, the whole of the progressive organization
of his religious sentiment is involved, including the
volitional factors already described, and intellectual and
emotional aspects of experience which were made apparent

---

[1] *J.W.J.* vol. i. p. 472.

[2] See Rivers, W. H. R., *Psychology and Politics*, p. 102, for a radical
criticism of Coué's methods.

[3] Baudouin, *op. cit.* part ii. chap. i.   Note that part of the difficulty
is due to the fact that the French *vouloir* means wish (not will).

n his conversion. And the dynamic significance of the conversion itself is directly related, not only to the suggestions of Peter Bohler, but to the Moravian and Lutheran tradition which he represented, and to the Christian Church, in which they had both been trained, and in the last resort to the New Testament, and to the personality of Jesus Christ, without which the New Testament would never have existed.

Psychoanalysis contributes to the understanding of the pathological element in Wesley's conversion. The repression which we have traced in his infancy was reinforced by his rigid self-discipline during the years 1725 to 1738, when he was attempting to conform his life to an absolute law, and to a legal conception of God. Through his own inner conflict, accentuated by the Moravian teaching, he gained a glimpse of a healthier and more normal self-development. He came to see that ' the faith which does not rely wholly upon God, but partly on exciting or disciplining its own soul, lives in valetudinarian anxiety about its spiritual health. To be perpetually feeling our own pulse is the surest way to rob ourselves of the self-forgetting vigour in which health is displayed.' [1] Consequently he was, in the days immediately preceding his conversion, abnormally sensitive to all warnings, consolations and moments of spiritual insight ; and messages peculiarly personal were recognized in all the conversations, reading, worship, and in the events of the day.

The relations of complex and sentiment are illustrated by Wesley's description of his experience on the day of his conversion. It would seem that the value of the term complex is best conserved if, following Dr. Rivers, re-

[1] Oman, John, *Grace and Personality*, p. 12.

pression is made the outstanding element in its meaning.
Both complex and sentiment are integrated systems of
mental elements, but, while both exist as largely unconscious tendencies, the complex is the result of repression
and to that degree a pathological condition, and the
sentiment is a progressive organization of emotional
systems which ultimately includes will and intelligence in
the formation of character.[1]   The tendencies in Wesley's
behaviour indicating the influence of a complex are very
marked, and will be best exhibited by an extract from his
own narrative in the *Journal*.

Wesley writes, ' I continued thus to seek it [2] (though
with strange indifference, dulness, and coldness, and
unusually frequent lapses into sin) till Wednesday,
May 24 (1738).   I think it was about five this morning,
that I opened my Testament on those words, Tὰ μέγιστα
ἡμῖν καὶ τίμια ἐπαγγέλματα, δεδώρηται, ἵνα γένησθε θείας
κοινωνοὶ φύσεως.[3]   Just as I went out, I opened it again
on these words, " Thou art not far from the kingdom
of God."   In the afternoon I was asked to go to St Paul's.
The anthem was, " Out of the deep have I called unto
Thee, O Lord : Lord, hear my voice.   O let Thine ears
consider well the voice of my complaint.   If Thou, Lord,
wilt be extreme to mark what is done amiss, O Lord, who
may abide it ?   For there is mercy with Thee ; therefore

---

[1] Freud's theory of the complex is inevitably bound up with that of
repression.   But in Jung's original use of the term, although he does
not define its meaning, the conception of complexes of presentations
toned with feeling (*gefühlsbetonte Vorstellungskomplexe*) is applied to the
structure of the normal mind.   See Jung, C. G., *Ueber die Psychologie
der Dementia Praecox*, Halle, 1907.   And compare the symposium by
Tansley, Rivers and Shand, ' The Relation of Complex and Sentiment,'
in the *British Journal of Psychology*, vol. xiii. part 2.   See Tansley,
N.P. p. 59.

[2] The ' saving faith ' referred to in the previous paragraph in the
Journal.

[3] 2 Peter i. 4.

shalt Thou be feared.   O Israel, trust in the Lord : for with the Lord there is mercy, and with Him is plenteous redemption.   And He shall redeem Israel from all his sins." '

' In the evening I went very unwillingly to a society in Aldersgate Street, where one was reading Luther's preface to the Epistle to the Romans.[1]   About a quarter before nine, while he was describing the change which God works in the heart through faith in Christ, I felt my heart strangely warmed.   I felt I did trust in Christ, Christ alone for salvation ; and an assurance was given me that He had taken away *my* sins, even *mine*, and saved *me* from the law of sin and death.   I began to pray with all my might for those who had in a more especial manner despitefully used me and persecuted me.   I then testified openly to all there what I now first felt in my heart.   But it was not long before the enemy suggested, " This cannot be faith ; for where is thy joy ? "   Then was I taught that peace and victory over sin are essential to faith in the Captain of our salvation ; but that, as to the transports of joy that usually attend the beginning of it, especially in those who have mourned deeply, God sometimes giveth, sometimes withholdeth them, according to the counsels of His own will.' [2]

The instantaneous change from ' dulness and coldness ' to the strange warmth of heart, marks the sudden rise into consciousness and consequent disappearance of the complex which had been buried by repression or dissociation. The presence of this complex was manifest in the seizing

---

[1] The Society was a Church of England society, not Moravian, though the reader was probably William Holland, a ' Congregation Elder ' in the Moravian Church.   See *J.W.J.* vol. i. pp. 475-6, note, on the reading.   But cf. Lockyer, T. F., *Religious Experience : its Reality and Value*, pp. 51-3, and *W.H.S.* vol. viii. p. 61.

[2] *J.W.J.* vol. i. pp. 472-476.

upon the chance Scripture passage as of such direct and vital significance, [1] though an element of unconscious selection may well be allowed for in that ; and in the abnormal sensitiveness to the meaning of every word of the anthem at St. Paul's. The unwillingness to go to the Society, the indifference, dulness and coldness, are symptoms of the resistance due to the system of repression, and an additional resistance would be set up by the fact that the discipline method had been so deeply identified with Wesley's self-sentiment. It is also typical of Wesley's mental attitude that he did not enter into any sudden access of joy. But this deferring of the elation led to a closer introspection, which, after a reference to recurring temptations, is recorded thus ; 'Herein I found the difference between this and my former state chiefly consisted. I was striving, yea, fighting with all my might under the law, as well as under grace. But then I was sometimes, if not often conquered ; now I was always conqueror.' [2] This is the dominant note of the new experience, and the subsequent records show a progressive integration of the instinctive and emotional factors in the formation of Wesley's character, with an increasing domination on the part of the joy and self-expansion tendencies. Wesley's mental discord and much of his unhappiness had been due to the repressions of early childhood. The natural buoyancy and delight in life which were his by temperament had been dammed up and ignored as long as he was under the influence of a legal and deistic theology. Wesley was psychologically accurate in the introspection just quoted. Conflict is lifelong. But mental discord due to repression means

---

[1] See Bernard Hart, *Psychology of Insanity*, chap. vi.
[2] *J.W.J.* vol. i. p. 477.

fighting a losing fight.   It is a segregation of vital forces
and a consequent wastage of personal power in more or
less conscious subjective strife.   But mental discord is
resolved by religious conversion.   On the pathological
side, the strange warming of heart symbolizes the emergence of repressions and the substitution of a normal for
a pathogenic conflict.[1]

A distinction must be drawn between the occasion and
the cause of conversion.   The religious explanation refers
the experience to an external dynamic.   And from the
point of view of the subject, whose distress is due to the
' sense of sin,' [2] this is the only satisfactory explanation.
' Forgiveness is a Divine miracle, something which in
its infinite marvel is inexplicable by the resources of nature
or humanity ; it presupposes the very grace and might
of the Eternal.' [3]   But this reference to an objective
reality goes beyond the scope of psychology, which is
limited to the description and interpretation of experience
in terms of the human mind and its activities.   And
from this standpoint, the experience of Wesley in the
Aldersgate Street Society can only be understood in the
light of the whole of the facts of his life up to that
moment.   Unconscious processes were maturing, by which
the old conflicts should be ended, and unification of mind
and character achieved.   But they needed the touch,
probably of emotion, in a moment of susceptibility, which
would bring them into full consciousness.   The whole
of the events of the day contributed to Wesley's sensitiveness, and the social sympathy in worship, the Lutheran

[1] See Freud, *Introd. Lectures on Psychoanalysis*, p. 110.
[2] The nature of this ' sense of sin ' will be discussed more fully in a
later chapter on conversion.
[3] Mackintosh, H. R., *The Doctrine of the Person of Jesus Christ* (1913),
p. 32.

message, the reader's voice, or a subtle and intimate process combining them all, provided the occasion. ' There are times in Alpine climbing when the stroke of an ice-axe or the shout of a climber will set an avalanche in motion. It was not the shout that was fit to move a thousand tons of snow ; it was the weight of the snow itself in equipoise so fine that the least vibration of the air could start it. So, too, thoughts and feelings gather until a word will give them life and force, to the over-throwing of spiritual dominions, principalities and powers.'[1]

The deeper significance of the conversion of John Wesley is more apparent when it is considered in relation to his religious sentiment as a whole. The instantaneous change is traceable to the release of repressions, and Wesley's experience included factors which have been described as sublimation and suggestion. But his conversion was not merely what would be psychoanalytically described as the re-orientation of the psyche ; it was the normal result of a development, conscious and unconscious, by which a powerful self-sentiment became identified, in ways too profound and secret for analysis, with a disinterested religious sentiment, the object of which was God as revealed in Christ. And into this system were woven Wesley's human passion, diverted from a satisfying human love, his filial affection, his loyalty to the Church, his social sentiment (which had developed through the Societies at Oxford, Savannah and London), and his strenuous pursuit of and passion for holiness.

Of Wesley's conversion, Lecky writes, ' It is, however, scarcely an exaggeration to say that the scene which took place at that humble meeting in Aldersgate Street forms

[1] Steven, G., *The Psychology of the Christian Soul*, p. 163.

an epoch in English history. The conviction which then flashed upon one of the most powerful and most active intellects in England is the true source of English Methodism.'[1] Lecky's use of the word ' conviction ' is important, indicating as it does the fact that the psychological origin of Methodism is not to be found in mere religious emotionalism. The system of Wesley's religious life moulded the mind of Methodism. His imperious will imparted to the movement a finely disciplined, if somewhat narrow morality. And the controlling emotion, the warming of the heart which Wesley described, touching as it did the very centre of his mental life, was associated with the attainment of a fixed idea of the nature of the Divine Being, which became the basis of Methodist doctrine.

An instructive contrast may be observed between the pages of the private Oxford diaries, and the manuscript hymn-book which was Wesley's constant companion on his evangelistic tours. The diary is a dreary account of the hopeless pursuit of a mechanical morality. There is little of rejoicing in any of the records before 1738. After Wesley's conversion, a new feature appears in the collections of hymns that he published from time to time. There is added a section entitled, ' Hymns for Believers Rejoicing.' The pages which show signs of most frequent use in Wesley's private manuscript volume are those where he found,

> ' Oh for a thousand tongues to sing,
>   My great Redeemer's praise,'

and

> ' Now I have found the ground wherein
>   Sure my soul's anchor may remain.'[2]

---

[1] Lecky, W. E. H., *History of England in the Eighteenth Century*, vol. iii. p. 48.

[2] The volume is in the Colman Collection. See also Curnock's Introduction, *J.W.J.* vol. i. p. 35.

Fear and anxiety are replaced by love and joy. The master sentiment is that of love to God, and all the fundamental emotions are co-ordinated and included within its system.

The psychological meaning of this emotional system cannot be understood except in relation to the intellectual content of the experience. This can perhaps be best indicated by turning again to the hymn-book. In November 1725, Wesley began his series of translations from the German Gesangbuch, which ultimately included the hymns of Scheffler, Lange, Gerhardt, Tersteegen, Zinzendorf, and Spangenberg. The majority of the hymns Wesley translated are in praise of the glory, goodness and mercy of God. But there is a change in his attitude, which can be illustrated by contrasting two translations : the first, made in 1737, from Lange ; the second, made in 1739, the year after his conversion, from Scheffler. The significance of the change may be sufficiently indicated by quoting the first verse of each.

> ' O God, Thou bottomless abyss !
>   Thee to perfection who can know ?
> O height immense !   What words suffice
>   Thy countless attributes to show ? '

The note of infinite divine perfection, and finite human failure pervades the whole hymn. Two years later, all Wesley's song is tuned to this new note :

> ' O God, of good the unfathomed Sea !
> Who would not give his heart to Thee,
>   Who would not love Thee with his might ?
> O Jesus, Lover of mankind !
> Who would not his whole soul and mind,
>   With all his strength, to Thee unite ? ' [1]

---

[1] *A Collection of Hymns . . . for . . . Methodists* (1769), pp. 231 and 185.

The emotional and intellectual aspects of the conversion are inseparable. The conception of God as the absolute law-giver and judge, had been replaced by a conception of God as in Christ the Redeemer and Saviour of His children. With the best of intentions, Wesley had been at war with his fate, his relations with ultimate reality had been strained almost to the point of hostility. At his conversion, this unavailing conflict gave place to reconciliation, the centre of which was a gracious personal relationship mediated through faith in Jesus Christ. And the growth of Wesley's character, its development through the stages of tradition and discipline, its attainment of mental harmony in conversion, and its place in history as the true source of English Methodism, can only be interpreted psychologically in its dependence upon this intellectual element, that is, in its essential relation to Wesley's conception of the object of his religious sentiment.

V

THE GENESIS OF THE REVIVAL

THE political, economic and social conditions which made possible the rapid growth of the Methodist movement were largely beyond the range of John Wesley's interest and vision. But he was well acquainted with the character and equipment of the national Church, and with the average level of moral and religious life, not only in the villages through his work at Wroote and Epworth, but also in the capital and in University circles. The significance of Oxford Methodism, and of Wesley's strenuous efforts along High Church lines in Savannah, lies in the fact that they indicate a vocational consciousness which centred in religion, and that they provided training for the task which awaited him after his conversion. Beginning simply in an attempt to preach in churches, in the Societies and in private houses, the truth to which his own religious experience had led him, this task evolved by unforeseen and inevitable stages. All the later developments were the result of his practical method of dealing with the difficulties and obligations inherent in the situation.

'Conversion often brings enhanced vitality, physical and mental, as well as spiritual.'[1] Wesley's behaviour

[1] Underwood, A. C., *The Psychology of Christian and Non-Christian Conversion*, Lectures at Leeds University, 1924.

immediately after his conversion exhibits a new mental autonomy and elasticity. His first convert was a condemned prisoner. Wesley and a friend prayed with the man at the Castle at Oxford, ' first in several forms of prayer, and then in such words as were given us at that hour. He kneeled down in much heaviness and confusion, having no rest in his bones by reason of his sins. After a space he rose up, and eagerly said, " I am now ready to die. I know Christ has taken away my sins ; and there is no more condemnation for me." ' [1] Three days later, Wesley was at prayer in one of the Societies, and he says, ' My heart was so full that I could not confine myself to the forms of prayer which we were accustomed to use there. Neither do I purpose to be confined to them any more ; but to pray indifferently, with a form or without, as I may find suitable to particular occasions.' [2] Tyerman suggests that Wesley's difficult experiences in Georgia had ' knocked the High Church nonsense out of him.' [3] But the truth is that, in the experience of conversion, Wesley gained an intellectual freedom such as he had never known before. And as the religious need of England became increasingly clear to him, and as his own realization of the emancipating power of his religious faith deepened, so he attained, by parallel steps, a capacity to vary his plans ; he acquired a freedom which included a new efficiency in dealing with men and movements, an ability to co-ordinate conflicting elements, and to transform or dispose of cramping or thwarting obstacles. After a discussion with his brother Charles on the nature and the fruits of faith, and on instantaneous conversion, concerning which Charles wrote, ' His obstinacy in favouring the

[1] *J.W.J.* vol. i. p. 448.   [2] *Ibid.* p. 449.
[3] Tyerman, *L.T.W.* vol. i. p. 168.

contrary opinion drove me at last out of the room,' [1] John entered in his *Journal*, ' My brother was very angry, and told me I did not know what mischief I had done by talking thus. And, indeed, it did please God then to kindle a fire which I trust shall never be extinguished.' [2] The last sentence indicates the way in which Wesley's consciousness at this time was dominated by a conviction of the vast and immeasurable significance of his experience and activity. His behaviour in relation to extempore prayer, to instantaneous conversion, and a few days later, to field preaching, together with his introspections in the *Journal*, are evidence of the new values of life and conduct for Wesley himself, which accompanied the historical beginnings of the Revival.

The Fetter Lane love-feast provides an important example of crowd psychology. ' On the first day of January, 1739, the two Wesleys, Whitefield, Ingham, Hall, and Kinchin, were present at a love-feast in Fetter Lane, with about sixty of the brethren. The year that was to witness the birth of the great Revival was commenced by them in mutual prayer. This meeting was, as Whitefield says, " a Pentecostal season indeed." Five days later they met again, to confer together as to what was best to be done. . . . They spent the day in fasting and prayer, and parted, " with a full conviction," as Whitefield says, " that God was about to do great things among them." ' [3] The reference to Pentecost gives a striking picture of the psychological unity which characterized the group. This like-mindedness is a pre-requisite of the suggestibility, emotional excitement, and absence of inhibition, which constitute a psychological crowd.

[1] *Charles Wesley's Journal*, vol. i. p. 85.   [2] *J.W.J.* vol. i. p. 456.
[3] Lelièvre, M., *John Wesley : his Life and Work*, p. 57.

The situation is deliberately compared with that described in the Book of the Acts. ' And when the day of Pentecost was fully come, they were all with one accord in one place.' [1]   It is very noticeable that in St. Luke's narrative the distinct assertion of like-mindedness comes before the description of the coming of the expected, when ' the clouds somehow burst, the old inhibitions which may have bound them to their old lives were gone, everything was surrendered to the will of God, and a tide of emotion and devoted loyalty swept over them which they had never known before, the results of which will only end with human history.' [2]

Wesley's first impression of English life after his absence in America, suggested to him the need for a revival of religion. He landed at Deal on Feb. 1, 1738, and he writes, ' After reading prayers and explaining a portion of Scripture to a large company at the inn, I left Deal, and came in the evening to Faversham. I here read prayers, and explained the Second Lesson to a few of those who were called Christians, but were indeed more savage in their behaviour than the wildest Indians I have yet met with.' [3]   Shortly after the Fetter Lane love-feast, Whitefield, during a visit to his native city of Bristol, learned that many people had said, ' If Whitefield will convert heathens, why does he not go to the colliers of Kingswood ? '   Finding his hands tied in the city by the opposition of the clergy, he decided to go to Kingswood, and on the 17th Feb. 1739, he preached to two hundred colliers from the brow of a hill. His second sermon in the open air was preached to a congregation of two

[1] Acts ii. 1.   [2] Pratt, J. B., *The Religious Consciousness*, p. 175.
[3] *J.W.J.* vol. i. p. 432.

thousand, and the numbers grew rapidly under the attraction of his emotional and rhetorical appeals.[1] A description of Whitefield's preaching appeared in the *Gentleman's Magazine* : ' On Saturday, the 18th inst., he preached at Hanham Mount to five or six thousand persons, and in the evening removed to the common, about half a mile farther, where Three Mounts and the plains around were crowded with so great a multitude of coaches, foot and horsemen, that they covered three acres and were computed at twenty thousand people.' [2] Hume described one of Whitefield's sermons, and added, ' This address was accompanied by such animated, yet natural action, that it surpassed anything I ever saw or heard in any other preacher.' [3] He also described the whole assembly as weeping, and declared that it was worth going twenty miles to hear Whitefield preach.

From Bristol, Whitefield wrote to Wesley, who had been preaching and teaching in the Societies, and in the churches in London until he was forbidden,[4] asking him to come to Bristol. ' Mr. Chapman brings a horse to London, which you may ride. I go away, God willing, next Monday se'enight. If you were here before my departure, it might be best. Many are ripe for bands. I leave that entirely to you.' [5] There was prolonged

[1] For an account of Whitefield's oratory and of the subject matter of his preaching, and its remarkable effects, see Lecky, *op. cit.* vol. iii. pp. 59-63. Cf. Doyle, J. A., *The English in America*, vol. v. pp. 232-42, for a criticism of Whitefield's preaching.

[2] *Gentleman's Magazine*, 1739, p. 162. Note that the estimate of the numbers is not Whitefield's.

[3] Hume, David ; see Gledstone's *Life of Whitefield*, pp. 378-9 ; quoted by Lecky, *op. cit.* vol. iii. pp. 62-3.

[4] Wesley's Journal for this period frequently records, *e.g.* ' Many here were, as usual, offended ' (ii. 144) ; ' I am to preach here no more ' (ii. 139).

[5] See Whitefield's letter ; Tyerman, *L.T.W.* vol. i. pp. 193-4.

discussion, concerning this invitation, at the Fetter Lane Society.[1] Charles Wesley was 'extremely averse' to his brother's going to Bristol. And a very forbidding series of Scripture passages was 'offered as often as we inquired touching the consequence of this removal'; 'And the children of Israel wept for Moses'; 'I will show him how great things he must suffer'; 'And devout men carried Stephen to his burial, and made great lamentation over him.' At last, they settled the question by casting lots, and by this method it was decided that Wesley should go to Bristol. Another dip into the Scriptures produced three more ominous passages. The Scripture references and the cipher exclamations inserted in the journal and private diary[2] for the days preceding his journey are indications of the extreme anxiety and apprehensiveness of Wesley.

The day after the lot was cast, Wesley went to Bristol met Whitefield, and heard him preach at Weavers' Hall, and in the open air at Hanham Mount and Rose Green. Whitefield departed for a tour in South Wales on Monday, April 2, 1739. 'Tongue cannot tell what a sorrowful parting we had. Floods of tears flowed plentifully; and my heart was so melted down that I prayed for them with strong cryings and many tears. The scene was very affecting, and, I think must have made an impression upon the most hardened heart.'[3] Wesley was thus left in Bristol to carry on a work which had already been established by Whitefield. He preached first in a little Society in Nicholas Street, taking as his subject the Sermon on the Mount, on which he comments in the *Journal*, 'one pretty remarkable example of field-

[1] See Wesley's letter to Church, *W.W.* vol. viii. p. 432.
[2] Private cipher diary. See *J.W.J.* vol. ii. p. 158.
[3] Whitefield's Journal, quoted Curnock, *Journal*, ii. 168.

preaching, though I suppose there were churches at that time also.' [1] On the following day he writes, ' At four in the afternoon I submitted to be more vile, and proclaimed in the highways the glad tidings of salvation, speaking from a little eminence in a ground adjoining to the city, to about three thousand people.' [2] His text on this occasion was St. Luke iv. 18-19 : ' The spirit of the Lord is upon me, because He hath anointed me to preach the gospel to the poor.' ' Is it possible,' he asks, ' that anyone should be ignorant that it is fulfilled in every true minister of Christ ? ' Thus Wesley's journey to Bristol, which had filled him with apprehension, committed him to the task which thenceforth occupied him for more than half a century.

Whitefield's remark, in his letter, ' Many are ripe for bands,' found its sequel on April 4, 1739, for on that date Wesley writes, ' In the evening three women [3] agreed to meet together weekly, with the same intention as those in London—viz. to confess their faults one to another, and pray for one another, that they may be healed.' [4] ' At eight four young men agreed to meet, in pursuance of the same design.' A description of the three bands which were formed on Sunday, April 8, is given in a letter to the Moravians.[5] Each ' band ' consisted of five men, of whom one was appointed leader. These were the first Bristol members of the Methodist Societies. The system thus established has been described as a Moravian graft upon an Oxford stock. It was a copy of the London Societies, but there was no antecedent

[1] *J.W.J.* vol. ii. p. 168.   [2] *Ibid.* vol. ii. pp. 172-3.

[3] *W.H.S.* vol. iii. pp. 40-41 ; vol. iv. p. 97 ; vol. vi. pp. 106-7.

[4] See No. 1 of Rules of the Fetter Lane Society. Quoted in *J.W.J.* vol. i. pp. 458-9.

[5] Printed in the *Moravian Messenger* for 1877.

religious society in Bristol upon which it could be founded.
On the 9th of May, a piece of ground was taken in the
Horse Fair, near to St. James' Church Yard, where a
room was to be built large enough to contain the Societies
which were meeting at Nicholas Street and Baldwin
Street, with their friends.   Three days later the foundation
stone was laid of a ' society room,' the first room built
for Methodist purposes, which afterwards became a
famous Methodist preaching-house.[1]

Wesley's activities soon extended, and similar Societies
were formed at Kingswood and Bath.   He preached in
the open air, on his return to London, at Blackheath, in
Upper Moorfields, and on Kennington Common.   His
brother Charles had been driven from his curacy at
Islington by the action of the churchwardens, and now
ventured to join Whitefield and John Wesley in preaching
out of doors.   ' Bands ' were formed in various parts of
London, and in less than three years there were eleven
hundred members of the Society scattered from Wapping
to Westminster.   The pastoral care of the Societies
depended entirely on the Wesleys.

The institution of the ' class-meeting,' which was the
next step in the organization of the movement, arose out
of some financial troubles at Bristol.   Discussing the
payment of the debt on the building in the Horse Fair, a
Captain Foy suggested to a number of the members that
each should give a penny a week until the debt was paid.
Some one objected that many people could not afford
to do this ; but he replied, ' Then put eleven of the poorest
with me ; and if they can give anything, well : I will
call on them weekly ; and if they can give nothing, I will
give for them as well as for myself.   And each of you call

[1] *J.W.J.* vol. ii. pp. 194-7.

on eleven of your neighbours weekly ; receive what they give, and make up what is wanting.' [1] The suggestion was adopted. The person who took charge of the contributions was called a ' leader,' and the company under his care a ' class.' [2] These leaders reported on the behaviour of the members, and several ' disorderly walkers ' were detected. Wesley at once saw that this was what was needed, and he introduced the new system in London. And when it proved inconvenient for the leaders to visit the members at their own homes, it was arranged that the members of each class should meet together for an hour or two every week. The class-meeting thus became a part of the system, the leaders became a lay pastorate, and Methodism was provided with an organization which remains practically unchanged to this day.

Within the first four years, the main lines of the developing organization of Methodism were determined. The field preaching aroused the curiosity of the crowd, and attracted great numbers wherever Wesley and his lay preachers went. But Wesley refused to preach in any place where he could not follow it up by organized Societies with adequate leadership. [3] The leaders met Wesley from time to time, and he instructed them, displacing unsuitable men where necessary. [4] Rooms were taken or buildings erected, and preaching services, society-meetings, band and class meetings held regularly. ' Stewards ' were appointed to receive subscriptions and to pay accounts. [5] The whole system emerged, not from any preconceived

---

[1] See Journal, vol. ii. p. 528 ; *W.W.* vol. viii. p. 243 ; Telford's *Life of Wesley*, p. 150.

[2] ' *Classis* ' : the class had no reference to teaching.

[3] *J.W.J.* vol. iii. p. 485.   [4] Telford, *Life of Wesley*, p. 152.

[5] *W.W.* vol. viii. p. 252 ; Telford, *op. cit.* p. 154.

plan, but through a readiness to adopt from time to time new measures which met the demands of the situation.

When Butler, who was then Bishop of Bristol, told Wesley, ' You have no business here : I advise you to go hence,' Wesley pleaded his college fellowship as giving him ' an indeterminate commission to preach the word of God in any part of the Church of England.' [1]   In this Wesley was in error.   His Master's degree gave him the *jus ubique docendi*, which Wesley seems to have mistaken for the *jus ubique praedicandi*.[2]   Hence his famous though irregular declaration, ' I look upon all the world as my parish.' [3]   The practical application of this aphorism was seen, not only in London, Bristol, Kingswood, Bath, Oxford, and Wales, but in 1742 in Newcastle-on-Tyne, and at many places on the roads between these already established strongholds of Methodism.   At Newcastle, eight months after Wesley's first visit, there were eight hundred members of the Society, besides many others in the surrounding villages.[4]   John Nelson, a stone-mason, who was converted under John Wesley's first open-air sermon at Moorfields, in London, returned to his home at Birstall, in Yorkshire, and his labours ' soon changed the face of the town.   So many came to hear him read and exhort that he had to stand at the door of his house and talk to the crowd that stood within and without.   Six or seven people were converted every week, and the greatest profligates and drunkards in the county were

[1] Eayrs, George, in *N.H.M.* vol. i. p. 323.

[2] See M'Cullagh, T., article in *London Quarterly Review*, Jan. 1902, p. 139 ; quoted Eayrs, *N.H.M.* vol. i. p. 323, note.

[3] Letter to Hervey, *J.W.J.* June 1739, vol. ii. pp. 216-8.

[4] Tyerman, *op. cit.* vol. i. pp. 392-3.

D.M.R.   P

changed.' [1] The first statistics of Methodism were
published in 1767. The total number of members then
was 25,911 ; of circuits 41 ; in nine instances a whole
county being covered by one circuit. Six of the circuits
were in Yorkshire, and eight in Ireland. The number of
itinerant preachers employed was one hundred and four.
And the majority of these travelling preachers followed
Wesley in adopting his principle, ' The world is my
parish ' ; but their activities were always directed by
Wesley himself.

Compared with the emotional oratory of Whitefield,
the preaching of Wesley was calm, argumentative, and
appealed to reason and conscience. The psychological
effects were in a large degree due to the fact that he
sought to produce in his hearers an experience similar
to his own in conversion. In his *Earnest Appeal to Men of
Reason and Religion* (1743), Wesley sets forth the essential
themes of his own preaching, and expounds the ruling
purpose of the Revival. To thoughtful men, brought up
in the school of Locke, or worshipping, as Deists, an
absentee God, and to ignorant and brutalized thousands,
beyond the reach of the ordinances of religion, there came,
through the Methodist preaching, an almost incredible
gospel. To all, ignorant and learned alike, was offered
as an instantaneous gift, such a faith in God as would cure
all the ills of life. The love of God and of all mankind,
' we believe to be the medicine of life, the never-failing
remedy for all the evils of a disordered world, for all the
miseries and vices of men. Wherever this is, there are
virtue and happiness going hand in hand. There is
humbleness of mind, gentleness, long-suffering, the whole
image of God, and at the same time a peace that passeth

---

[1] Telford, *op. cit.* pp. 159-160.

all understanding, and joy unspeakable and full of glory.
. . . This religion we long to see established in the world, a
religion of love, and joy and peace, having its seat in the
inmost soul, but ever showing itself by its fruits, continually springing forth, not only in all innocence (for love
worketh no ill to his neighbour), but likewise in every
kind of beneficence, spreading virtue and happiness all
around it.' The *Appeal* then describes how Wesley
and his friends had wandered long in darkness, having no
man to guide them into ' the straight way to the religion
of love, even by faith.' The blessed change it had wrought
in their own souls gave them confidence in urging all to
seek the same joy. ' By this faith we are saved from all
uneasiness of mind, from the anguish of a wounded spirit,
from discontent, from fear and sorrow of heart, and from
that inexpressible listlessness and weariness, both of the
world and ourselves, which we had so helplessly laboured
under for many years, especially when we were out of the
hurry of the world and sunk in calm reflection. In this
we find that love of God and of all mankind which we
had elsewhere sought in vain. This, we know and feel,
and therefore cannot but declare, saves every one that
partakes of it both from sin and misery, from every
unhappy and every unholy temper.'

Wesley's general practice was to speak strong and stern
words in churches where he had wealthy and critical
congregations, and to choose Scripture passages of the
most tender and affectionate type for exposition to the
ignorant and debased crowds in the colliery and industrial
areas. His written sermons are logical, argumentative,
and many of them reflect the spirit of the *Earnest Appeal*.
But in his field preaching, Wesley frequently opened the
Bible at random, believing that the Holy Spirit would

guide him infallibly in the choice of a text.   And while
his written sermons are short,[1] and his instructions to
his preachers were that they should ' Be temperate in
speaking ; never too loud, never too long,' and ' begin
and end at the time appointed,' [2] his own sermons occasionally lasted two or three hours.[3]   He regularly preached
three times every week-day and five times on Sunday,
and he attributed his good health at eighty-five years of
age partly to the fact that for fifty years he had constantly
preached at five o'clock in the morning.   This practice he
commenced in order not to interfere with the working
hours of his hearers.   The miners of Newcastle came to
hear him at night, and slept in the old meeting house, on
the benches, so that they might hear him again at five
in the morning before they went to their work.[4]

Either unintentionally or deliberately, Wesley evoked
the mental conditions which are necessary for a successful
revival.   These are the states of tension, expectancy and
subdued excitement which transform collections of
individuals into a psychological crowd.   Wesley's description of the beginning of his work in Newcastle is an
example of this process.   ' Standing at the end of the
street with John Taylor,' Wesley writes that he ' began to
sing the hundredth psalm.   Three or four people came out
to see what was the matter, who soon increased to four or
five hundred.   I suppose there might be twelve to fifteen
hundred before I had done preaching. . . .   Observing
the people, when I had done, to stand gaping and staring

---

[1] The average number of pages to a sermon in *Wesley's Works* is less
than ten and a half, with approximately 380 words to a page.

[2] *The Wesleyan Methodist Magazine*, 1833, pp. 420-421.

[3] See Rigg, *The Living Wesley*, pp. 139 ff.

[4] Manscripts.   See Tyerman, *L.T.W.* vol. i. p. 394.

upon me with profound astonishment, I told them, If you desire to know who I am, my name is John Wesley. At five in the evening, with God's help, I design to preach here again.' [1] The manifestations of curiosity and wonder indicate the state of expectation and excitement which was induced, and which prepared the minds of Wesley's hearers for the unquestioning acceptance of wonderful messages, and for belief in mysterious and supernatural power.

The aim of the revivalist is to create an atmosphere of contagious emotion and suggestibility, in which worldly reason, the counsels of selfish prudence and material welfare are inhibited, and the audience reduced to a state of relative primitive credulity.[2] The mental condition desired in the congregation is akin to that induced by the romantic poet, who seeks to create in the minds of his readers ' that willing suspension of disbelief for the moment, which constitutes poetic faith.' [3] The element of suggestion which contributed to the influence of the Moravians in Wesley's conversion, appears in the case of many of his converts. ' Make the individual *want* to believe with all his heart, make him feel that he *ought* to believe, and also that others around him are believing, and he will believe.' [4] Where this inhibition of critical reason was not achieved, Wesley had to record failure. Thus he writes of Tanfield Lea, ' So dead, senseless, unaffected a congregation have I scarce seen, except at Whickham. Whether gospel or law, or English or Greek, seemed all one to them.' [5] This is a case in which ' in the phrase of evangelical theology, the heart is not awakened and there is no overmastering sense of sin and no

---

[1] *J.W.J.* vol. iii. p. 14.   [2] Cf. Pratt, *R.C.* p. 190.
[3] Coleridge, S. T., *Biographia Literaria*, p. 161 (Everyman edition).
[4] Pratt, *op. cit.* p. 190.   [5] *J.W.J.* vol. iii. p. 53.

"conversions"; in psychological terms there is no increased suggestibility and loss of inhibition.' [1]

Closely associated with the sensitiveness and suggestibility manifest in crowds, which was an elementary factor in the Revival, was the complex effect of an intensified responsiveness to rhythm.[2] The Revival itself is an example of the wider recurring rhythms of human life, which correspond with the inevitable rhythms of organic and inorganic nature.[3] Group movements in religion, subject to the same laws as individual religious experience, oscillate from times of compelling emotional intensity to periods of emotional coldness and of matter-of-fact routine. Examples of this rhythmic recurrence of religious revival occur in the Christian year, with its great emotional seasons and sacred days, unconsciously adapted to the seasons of the year, and in the Hindu, Mohammedan and Hebrew holy days. The same phenomena are found among very primitive peoples. Davenport gives examples from the Ghost Dance among the North American Indians.[4] Pratt also points out that the ancient Greeks, who were surely far removed in culture from the primitive natives of North America, showed an equal propensity to revivals of an exceedingly emotional type. 'The cult of the Thracian Dionysos seems to have been introduced into central Greece and nourished there largely through the use of what might be called "revival meetings," and these of

[1] Pratt, *op. cit.* p. 174.

[2] See Fechner; quoted by Royce, *The World and the Individual,* vol. ii. p. 221. Compare Von Hügel, *The Mystical Element of Religion,* vol. i. p. 189; and Underhill (Evelyn), *Mysticism,* p. 95.

[3] Spencer, H., *First Principles,* part ii. chap. x. (4th ed.), especially sections 85, 86 and 87. For the physical basis of rhythm in human nature, in heart beat, breathing, day and night, and the seasons, see Pratt, *op. cit.* pp. 165-7.

[4] Davenport, F. M., *Primitive Traits in Religious Revivals,* chap. iv.

a very emotional and exciting sort.'[1] Comparison may also be made with the celebration of the Eleusinian Mysteries, with the work of Chaitanya,[2] the Vaishnava reformer and missionary of sixteenth century India, and with the 'retreats' of the Roman Catholic Church. In all these group movements the laws of rhythm combine with the psychological factors already described, in stimulating the religious life of the community and of the individual.

This rhythmic element in human nature was one of the most potent forces displayed in the technique of the Methodist Revival. Charles Wesley's hymns followed the rotation of the Church feasts and holy days in the Christian year, and thus, as a guide to the devotion of organized Methodism, they utilized the old traditional festivals of English religious life. But the significance of the singing, and of the words and music, of the hymns of Methodism for the psychology of the movement is manifold. It is important to remember that before 1736 the Church of England had no hymn-book. The Psalms, metrically rendered by Sternhold and Hopkins, or Tate and Brady, George Herbert's *Temple*, and Jeremy Taylor's *Golden Grove*, were in circulation, together with devotional books in which hymns were included, but there were no hymn-books. Consequently the congregational singing, which the Wesleys had learned from the Moravians, appealed to the people with all the attractiveness of complete novelty. The hymns stimulated curiosity and helped to create the attitude of wonder, surprise and

---

[1] Pratt, *op. cit.* p. 167.

[2] Sarkar, Jadunath, M.A., *Chaitanya's Pilgrimages and Teachings*, 1913. See also Rai Sahib Dineschandra Sen, B.A., *The Vaisnava Literature of Medieval Bengal*, Univ. of Calcutta, 1917, pp. 128-134, and 203 *et seq.*

astonishment among those by whom they were heard for the first time.

The hymns of Charles Wesley rank high among the productions of the creative imagination ; and it is almost impossible to estimate the importance of his work in the genesis and development of the Revival. Have we any equal example of a great genius of John Wesley's eminence in leadership associated with another genius in a different mode of expression, and forming such a powerful combination ?

Many of the Wesley hymns were a transcript from life. Of all the six thousand five hundred hymns attributed to Charles, none surpass, if any equal, those produced in the first few years of the Revival. The *Hymns and Sacred Poems* published in 1742 reflect the stirring experiences of the two brothers. And the very fact that John and Charles were composing verses expressive of their religious experiences reacted on them, and, by the expression it necessitated, led to a clearer definition of their doctrine. ' The artist intensifies his own sentiment by the mere fact of expression.' [1]   Many of the hymns that were written by Charles are evidently based upon the experience of John. The conversion of John Wesley, as it is described in his introspections after the event, is the obvious background for the stanza,

> ' I wrestle not now, but trample on sin,
>   For *with* me art Thou, and shalt be *within*,
>   Whilst, stronger and stronger in Jesus's power,
>   I go on to conquer, till sin is no more.' [2]

The autobiographical element in hymns of this type added to their emotional power of suggestion when sung by a congregation.

[1] Baudouin, *S.A.* pp. 70, 75.   [2] See *J.W.J.* vol. i. pp. 477-479, note.

The range of experience covered by the singing of the early Methodists is indicated by the contents list in Wesley's hymn-book. The topics include, ' Exhorting Sinners to return to God ; Describing, 1. The pleasantness of Religion ; 2. The Goodness of God ; 3. Death ; 4. Judgment ; 5. Heaven ; 6. Hell (one only) ; Praying for Repentance ; For Mourners convinced of Sin ; For Believers Rejoicing ; Fighting ; Groaning for a Full Redemption ; Saved ; Interceding for the World.' [1] The emphasis on joy and praise, the elements of elation and self-expansion in Wesley's hymns have not received full recognition. The hymns are of great value as a record of the introspections and suggestions which have been used by the Methodist people from the early days of the movement.

In the organization of the Revival itself, the hymns were of value in three directions. Their power of suggestion, their educational value, and the effect of the music with which they were associated, contributed in a marked degree to the creation of the desired emotional experience, and to the permanent influence of the religious ideas and impulses which were the psychological centre and soul of the movement.

The fact that the whole congregation could take part in singing made the hymn a means for the expression of the violent emotions aroused by the revival experiences ; and at the same time the emotion was intensified by its expression. Thus it is that ' the hymn is especially valuable for both suggestion and auto-suggestion.' [2] While singing lustily in rhythmic phrases the ideas and sentiments which the Wesleys desired to instil into him,

[1] See *A Collection of Hymns for the Use of the People called Methodists.* By the Rev. John Wesley, A.M.   London, 1769.

[2] Pratt, J. B., *op. cit.* p. 176.

each member of the congregation suggested them to
himself in the technical meaning of that phrase.   And at
the same time he was passing on the suggestion to his
neighbour.   ' The whole audience thus acts upon each
individual in the audience and so acts and reacts upon
itself, thus spreading the desired suggestion by geometrical
progression.' [1]   Consider, for example, the revival value of
these verses sung by a large congregation,

> ' For you and for me
> He prayed on the tree :
> The prayer is accepted, the sinner is free.
>
> That sinner am I,
> Who on Jesus rely,
> And come for the pardon God cannot deny.' [2]

The dramatic passage from the second to the first person
identifies the poet with the audience, and by a perfect
combination of suggestion and auto-suggestion the hymn
conveyed from one individual to another an immediate
and vital experience.

The themes of the hymns were doctrinal and experimental, and thus their educational value was considerable.
Singing these songs frequently gave definition to the
various phases of religious experience, and the repetition
provided the new converts with a range of religious ideas
which formed a basis for theological construction.   The
Methodist was compensated for his lack of ancient liturgy
by a hymn-book which was at once creed and catechism.

When these hymns were sung to the old English Church
tunes of the sixteenth and seventeenth centuries, or to
the German chorales, or in several cases to popular song

[1] Pratt, *op. cit.* pp. 176-7.   Professor Pratt's chapter on ' Crowd
Psychology and Revivals ' is a valuable contribution to this subject.

[2] On the hymns, see Wiseman, in *N.H.M.* vol. i. pp. 235 ff.

tunes of the day,[1] their power of producing and com-
municating emotion was enhanced by the effect of the
music.   One-fifth of the hymns in the *Standard Hymn
Book* are hymns of penitence, and one-third of the tunes
in *Sacred Melody* (1761) are in the minor key.   Many of
these tunes have virility and jubilant qualities, but they
were peculiarly calculated to kindle the emotions of awe
and wonder, and an attitude of repentance and hope.
The heightening of emotion by means of the music was
one of the most effective agencies in creating the atmosphere in which conversions were to be expected.   A
clergyman, writing at the end of the eighteenth century,
says, ' For one who has been turned away by doctrine,
ten have been induced by music.' [2]   M. de Fursac,
witnessing the scenes which occurred during the Welsh
Revival, and observing them with a detached and scientific
purpose, felt the power of the ' musique religieuse.'   He
says, ' Dans cette atmosphère de mysticisme, chanté par
des centaines de voix, l'effet est prodigieux.   On a
l'impression de quelque chose qui vous prend tout entier,
vous éteint et vous pénètre ; on éprouve le sentiment
religieux par excellence, le sentiment   d'une réalité
superieure dépassant les réalités sensibles ; il semble que
la conscience affranchie de l'espace et du temps prenne
contact avec l'absolu. . . .   Tout cela est d'une méta-
physique peut-être bien prétentieuse.   En tout cas c'est
terriblement vague.   Je le sais ; ce n'est pas ma faute, les
émotions musicales ne se laissent guère décrire.   Ce sont
de purs états affectifs qui ne peuvent se traduire en idées
et que les mots sont impuissant à rendre.' [3]   The novelty

---

[1] In order to win some sailors who were in the habit of singing a
popular music hall song called ' Nancy Dawson,' Charles Wesley wrote
words to fit the tune.   See *N.H.M.* vol. ii. App. C, p. 558.

[2] *N.H.M.* App. C, p. 560, vol. ii.   [3] De Fursac, *M.M.C.* p. 55.

of congregational singing in the eighteenth century makes these words even more applicable to the religious music of the Methodist Revival.

By the middle of the eighteenth century the system of Methodist Societies and classes had developed a collective loyalty or group spirit which was a very potent force in the growth of the movement.[1] But in the beginnings of the movement, the novelty of the field preaching, the wonderful gospel of faith as an instantaneous gift which would cure all the ills of life, and the suggestibility and emotional excitement peculiar to the crowd, together with the indefinable power of the hymns and music, were the principal psychological features in the genesis of the Revival.

[1] The group spirit in Methodism is discussed in Chap. XI.

VI

CROWD PSYCHOLOGY

THE abnormal physical effects which frequently occur in connection with religious revivals have been the subject of much psychological research. Elemental forces are displayed in these primitive traits which may indicate the relative importance of social suggestion and instinctive tendencies for the psychology of religious experience. Two lines of research in recent psychology make it possible to examine the abnormal phenomena of the Methodist Revival in a new light ; first with reference to the psychology of crowds, and second with reference to the primary instincts.

The facts concerning the origin of Methodism have been briefly set forth in the previous chapter. In such a setting there occur peculiar phenomena, which illustrate many of the varied phases of the psychology of crowds and religious revivals. Some of the extreme physical effects, such as ' barking,' ' jerks,' and glossolalia or ecstatic utterance, which have been observed in other revivals,[1] are absent from the Methodist records. But the *Journal* of John Wesley contains detailed descriptions of experiences ranging from instantaneous conversion followed by immediate elation and joy, to pathological

[1] Davenport, *Primitive Traits in Religious Revivals*, pp. 77-80.

tortures both mental and physical, some of which cul-
minated in permanent mental derangement.[1] Abnormal
physical effects attended Wesley's preaching only for a
short period in his long ministry, and they are chiefly
confined to the years 1739 and 1742. Similar incidents
occurred in connection with the camp meetings of early
Primitive Methodism, and examples are to be found in
the *Journal* of Hugh Bourne.[2] These ' extravagances of
the Methodists,' as Southey called them, were almost
entirely absent from the services conducted by Whitefield[3]
and Charles Wesley. Those who attempted to interrupt
the preaching of Charles were dealt with in very summary
fashion. He ordered them to be carried out, and adds
in his *Journal*, ' My porters had no employment the whole
night.'[4]

The physical phenomena recorded in John Wesley's
Journal are described in considerable detail. Miss
Wedgwood refers to the ' monotonous formulae made use
of by Wesley to describe the symptoms of his penitents,'
and says that ' they effectually conceal from us all that
may have been individual or characteristic in them.'[5]
She continues, ' It is evident that many of Wesley's
patients were affected by causes which had nothing to
do with religion.'[6] But the *Journal* gives singularly
detailed observation and precise description, and provides
data from which inferences can be drawn that have

[1] *J.W.J.* vol. ii. pp. 331, 379, 385, 459-60.

[2] See Humphries, *Holy Spirit in Faith and Experience*, pp. 230-8. Cf.
also Bourne, F. W., *Billy Bray* (1890), p. 30.

[3] Southey, *Life of Wesley*, p. 166.

[4] *Charles Wesley's Journal*, June 4, 1743. See *J.W.J.* ii. 299 *n.*

[5] Wedgwood, Julia, *John Wesley and the Evangelical Reaction of the
Eighteenth Century*, p. 200.

[6] *Ibid.* p. 202.

a very definite bearing on the psychological interpretation of the facts, and this interpretation will not
remove the phenomena from the category of religious
experience.

The classification and the distribution of the cases
described in the *Journal* are important for the purposes
of a psychological explanation. Apart from the instances
in which the whole congregation is described as breaking
forth into tears or cries or groaning, and those cases in
which ' many ' and ' several ' are described as being
affected in various ways, I have examined two hundred
and thirty-four cases enumerated and reported on during
the years 1739-1743. The detailed descriptions given by
Wesley indicate that out of eighty-five cases enumerated
of persons who ' dropped as dead,' fifty-six occurred in
Bristol, nineteen in London, seven in Newcastle, and
three in Cornwall. Two cases of persons struck blind
(psychogenic blindness) are reported from Newcastle.
Convulsive tearings, violent trembling, groaning, strong
cries and tears, and other physical effects are frequently
recorded throughout the second and third volume of
Wesley's *Journal*. There are fourteen cases of madness
and restoration, and nine of incurable madness. These
figures do not include the incidents of a similar nature
occurring under the ministry of Berridge, Vicar of
Everton, which were reported to Wesley, and referred
to in his *Journal* in 1759.[1] All the cases examined
for our purpose were observed and described by John
Wesley.

There is not sufficient evidence on which to base estimates of the relative number of men and women involved.
In the majority of cases the word ' persons ' is used. Out

[1] *J.W.J.* vol. iv. pp. 291, 300, 317-22, 334-343.

of the total of 69, where the sex is mentioned, there were
40 women, 22 men, 3 boys, and 4 girls. These figures
yield an average of 64.5 per cent. women. Of the several
cases which are given in great detail, with the exception
of John Haydon,[1] all are women.

The distribution of the cases is remarkable, and suggests
an unexpected relation of abnormal reactions to racial
stock. In the case of the Methodist Revival it seems that
the traditional Celtic excitability was untouched by the
logical and ethical appeals of Wesley, either in Wales or
Cornwall, or in the North. In Cornwall, Wesley found,
at least during his first campaigns, 'huge approbation
and absolute unconcern,' 'earnest stupid attention,' and
'goodwill but no life.'[2] The most notable examples of
motor impulses are confined to Bristol and Newcastle.
London witnessed the first Methodist preaching, but
physical effects rarely occurred there after 1739. The
figures for Newcastle are misleading, as Wesley gives very
little detail of individual cases in the North, but he
describes many scenes similar to those which occurred at
Kingswood.[3] Tyerman, who carefully collated the phenomena, noted also the distribution, which, he says, adds
to the strangeness and mysteriousness of the facts, but he
offers no explanation. The key to a psychological solution
of the problem is to be found in the pages of John Wesley's
Journal. Bristol and Kingswood at that time contained
a population the most primitive, brutal and ignorant in
all England. Wesley himself spoke of the colliers as 'a
people famous from the beginning hitherto for neither
fearing God nor regarding man, so ignorant of the things

[1] *J.W.J.* vol. ii. pp. 188-191, 240, 254, 289.
[2] *Ibid.* vol. iii. pp. 88-9.
[3] *Ibid.* vol. iii. pp. 60-69.

of God that they seem but one remove from the beasts that perish, and therefore utterly without desire of instruction as well as without the means of it.'[1] Davenport writes, ' From what we know of the primitive nature of man unmoulded by experience and civilized environment, where more certainly would the peculiar phenomena be likely to appear in the England of the eighteenth century than in the neighbourhood of Bristol and Kingswood ? '[2] It is all the more striking that, after a lull of four years in the storm of phenomena, they suddenly appear again at Gateshead Fell and Chowden, which Wesley characterizes as ' the very Kingswood of the North.' As he entered the village for the first time, he says, ' Twenty or thirty wild children ran round us, as soon as we came, staring as in amaze. They could not properly be said to be either clothed or naked. One of the largest, (a girl about fifteen) had a piece of a ragged, dirty blanket, some way hung about her, and a kind of cap on her head, of the same cloth and colour. My heart was exceedingly enlarged towards them ; and they looked as if they would have swallowed me up.'[3] Among such savage and demoralized types the Kingswood scenes were repeated. ' Experience and environment had never developed the inhibitions of civilization,' and these peculiar phenomena occurred among the primitives of England, in the Kingswood of the West, and the Kingswood of the North.[4]

The stimulus which provoked these physical reactions was due in the first place to conscious or unconscious

[1] *J.W.J.* vol. iii. pp. 60-69.
[2] Davenport, F. M., *Primitive Traits in Religious Revivals*, pp. 164-5.
[3] *J.W.J.* vol. iii. p. 68.
[4] Davenport first pointed out the bearing of these facts on the primitive traits, *op. cit.* p. 166.

suggestion on the part of John Wesley. He had been reading Jonathan Edwards's account of the great revival in New England. While walking alone from London to Oxford, he says, he ' read the truly surprising narrative of the conversions lately wrought in and about the town of Northampton, in New England. Surely " this is the Lord's doing, and it is marvellous in our eyes." ' [1] Extraordinary physical symptoms accompanied these conversions, and Wesley, at that time, accepted quite uncritically the view of Edwards that ' the unavoidable manifestations of strong religious affections tend to a happy influence on the minds of the bystanders, and are found by experience to have an excellent and endurable effect ; and so to contrive and order things that others may have opportunity and advantage to observe them, has been found to be blessed as a great means to promote the work of God.' [2] Wesley argued that, ' perhaps it might be because of the hardness of our hearts, unready to receive anything unless we see it with our eyes and hear it with our ears, that God, in tender condescension to our weakness, suffered so many outward signs of the very time when He wrought this inward change to be seen and heard among us.' [3] And Wesley appealed to the ethical fruits of conversion as a proof of the Divine origin of the bodily disturbances.[4]

Wesley's responsibility for these phenomena is apparent from the fact that when he encouraged them they appeared and when he discouraged them they ceased. It was

[1] *J.W.J.* vol. ii. p. 84.

[2] Edwards, Jonathan, *Thoughts on the Revival of Religion in New England*, p. 260.

[3] *W.W.* vol. i. p. 184 ; *J.W.J.* vol. ii. p. 202. See Tyerman, *L.T.W.* vol. i. p. 267.

[4] *J.W.J.* vol. ii. p. 202.

not until he had expressed regret that the ' grace of God '
did not sink so deep at Newcastle as it did at Bristol
and Kingswood,[1] that bodily effects followed his preaching.
Then, after six or seven had dropped as dead, he writes,
' There seemed in the evening to be a deeper work in
many souls than I had observed before.' But after
inquiring into the cases of those who cried out aloud
at Gateshead Fell, and finding that ' Some said they felt
as if a sword was running through them ; others, that
they thought a great weight lay upon them, as if it would
squeeze them to the earth. Some said they were quite
choked, so that they could not breathe ; others that
their hearts swelled ready to burst ; and others that it
was as if their heart, as if their inside, as if their whole
body, was tearing to pieces,' [2] Wesley revised his opinion
as to the significance and as to the cause of these disturbances. He writes, ' These symptoms I can no more
impute to any natural cause than to the spirit of God.
I can make no doubt but that it was Satan tearing them,
as they were coming to Christ. And hence proceeded
those grievous cries, whereby he might design both to
discredit the work of God and to affright fearful people
from hearing that word whereby their souls might be
saved.' [3] After forming this judgment as to their origin,
it is not surprising that Wesley refrained from· evoking
these bodily effects, and that in fact from this point in
the narrative extreme physical disturbances are a
diminishing quantity, and rarely appear in any part of
the country after the year 1743.

If we admit that a crowd is the primitive biological

[1] *J.W.J.* vol. iii. p. 51.
[2] *Ibid.* vol. iii. pp. 69-70 ; cf. vol. vii. p. 153.
[3] *Ibid.* p. 69.

herd,[1] Wesley was an eminently skilful herd leader. Le
Bon, in his *Psychologie des foules*, describes the methods
of the crowd leader. ' Les moyens d'action des meneurs,'
he says, are ' l'affirmation, la repetition, la contagion.' [2]
This is peculiarly true of Wesley. Familiar features in
the *Journal* from beginning to end are the confident
affirmation of certain beliefs, the repetition of particular
phrases, and the evident influence of contagion among
his hearers. But the work of M. Le Bon, together with
Tarde's *Laws of Imitation*,[3] has been responsible for
popularizing a doubtful distinction between the psychology
of the crowd and the psychology of the individual.
Imitation and suggestibility are not the creation of a
spirit peculiar to crowds. They are as plainly characteristic of the individual out of the crowd as in it. M. Le Bon
describes, ' l'impulsivité, l'irritabilité, l'incapacité de rai-
sonner, l'absence de jugement, et d'esprit critique,
l'exagération des sentiments,' as ' caractères spéciaux des
foules,' and relates them to ' des formes inférieures
d'évolution, comme le sauvage et l'enfant.' [4] And in his
chapter on the ' Suggestibilité et crédulité des foules,' he
writes, ' La qualité mentale des individus dont se compose
la foule ne contredit pas ce principe. Cette qualité est
sans importance. Du moment qu'ils sont en foule,
l'ignorant et le savant deviennent également incapables
d'observation.' [5] Thus it is assumed that ' the individual
left to himself is reflective and rational, while man's
emotional obsessions and irrationalities are to be accounted
for by the psychology of association with others.' [6] But

[1] See Tansley, *N.P.* pp. 231 ff.   [2] Le Bon, P. F., chap. iii. p. 103.
[3] Published 1892. See Pratt, *op. cit.* p. 169.
[4] Le Bon, *op. cit.* p. 23.   [5] *Ibid.* p. 28.
[6] Dewey, John, ' The Need for Social Psychology,' *Psy. Review*, xxiv.
July 1917, p. 268. Quoted Pratt, *op. cit.* p. 171.

individual and social psychology are not antithetic ; and the low estimate of the mentality of the crowd is not based upon scientific observation. The facts under discussion in the present chapter cannot be explained by ' l'âme des foules,' [1] nor by the ' besoin instinctif de tous les êtres en foule d'obéir à un meneur.' [2] A valid social psychology demands a more exact explanation. Neither the suggestion of a ' meneur des foules,' nor the impulsivity of the crowd can account for the revival phenomena. ' Suggestion, domination, etc., are, until they are empirically defined, sheer abstractions used as agents or forces. They are precisely analogous to the *faculties* of the eighteenth century.' [3]

Among the 234 cases of pathological symptoms which I have analysed, there are many in which unconscious imitation is obviously a potent factor.[4] Some were probably due to that form of self-display which expresses itself in love of producing a sensation. But there are many shades of behaviour between perfect honesty and conscious acting.[5] In the majority of instances the imitation followed upon an absorbed observation of other cases. Neither conscious imitation nor suggestibility is an ultimate factor in the psychology of these experiences. The chief agent is probably the tendency for any mental content upon which spontaneous attention is fixed, to gain control of the motor centres apart from the will, and thus to work itself out into the activity of the muscular system. This element of dynamogenesis or ideo-motor action is evident in nearly all the cases considered. Many

[1] Le Bon, *op. cit.* pp. 11-61.   [2] *Ibid.* p. 97.
[3] Bentley, ' A Preface to Social Psychology,' *Psy. Review*, June 1916, p. 11.   Quoted Pratt, *op. cit.* p. 169.
[4] See for example, *J.W.J.* vol. ii. pp. 298, 187, 203, 377.
[5] See Wedgwood, Julia, *op. cit.* p. 202.

instances might be quoted, of which one may suffice.
' Another person dropped down, close to one who was a
strong asserter of the contrary doctrine. While he stood
astonished at the sight, a little boy who stood near him
was seized in the same manner. A young man who stood
up behind fixed his eyes on him, and sunk down himself
as one dead ; but soon began to roar out and beat himself
against the ground, so that six men could scarcely hold
him.' [1]

The majority of these phenomena occurred in Societies
or during services held in private houses ; consequently
the intensified suggestibility manifest under crowd conditions is one of the elements in a psychological interpretation. There is a cumulative effect in social
suggestion which is due to the fact that man is by nature
and instinct a gregarious creature. But whether this
can be traced to a single specific ' herd instinct ' is doubtful. The physical proximity of others, especially in a
closely packed throng or room, diminishes the sense of
independence, and produces a feeling of helplessness.
There is a purely mechanical aspect of this experienced
in the restriction of movement consequent upon the
pressure of the crowd. More important is the increased
sense of power invested in a throng. Security is felt to
be in companionship. But Galton's ox [2] has been made
to bear an almost intolerable load in recent popular
psychology. The other side of the same truth is the

---

[1] *J.W.J.* vol. ii. p. 203. Thomas Maxfield ; see *J.W.J. passim.*

[2] ' Although the ox has little affection for, or interest in, his fellows,
he cannot endure even a momentary separation from his herd. If he
be separated from it by stratagem or force, he exhibits every sign of
mental agony ; he strives with all his might to get back again, and
when he succeeds he plunges into its middle to bathe his whole body
with the comfort of closest companionship ' (Galton, Francis, *Inquiries
into Human Faculty,* p. 72) [quoted by James, *P.P.* vol. ii. pp. 430-431].

corresponding diminution of individual responsibility. In M. Le Bon's chapter on juries, he omits any reference to the fact that in pooling responsibility its weight for individuals is lessened. John Wesley was familiar with this mental peculiarity. He refers to the addition of twenty-four to the jury which was to try him in Georgia, and remarks, ' so many being engaged in the same work they would encourage one another to take bolder steps than a few would dare to venture on.' [1] These three factors in crowd mentality, the loss of individual inde-pendence, the sense of corporate power, and the diminished consciousness of responsibility, contributed in a marked degree to the creation of revival conditions, and they are also a partial explanation of the abnormal phenomena.

Ordinary inhibitions are broken down under crowd conditions in many ways, but there are three main types in the data before us. The experiences may be classified as the breakdown of inhibitions to emotion, to action, and to belief.[2]

In the release of emotion to the point of violence, the Methodist Revival conformed to the type of all religious revivals. Ample illustration of this characteristic with special reference to ' instinct experience ' will be given in the following chapter. The distinctive feature of Wesley's work, when it is viewed in relation to the history of revivals, is the marked *ethical* quality both in his preaching and in his life, which made the emotional disturbance in the vast majority of cases a decisive force in the formation of a higher type of character. Wesley could not tolerate the hysterical behaviour of the Camisards, or French

[1] *J.W.J.* vol. i. p. 382.
[2] Pratt, J. B., *op. cit.* pp. 182-191, gives a very full and suggestive discussion of these three characteristics.

prophets, whom he met from time to time in various parts
of England, and his criticism was not withdrawn after
he had witnessed the peculiar effects sometimes produced
by his own preaching.[1]   The element of will in disciplined
morality, and the use of a shrewd critical judgment,
safeguarded the Revival against unbridled emotionalism.

Closely associated with the absence of restraints on
emotion, is the breakdown of inhibitions to action, and
the parallel intensifying of various motor impulses.   All
the varieties of peculiar behaviour which have been
described illustrate this tendency.   The weakening of
moral control, which has so frequently led, in the reaction
from emotional excitement, to outbreaks of immorality,
was manifest in the case of Westley Hall, who married
Wesley's sister ;   and the Methodists of Salisbury were
' loaded with insults and infamy on his account.'[2]   But
the movement as a whole was remarkably free from this
danger, and the Puritan strain in Methodist character
was manifest from the first.

The breakdown of inhibitions to belief is exemplified in
a remarkable way by the experience of those whose
recovery of mental balance was associated with hallucinations.   Wesley examined a number of converts in London,
and they described their experience as ' feeling the blood
of Christ running upon their arms, or going down their
throat, or poured like warm water upon their breast or
heart.'   Wesley writes, ' I plainly told them the utmost
I could allow, without renouncing both Scripture and
reason, was, that these circumstances might be from God
(though I could not affirm that they were) working in an

[1] See *J.W.J.* vol. ii. pp. 136, 226 ; vii. p. 153.

[2] Tyerman, *L.T.W.* vol. ii. p. 88 ; vol. i. pp. 561-2 ; *J.W.J.* vol. iii.
pp. 531-3.   Cf. *Gentleman's Magazine*, 1747, p. 531.

unusual manner, no way essential either to justification or sanctification, but that all the rest I must believe to be mere empty dreams of an heated imagination.' [1] In his first-hand examination of the facts of the Welsh Revival of 1904-5, M. de Fursac discusses the visions and sensations which were described by the converts. The experiences of sight and touch and hearing correspond very closely to those recorded by Wesley, and M. de Fursac's description of the psycho-physiological processes involved, which mainly follows that of James, may be accepted. M. de Fursac writes, ' En effet, parmi les illusions nombreuses auxquelles l'esprit humain est exposé, il en est une que la psychologie des foules et la psychiatrie courante ont bien mise en lumière. Elle consiste dans ce fait que l'esprit concentré sur une idée a une grande tendance à transformer cette idée en sensation.[2] C'est surtout dans le mysticisme que les faits de cet ordre se rencontrent. Mais ils ne sont pas absolument rares dans la vie ordinaire. On se rappelle qu'en 1870 des populations terrorisées ont vu des régiments entiers de Prussians imaginaires. L'explication psycho-physiologique du phénomène est très simple. La fatigue due à l'attente paralyse les fonctions psychiques supérieures, affaiblit le jugement et lâche la bride à l'automatisme mental. Les centres sensoriels fonctionnent indépendamment de toute excitation extérieure et l'hallucination est créée.' [3] James, in his treatment of the neural process of hallucination, writes, ' It must, of course, consist of an excitement from within of those centres which are active in normal perception,

[1] *J.W.J.* vol. iii. pp. 43-4.
[2] Cf. *supra*, p. 158, and see Baudouin, *S.A.* p. 114.
[3] De Fursac, *M.M.C.* pp. 147-8. Cf. the story of Russian troops passing through England during the war ; cf. also the story of the angels at Mons.

identical in kind and degree with that which real external objects are usually needed to induce.' [1] Binet's theory is that hallucinations can only occur through peripheral initiation.[2] James rejects this explanation and infers from a regular series of facts that, ' it seems probable on the whole, therefore, that centrally initiated hallucinations can exist.' [3] This view is empirically justified by the cases described by Wesley ; and the conditions favourable to these fallacies of perception are those mentioned by M. de Fursac. The weakening of the judgment as a result of mental fatigue gives the rein to what would now be explained as unconscious activities of the mind ; and social suggestion and contagion determine the form which these hallucinations assume.

Methodism has been adversely criticised on account of the strange scenes and emotional excesses which accompanied its origin under the early Revival preaching. A common result of crowd emotion and religious excitement is chronic mental derangement; and it is notable that out of fourteen cases of insanity which Wesley reports in the *Journal*, nine were incurable. Lecky refers to the ' religious terrorism ' and ' religious madness ' which were characteristic of Methodism, and says, ' A more appalling system of religious terrorism, one more fitted to unhinge a tottering intellect and to darken and embitter a sensitive nature, has seldom existed.' [4] ' The Methodist preached especially to the nerves.' But ' by their fruits ye shall know them,' and Methodism may well be content to accept the verdict of history as to the health and sanity of its

---

[1] James, *P.P.* vol. ii. p. 122.
[2] Binet and Féré, *Animal Magnetism*, ch. ix. quoted by James, *op. cit.* vol. ii. p. 128.
[3] James, *P.P.* vol. ii. p. 130.
[4] Lecky, W. E. H., *op. cit.* vol. iii. pp. 77-8.

influence on the life of the people. In the period of the Welsh Revival, the cases of insanity reported from the Glamorgan County Asylum show an increase above normal of only one per cent. ; and during the same period, the number of cases of insanity in Wales due to alcoholism decreased from seventy-one to forty-two, or from sixteen per cent. of the total number of cases in 1904 to twelve per cent. in 1905. De Fursac's comment on this fact is equally applicable to the Methodist Revival. He concludes,[1] ' Cependant, si l'on prend un critérium quantitatif, si l'on considère le nombre absolu de ceux que le Réveil a sauvés de la folie alcoolique, et le nombre absolu de ceux que le Réveil a jétes dans la folie mystique, la société y trouve son bénéfice. Il vaut mieux, disait quelqu'un, qu'un homme devienne fou par la religion que cent par l'alcool.'

[1] De Fursac, *op. cit.* p. 125.

VII

THE PRIMARY INSTINCTS

THE place of the primary instincts in religious experience has been recognized by contemporary writers on psychology, and attempts have been made to determine their relative importance for the evolution of religion. Fear has frequently been given the first place by both ancient and modern writers. The line from Petronius is often quoted : *Primus in orbe timor fecit deos*.[1] Ribot,[2] Leuba,[3] and McDougall [4] agree in their estimates of the importance of fear, although McDougall adds reverence and admiration, and supplements fear with awe. Robertson Smith, in his *Religion of the Semites*, points out that religion in the only true sense of the word, is rooted not in a vague fear of unknown powers, but in a loving reverence for known gods who are knit to their worshippers by strong bonds of kinship.[5] Similarly, Jevons, in his *Introduction to the History of Religion*, presents a strong case against the fear-origin of religion.[6] Marett argues that if *Timor*

---

[1] Petronius Arbiter, *Saturae,* quoted Pratt, *R.C.* p. 71.

[2] *The Psychology of the Emotions,* part ii. chap. ix.

[3] ' Fear, Awe, and the Sublime in Religion,' *American Journal of Religious Psychology,* ii. 1-13. See also *A Psychological Study of Religion,* chap. vii.

[4] *S.P.* chap. xiii.   [5] p. 55.

[6] Jevons, Frank Byron, *An Introduction to the History of Religion* (1896), pp. 106-9, cf. p. 20.

means awe we are nearer the truth, but that we must admit wonder, admiration, interest, respect, even love perhaps, to be, no less than fear, essential constituents of the elemental mood of religion.[1] Ribot makes love predominant in the second stage of the evolution of religion, and McDougall makes a very vital suggestion to the effect that in the development of morality, fear and pugnacity were in the later stages supplemented by curiosity and subjection, and at a still later stage, ' by the tender protective impulse principally evoked in the form of gratitude towards the protecting deities.'[2] The significance of this last phrase will become apparent after a detailed study has been made of the psychological factors involved in the early Methodist conversions. Dr. Wright finds evidence of the activity of the gregarious, reproductive, and food-seeking tendencies ;[3] and Mr. A. S. Woodburne traces also the influence of the self-preservation tendencies.[4] It seems to be indubitable that religion, instead of being, as is so frequently assumed, the manifestation of a single religious instinct, is an experience which involves, at least in its fully developed stages, all the instinctive propensities. The extent to which this is true of Methodism may be tested by an examination of the documents.

It is notable that the physical effects of the early Methodist preaching have been explained in such diverse ways by Wesley and his friends, and by psychologists.

[1] Marett, R. R., *The Threshold of Religion*, p. 13. For a very suggestive treatment of fear and fascination side by side as two factors, see Otto, Rudolf, *The Idea of the Holy*, chap. iv. on ' Mysterium Tremendum,' and chap. vi. on ' The Element of Fascination.'

[2] *S.P.* pp. 314-5.

[3] ' Instinct and Sentiment in Religion,' *Phil. Rev.* xxv. 1916, p. 34.

[4] ' The Relation of Religion to Instinct,' *American Journal of Theology*, xxiii. 1919, pp. 319-44.

As we have seen, Wesley attributed them to God and to the devil. As late as 1759, he regarded the physical convulsions under Berridge of Everton as ' the work of God.' His enemies made full use of the facts as a proof of the ' enthusiasm ' and fanaticism of the Methodists.[1] Some critics said that they were ' natural effects, due to the heat and closeness of the rooms, others were sure it was all a cheat.' [2] Davenport classifies the phenomena as primitive traits, and regards ignorance and brutality as the main psychological explanation, while many psychologists have treated all such revival occurrences as entirely due to the peculiar conditions created by crowd contagion and excitement. Meanwhile the descriptions of their own experiences by the persons involved have been ignored, and very little attention has been paid to the particularly detailed account which Wesley himself gives of their symptoms. Both the introspections and the behaviour of the Methodist converts reveal very definite evidence of the stimulation of specific natural propensities. The instinctive factors combine with the other elements in the situation, but there are marked features characteristic of the phenomena as a whole which can only be explained psychologically in terms of ' instinct experience.'

Two of the primary instinct tendencies have already been indicated as factors in the religious experiences of the Revival. Apart from the case of Wesley, who has given very full accounts of his love affairs, there is very little material on which to base an estimate of the direct relation of the sex instinct to conversion. The gregarious or herd instinct may possibly be discerned in the characteristics of crowds which have been discussed, and in the

[1] See Green, Richard, *Anti-Methodist Publications* (1902).
[2] *J.W.J.* vol. ii. pp. 202, 222.

development of the group spirit which will be examined in a later chapter. Sufficient recognition has been given to the social influences which contributed to the creation of revival conditions, and to the production of abnormal states. The social explanation is not an adequate interpretation of the facts : the breakdown of inhibitions can of itself produce no activity, mental or physical. And the laws and tendencies of social and crowd behaviour leave a large part of individual religion unexplained.

I have tabulated some hundreds of cases described by Wesley, exhibiting forty-two distinct physical phenomena, and they correspond in every detail with the physical manifestations of certain instincts as these are classified by Darwin,[1] James,[2] McDougall,[3] Drever,[4] Stout,[5] and Shand.[6] Of the total number of symptoms analyzed, two correspond with the bodily expressions or symptoms of Curiosity, twenty-four are characteristic of Fear, fourteen of Anger, and two of Repulsion or Disgust. The evidence of the parallels in my table[7] is very clear, and justifies the inference that marked instinctive activity was excited by the Revival meetings. The close observation of the behaviour of animals on which the psychology of the instincts is based has provided ample support for the common-sense view that emotion plays a large part in determining action. Emotion and motive are very closely related, because the peculiar quality of experience which may be called a primary emotion is brought into play by the working within us of instinctive impulses.

[1] *The Expression of the Emotions in Man and Animals*, 1872.
[2] *Principles of Psychology*, vol. ii. chaps. xxiv-xxv.
[3] *Social Psychology*, chap. iii. ; *Outline of Psychology*, chap. v.
[4] *Instinct in Man*, chap. viii.
[5] *Manual of Psychology*, bk. iii. chap. iv.
[6] *The Foundations of Character*, bk. ii.   [7] See Appendix II.

It is not necessary to follow McDougall and say that when we see signs of the emotion of fear, we must conclude that the instinct of flight is indicated, or that anger points to the fighting instinct. The terms will be simplified by describing the impulses as specific instinct tendencies of the emotional type, thus following Drever, and in the cases under discussion we shall use the words Curiosity, Fear, Anger, and Disgust or Repulsion to describe the whole experience.[1]

Curiosity is described by McDougall as ' the impulse to approach and examine more closely the object that excites it.'[2] The element of surprise, as the emotional response to ' unexpectedness,' was of great importance in the beginnings of the Revival, and the natural tendency would be for it to pass into curiosity. McDougall's technical use of the term ' wonder ' cannot be retained, and he himself has abandoned it in his most recent work.[3] Wonder is more than the concomitant emotion of the instinct ' curiosity.' The definition of Dr. Drever is most in accord with the data under discussion. ' Wonder is developed, as the consciousness of a baffled enquiring impulse develops, but curiosity still persists in wonder. . . . Wonder, in its simplest and most elementary form, is baffled curiosity. It is therefore hardly to be regarded as a primary emotion in the strict sense.'[4] But wonder survives when curiosity has made the most marvellous discoveries. It is much more than baffled curiosity. This compound emotional tendency develops in two directions. It became, in the later experience of these converts, the

---

[1] See McDougall, W., *O.P.* chaps. ii-v ; Drever, *I.M.* p. 171. Cf. Laing, B. M., *A Study in Moral Problems* (1922), p. 91.

[2] *S.P.* p. 57. [3] McDougall, *O.P.* p. 324.

[4] Drever, *op. cit.* p. 200.

source of that ' intellectual curiosity ' which is the driving power in theological discussion.[1] The correspondence of Wesley and his followers, and the history of Methodist doctrine with its controversies, are instances of this intellectual exploration, the joy of which is largely in the satisfaction, in higher and more comprehensive ways, of the curiosity impulse. ' For no other instinct gives so great scope for the exercise of discrimination and the co-operation of the reflective judgment. The attitude of curiosity is essentially one of suspended judgment ; and that is the beginning of wisdom, of questioning, of further examination, and of explicit judgment.' [2]

In the earlier stages of the Revival, the tendency observed most frequently was that of curiosity passing into astonishment, which, as Darwin pointed out, is usually found to precede fear. Fearful curiosity is a very familiar experience.[3] The opposed impulses of approach and retreat in animals and young children are commonly excited in rapid alternation. ' The horse approaches the strange ill-defined object on the ground, circling round it, with eyes, ears, and nose on the alert, starting away in retreat and again approaching.' [4] In the case of the persons who were drawn by curiosity to listen to the sermons of Wesley, or to join in a Methodist gathering, the most common result observed, at least in the early years of the movement, was a transition through the stages already mentioned, curiosity, astonishment, and

---

[1] The view here adopted is supported by McDougall, S.P. p. 315, and by Drever, p. 201 ; but James held that ' with what is called scientific curiosity, and with metaphysical wonder, the practical instinctive root has probably nothing to do. The stimuli here are not objects, but ways of conceiving objects ' (P.P. vol. ii. pp. 429-30).

[2] McDougall, W., O.P. p. 144.　　　[3] Ibid. p. 143.

[4] Ibid. Cf. James, P.P. vol. ii. p. 429.

fear, the last of these in turn becoming either the awe which is a primary factor in normal religious life, or the terror which is, on the evidence of the symptoms described in Wesley's *Journal*, the principal agent in the production of pathological phenomena.

The variety of the manifestations of fear, which have been observed by Wesley, might seem to justify the analysis of the fear impulse into a number of distinct varieties.   Mr. Shand distinguishes eleven different types of fear,[1] but his classification is based on the reactions, such as flight, concealment, silence, immobility, clinging for protection.   And his second, third, fifth, and sixth are all varieties of the same type of response ; while several of the others are ambiguous and suggest the presence of something more than fear.   All these motor impulses are included in the phenomena of the Revival, but distinctions of this kind are out of place in a psychological analysis, because they fail to distinguish between motor mechanisms and instincts.   And the danger of such a method of classification is that the number of types would only be limited by the introspective vocabulary of the investigator.[2]   The facts considered and tabulated conform to the general law of the behaviour of fear. ' Fear in all its varieties strives to escape danger.'[3]

The question arises as to the nature of the stimulus to fear, which was such a marked feature of the Revival experiences.   The descriptions given by the converts themselves must be accepted with a certain reserve. Religious experience, however recorded, does not come to us in perfectly pure form, and it cannot therefore be regarded as immediate data.   Fact and meaning are

[1] Shand, *op. cit.* pp. 199-210.   [2] See James, *P.P.* vol. ii. p. 485.
[3] Drever, *op. cit.* p. 176.

confused ; and the facts of inner religious history are fashioned and coloured by interpretation through a system of religious ideas and beliefs. ' Unconscious interpretation is always present in introspection. " Percepts without concepts," as Kant remarked, " are blind." And those who study religious experience and its phenomena are irresistibly led to the conclusion that the same process is constantly present there.' [1] It is necessary therefore to attempt to get behind the phrases used, to the ' instinct experience ' which is the subject of doctrinal interpretation.

The inference that the physical manifestations are due to instinctive activity is definitely confirmed by the account of various experiences elicited by Wesley's inquiry at Newcastle. Some of the converts examined said that ' they were in fear ' ; they were ' afraid of the devil.' Others ' could not tell what they were afraid of.' ' A few gave a more intelligible account of the piercing sense they had of their sins, both inward and outward, which were set in array against them round about ; of the dread they were in of the wrath of God and the punishment they had deserved, into which they seemed to be falling, without any way of escape. One of them told me, " I was as if I was just falling down from the highest place I have ever seen. I thought the devil was pushing me off, and that God had forsaken me." Another said, " I felt the very fire of hell already kindled in my breast ; and all my body was in as much pain as if I had been in a burning fiery furnace." ' [2] Similar phrases occur in the introspections of the converts Wesley examined at Gateshead Fell. They were ' convinced of inward

[1] Galloway, George, *Philosophy of Religion*, p. 254.
[2] *J.W.J.* vol. iii. p. 60.

and outward sin '; they ' felt the wrath of God '; they
were ' afraid of his judgments '; ' the accuser came
telling them that there was no hope . . . that they were
lost for ever.' [1]

At the purely instinctive level, the references to fire and
the furnace suggest the theory of Spencer that fear
consists in a revival of painful sensations produced by
the object feared. ' Everyone,' he says, ' can testify
that the psychical state called fear consists of mental
representations of painful results.' [2] ' Fear, when strong,
expresses itself in cries, in efforts to escape, in palpitations,
in tremblings ; and these are just the manifestations that
go along with an actual suffering of the evil feared.' [3]
In so far as the fear of hell as a place of physical torment
may account for a small proportion of the cases, this view
would seem to be supported. But it is not an adequate
explanation of the actual bodily symptoms of fear, as
James points out,[4] nor does it account for the difference
between the experience of fear and the experience of
burning, the former of which may be much more intolerable than the latter.[5] The facts before us demand a
different and a deeper interpretation. Psychology here
sustains the evidence of the documents, to the effect that
Wesley did not make use of the appeal to fear as the terror
of physical torment in hell. Such a fear could not have
produced the symptoms enumerated, and no valid
psychology can describe fear as a mental representation of
painful sensations.

[1] *J.W.J.* vol. iii. pp. 69-70.
[2] Spencer, H., *Psychology*, sec. 213, quoted Stout, *Manual of Psychology*, p. 315.
[3] *Ibid.*, quoted James, *P.P.* vol. ii. p. 479.
[4] James, *P.P.* vol. ii. p. 482.
[5] See also Stout, *Manual of Psychology*, pp. 315-6.

What was the danger which aroused such terror ? After allowing for a certain implicit judgment of value on the part of the writers, and in Wesley's interpretation and editing of the replies, there is a close correspondence between these introspections and the behaviour they are intended to explain. The root of the horror and fear is in the danger envisaged of loss to the essential self.[1] This dread of final condemnation is one of the factors in normal conversion, as we shall see in a later chapter, but apart from its religious implications which are there discussed, there is a biological foundation for this terrifying sense of danger. ' The moral character in its contrast with the immoral one is a particular instance of the contrast established within the organic world between the successful type and the individuals which conform to it, and that which fails in competition with it and in nature tends to destruction. The terms of moral disapproval indicate the process by which the unsocial type is discarded in human life.' [2] The fear of moral dereliction, however it may be defined, is a quite adequate explanation of the physical symptoms described.

Closely related to fear, and consequently merging into anger, is the attitude of submission [3] or self-despising, which is responsible, in the introspections, for the most abject self-condemnatory phrases. Dr. McDougall refers to the diminution of muscular tone which accompanies, in pathological cases, a self-abasement in which the patient thinks himself a most wretched, useless, sinful creature.[4] Although the physical manifestations of this tendency are not included in my parallel table, there is evidence of very

[1] *Vide infra*, pp. 201-3.
[2] Alexander, S., *Space, Time, and Deity*, vol. ii. p. 285.
[3] See McDougall, *O.P.* p. 324.   [4] McDougall, *S.P.* p. 66.

marked ' negative self-feeling ' in many of the abnormal cases under review.[1]   In some cases there appears to be an extreme reaction from this attitude of subjection, manifest in indignation against the preachers who have aroused it, and expressed in the various degrees of avoidance, repulsion, or disgust.[2]   It is doubtful if either self-abasement or repulsion can be accurately described as primary instincts.   A wider range of inquiry is necessary in order to arrive at a satisfactory classification of instincts. But in the religious experience of Methodism, it is difficult to define the point at which instinctive self-abasement becomes the ethical self-reproach which forms part of the sentiment that is connected with the pursuit of virtues, ideals and duties.[3]   Disgust or repulsion seems to have a more primitive instinctive basis, and forms a link between self-abasement and anger.

The symptoms of anger are not so complete and well defined as the manifestations of fear.   But at least seven of the organic indications of the presence of anger are included in Wesley's observations.   And these have the more weight because the idea of anger as a cause of the physical condition seems never to have occurred to Wesley.   The resentment at interference with habitual and largely instinctive activities would account, in part, for the excitement of the pugnacious instinct.   ' The condition of its excitement is rather any opposition to the free exercise of any impulse, any obstruction to the activity to which the creature is impelled by any one of the other instincts.' [4]

[1] ' Lowness of spirits,' *J.W.J.* vol. ii. p. 242 ; cf. vol. iii. pp. 23-24 ; and *J.W.J. passim.*

[2] See McDougall, *O.P.* pp. 147-149, and 324.

[3] See Shand, *op. cit.* pp. 113-115.   [4] McDougall, *S.P.* p. 59.

Another stimulus to the fighting impulse would be found in the intensity of the fear of sin or of the moral law as represented in God, and in the impossibility of escape. The experience, prior to the relieving of the emotional situation by a new and more powerful emotion, may be compared with that of animals at bay. ' The fear-impulse, the most opposed to the pugnacious, may on obstruction, give place to it ; for the hunted creature when brought to bay—*i.e.* when its impulse to flight is obstructed—is apt to turn upon its pursuers and to fight furiously, until an opportunity for escape presents itself.' [1] Unless the fear became excessive, and involved so great a nervous disturbance as to defeat the ends of the instinct by inducing convulsions or paralysis, it was, in many of the cases observed by Wesley, supplanted by the instinct of aggression. This general tendency has been formulated by Mr. Shand : ' Fear tends to elicit anger in support of its end when its impulse is obstructed.' [2] The anger thus elicited, was sometimes directed towards the preacher as its object,[3] sometimes towards the devil,[4] and sometimes towards God.[5] In each case the object of the anger was regarded as the source of the danger, and therefore the enemy to be attacked.

Anger against the preacher is illustrated frequently in the *Journal*. From Wesley's narrative it is clear that in some of the cases anger is directed against God and the preacher, and is combined with the instinct of repulsion or disgust. For example, he writes, ' I was sent for to one

---

[1] McDougall, *S.P.* p. 59.

[2] Shand, *op. cit.* bk. ii. chap. v. p. 261.

[3] *J.W.J.* vol. ii. p. 300 ; iii. pp. 155, 483. See also letters from Eliz. Spring and Mary Purnell (Colman Collection).

[4] *J.W.J.* vol. ii. p. 191.

[5] *Ibid.* vol. ii. pp. 300, 347 ; vol. iii. p. 242.

in Bristol, who was taken ill the evening before. She lay on the ground furiously gnashing her teeth, and after awhile roared aloud. It was not easy for three or four persons to hold her, especially when the name of Jesus was named. We prayed ; the violence of her symptoms ceased, though without a complete deliverance. In the evening, I was sent for to her again. She began screaming before I came into the room ; then broke out into a horrid laughter, mixed with blasphemy. One, who apprehended a preternatural agent to be concerned in this, asking, " How didst thou dare to enter into a Christian ? " was answered, " She is not a Christian—she is mine." This was followed by fresh trembling, cursing, and blaspheming. My brother coming in, she cried out, " Preacher ! Field preacher ! I don't love field preaching." This was repeated two hours together, with spitting, and all expressions of strong aversion. We left her at twelve, and called again at noon the next day. And now it was, that God showed He heareth prayer. All her pangs ceased in a moment ; she was filled with peace, and knew that the son of wickedness was departed from her.' [1] The symptoms in this case show how the excitement produced by the Revival stimulated violent instinctive and emotional tendencies almost to the point of insanity. Some of the features exhibited can only be explained psychoanalytically, notably the evidence of a repressed complex centring in the name of Jesus, and the dissociation of personality involved in the patient's reply, ' She is not a Christian—she is mine,' spoken on behalf of the devil. But the physical effects unmistakably point to the determining influence of instinctive activity.

The manifestations of anger against the Deity are

[1] *J.W.J.* vol. ii. p. 300.

usually described as 'blasphemy,' and the word occurs frequently in the *Journal* for the years 1739-1742. But no detail is available as to the phrases used or the special forms taken by the rage and fury against God.

Anger against the devil is illustrated by the case of John Haydon, which is of special importance as an example of extraordinary physical phenomena induced without any possibility of crowd contagion or loss of inhibition through social sympathy and suggestion. Wesley writes, ' I did not mention one John Haydon, a weaver, who was at Baldwin Street the night before. He was (I understood) a man of regular life and conversation, one that constantly attended the public prayers and sacrament, and was zealous for the Church and against Dissenters of every denomination. Being informed that people fell into strange fits at the societies, he came to see and judge for himself. But he was less satisfied than before ; insomuch that he went about to his acquaintance, one after another, till one in the morning, and laboured above measure to convince them it was a delusion of the devil. We were going home, when one met us in the street, and informed us that John Haydon was fallen raving mad. It seems that he had sat down to dinner, but had a mind first to end a sermon he had borrowed on " Salvation by Faith." In reading the last page [1] he changed colour, fell off his chair, and began screaming terribly, and beating himself against the ground. The neighbours were alarmed, and

---

[1] The paragraph was from John Wesley's ' Sermon in Univ. Church, Oxford ' ; see *J.W.J.* vol. ii. p. 190, note ; and reads thus, ' For this reason the adversary so rages whenever " salvation by faith " is declared to the world : for this reason did he stir up earth and hell, to destroy those who first preached it. And for the same reason, knowing that faith alone could overturn the foundations of his kingdom, did he call forth all his forces, and employ all his arts of lies and calumny, to affright Martin Luther from reviving it ' (*W.W.* vol. v. p. 13).

D.M.R. U

flocked together to his house. Between one and two I came in, and found him on the floor, the room being full of people, whom his wife would have kept without ; but he cried aloud, " No ; let them all come ; let all the world see the just judgment of God." Two or three men were holding him as well as they could. He immediately fixed his eyes upon *me*, and, stretching out his hand, cried, " Aye, this is he who I said was a deceiver of the people ; but God has overtaken me. I said it was all a delusion ; but this is no delusion." He then roared out, " O thou devil ! thou cursed devil ! yea, thou legion of devils ! thou canst not stay. Christ will cast thee out. I know his work is begun. Tear me to pieces, if thou wilt ; but thou canst not hurt me." He then beat himself against the ground again, his breast heaving at the same time, as in the pangs of death, and great drops of sweat trickling down his face. We all betook ourselves to prayer. His pangs ceased, and both his body and soul were set at liberty.' A little later, ' Returning to John Haydon, we found his voice was lost, and his body weak as that of an infant ; but his soul was in peace, full of love, and " rejoicing in hope of the glory of God." ' [1]

The subsequent history of many of the pathological cases is difficult to trace, but in the case of John Haydon the crisis seems to have been succeeded by normal religious development.[2]

The evidence of instinctive activity is complicated by the influence of a resistance due to Haydon's traditional churchmanship, but the presence of powerful primary instinctive tendencies is manifest. The symptoms of

[1] *J.W.J.* vol. ii. pp. 189-191.
[2] Moravian Letter ; see *J.W.J.* vol. ii. p. 211. Cf. also Wesley's manuscript cipher diary ; see *J.W.J.* vol. ii. pp. 240, 254, and 289.

anger are typical of the majority of Wesley's cases, and
are clearly signs of anger associated with fear, or at least of
anger in its protective function. It is noisy, ferocious in
aspect, as if to strike terror to the heart of the enemy, and
so remove some part of the fear from its own ; and it must
be distinguished from the anger which is allied with the
hunting instinct, and is ' stern, silent, and remorseless,
pursuing its enemy, not frightening him away.' [1] Dr.
Drever points out that the animal at bay presents several
very interesting psychological phenomena. [2] It illustrates
the fact that the stronger the impulse which meets with a
check, the fiercer as a rule is the anger aroused. Haydon's
regular and habitual loyalty to the Church of England was
at stake, and all the emotional ties of the social group
would constrain him to reject the Methodist teaching and
fellowship. The combination of fear, anger, and a
vigorous self-assertion in defence of the new faith and
its preachers, illustrates the general characteristic of
emotional life ; the motive which finally determines
action may draw a large part of its driving force from
emotions experienced simultaneously, or so short a time
previously, that the emotional disturbance has not had
time to subside—emotions, which do not themselves
issue in action at all, but which thus lend their force to
an impulse, sometimes of a totally different kind. [3]

By comparing these narratives in which physical
phenomena are prominent, with the record of conversions
presented all through the *Journal* of Wesley, it is clearly
seen that the same instinctive activity enters into the
religious crisis in the majority of normal conversions.
The disappearance of the excessive emotion after the

[1] Drever, *I.M.* p. 181.   [2] *Ibid.* p. 180.
[3] *Ibid.* p. 179-180.

physical phenomena had been condemned by Wesley, gives an interesting example of the degree of truth inherent in the James-Lange theory of emotion.[1] But against this must be set the equally apparent emotional experience of many of the converts, in whom the bodily changes were almost, if not entirely, imperceptible. There is a very close parallel between the instinctive activity revealed in the abnormal phenomena, and the instinctive elements in normal religious life. And the biological value of the instincts is comparable with their value in the later and higher organization of the religious sentiment. The reinforcing character of fear will be referred to later as one of the potent forces at work in conversion. But in the case of the human being, the primitive basis in instinct is made the foundation for a complex apprehension of danger, which includes the retrospective and prospective emotions of desire. The element of anger would seem to have two main functions. Like fear, but not to the same extent, it is protective ; like fear, but to a much greater extent, it is reinforcing. ' As a reinforcing agent, when difficulties have to be faced and overcome, its value, both to the individual and to society, is incalculable. Weaklings are what they are, as often through lack of anger in their constitution, or of its developed forms as organized forces in their character, as through excess of fear. By lack of anger we mean, not so much lack of the emotion, which is rather rare, as weakness in the instinctive driving force, the fighting instinct itself, of which anger is merely the emotional manifestation.' [2]

[1] James, *P.P.* vol. ii. pp. 449-467. The bodily changes come first and are the causes of the mental disturbance. You are afraid because your hair stands on end, and sorry because you cry.

[2] Drever, *I.M.* p. 184.

From the point of view of biology, these natural propensities have meaning and value in relation to the preservation of the individual. For the psychology of religion, curiosity, fear and anger are the primitive basis from which are organized the intellectual exploration of religious truth, or the development of theological doctrine ; the awe or attitude of reverence which is sensitive to spiritual values ; and the intensity of purpose which expresses itself in moral indignation, or in passionate dedication to religious activity.

VIII

CONVERSION

THE achievement of mental harmony through conversion is not necessarily a process that is confined to religious experience. Roberto Ardigo, the leading philosopher in Italy at the end of last century, is an instance of counter-conversion. His conflict was resolved and unification of character attained by a sudden conversion from Scholasticism and the doctrines of the Roman Catholic Church to a scientific positivism.[1] Ardigo's experience is paralleled by several cases described by Starbuck and James,[2] which illustrate the thesis that ' to find religion is only one out of many ways of reaching unity ; and the process of remedying inner incompleteness and reducing inner discord is a general psychological process, which may take place with any sort of mental material, and need not necessarily assume the religious form.' [3]   ' Conversion is a natural human phenomenon, independent alike of supernatural interference and of theological prepossession.'[4]

Emphasis on the radical nature of the change, and the use of the term ' regeneration ' have resulted in over-estimation of the completeness and suddenness of the

---

[1] Quoted by Höffding, *Modern Philosophers*, pp. 42-3 ; see Pratt, *op. cit.* pp. 126-9.

[2] James, *V.R.E.* pp. 176-9.   [3] *Ibid.* p. 175.

[4] Pratt, *op. cit.* p. 128.

158

mental revolution, and an under-estimation of the mental
continuity which operates in conversion.   It is important
to maintain the essential unity of the self through all its
crises.   ' The Becoming or Change of qualities consists in
one quality disappearing in order to give place to another
which comes after it ; the thing, the individual, does not
in changing simply cease to be,—it ceases to be in one
respect or mode in order to be in another.   There is no
contradiction in that a thing may both be and become.' [1]
And ' even when the prevailing elements of consciousness
are not the same throughout the whole of life, but different
at different stages of development, the formal unity may
still be preserved, if the transition from one standpoint
to another is *continuous and consequent*. A mental
revolution does not destroy the unity of the self if (like
most revolutions) it is but the outcome of a process
long carried on in secret.' [2]   The conversion of John
Wesley, already described, provides a concrete example of
this psychological continuity.

It has been too readily assumed by some writers on the
psychology of religion that conversion as a religious
experience is peculiar to certain sects.   Thus Professor
Ames writes of conversion, ' It is the result of immediate,
direct control and suggestion on the part of evangelists,
parents, teachers.   It is common among certain evangelical protestant denominations.   It occurs chiefly in
those communions which have cultivated an elaborate
technique to produce it.' [3]   The truth of this statement

[1] Mellone, *Philosophical Criticism and Construction*, p. 162 ; quoted
by Mark, H. Thiselton, *The Unfolding of Personality*, p. 38.
[2] Höffding, Harald, *Outlines of Psychology*, Eng. tr. p. 140 ; quoted
by Mark, *op. cit.* p. 38.
[3] Ames, Edward Scribner, *The Psychology of Religious Experience*,
p. 257.

can only be maintained on the basis of a very narrow definition of conversion. But the significance of conversion for psychology depends upon its universality ; and on this point the studies of James have a direct bearing. ' Is there,' he asks, ' under all the discrepancies of the creeds, a common nucleus to which they bear their testimony unanimously ? ' He answers immediately in the affirmative. ' The warring gods and formulas of the various religions do indeed cancel each other, but there is a certain uniform deliverance in which religions all appear to meet. It consists of two parts :

1. An uneasiness ; and
2. Its solution.

1. The uneasiness, reduced to its simplest terms, is a sense that there is *something wrong about us* as we naturally stand.

2. The solution is a sense that *we are saved from the wrongness* by making proper connection with the higher powers.' [1]

Thus James relates the experience of conversion to the mental processes which are characteristic of universal religion. Recent research on the subject of conversion in non-Christian religions abundantly confirms the view adopted by James. The psychological process of conversion is common to Hinduism, Buddhism, Mohammedanism, and to the religions of Greece and Rome, Egypt and Japan.[2] It is not limited to Protestantism or to Christianity, but is found in all the great religions of the world.

Two recent definitions of religious conversion may be

[1] James, *V.R.E.* pp. 505-6.
[2] Underwood, A. C., *Conversion : Christian and Non-Christian* (1925), *passim.*

considered as typical of the modern psychological point
of view. Professor Pratt regards the ' moral self as a
group of powers united in the service of a harmonious
system of purposes,' and conversion is identified with
the ' new birth ' or ' regeneration,' ' by which a man ceases
to be a mere psychological thing, or a divided self, and
becomes a unified being with a definite direction under
the guidance of a group of consistent and harmonious
purposes or ideals.' [1] Dr. Thouless approaches religious
experience with more definitely psychoanalytic presuppositions, and he defines conversion as 'an outbreak
into consciousness of something, such as a system of
beliefs, which seems to have had no period of development
in the mind.' [2] The weakness of these definitions from
the point of view of psychology is that in the first case
the emphasis is almost entirely on the ethical aspect of
the crisis, and in the second case the reference to a system
of beliefs gives undue prominence to the intellectual
factor. These definitions cover particular types of
conversion ; they are not true of conversion in general.
Both the types defined are found in the narratives of
Methodism, but the typical Methodist conversion must
be more accurately defined. Such a definition must
necessarily be broad and abstract, in order to cover the
wide variety of experiences under review. Conversion
denotes ' the process, gradual or sudden, by which a self
hitherto divided, and consciously wrong inferior and
unhappy, becomes unified and consciously right superior
and happy,' [3] through the establishment of a right
relationship with the object of the religious sentiment.
This unification is more than the attainment of moral

[1] Pratt, *op. cit.* p. 123.   [2] Thouless, *op. cit.* p. 188.
[3] James, *V.R.E.* p. 189.

D.M.R.   X

self-hood, and more than the outcropping of unconscious
elements. It includes both these, but it also involves
attention and will, and, even more essentially, rational
and emotional experiences. Defined in this way, the
experience of conversion in Methodism may be regarded
as typical of religious conversion in general, as a normal
experience of human nature.

Certain features are distinctive of the conversion narratives of Methodism, and from some of these a wider inference
may be drawn. The cases examined for our purpose in
John Wesley's *Journal* and in other contemporary documents provide empirical grounds for several generaliza-
tions. In Methodism, conversions are mainly instantaneous;
they are marked by a combination of emotional and ethical
elements; a large proportion of the subjects are adults,
and they are not unstable or neurotic types; and the crisis
varies in the stage which it represents in the organization
of the religious sentiment.

In his sermon on ' Patience,' Wesley writes, ' Not
trusting to the testimony of others, I carefully examined
most of these myself; and in London alone I found six
hundred and fifty-two members of society who were
exceedingly clear in their experience, and of whose
testimony I could see no reason to doubt. I believe no
year has passed since that time wherein God has not
wrought the same work in many others . . . and every
one of these (after the most careful inquiry, I have not
found one exception either in Great Britain or Ireland)
has declared that his deliverance from sin was *instantaneous*; that the change was wrought in a moment.
Had half of these, or one third, or one in twenty, declared
it was gradually wrought in them, I should have believed

this, with regard to them, and thought that *some* were gradually sanctified and some instantaneously. But as I have not found, in so long a space of time, a single person speaking thus ; as all who believe they are sanctified, declare with one voice, that the change was wrought in a moment ; I cannot but believe that sanctification is commonly, if not always, an *instantaneous* work.' [1] The only qualification of this statement which psychological analysis would necessitate has reference to the unconscious process of preparation for conversion, which is evident in nearly all the cases where full information as to the history of the convert is available.

John Wesley

The blending of emotional and ethical factors in the conversions of Methodism is characteristic and almost constant. I have examined one hundred and thirty-two cases described in considerable detail in the first five volumes of the *Journal*, and while eight only of these are concerned with a specific moral issue, the desire to be freed from moral reprobation, or the experience usually named ' conviction of sin ', is strongly emphasized in one hundred and twenty-two out of the total. The affective element dominates the situation in one hundred and eighteen cases. Thus, out of the total number of conversion narratives scrutinized, the emotional experience is emphasized in 89.4 per cent. of the cases, and 92.4 per cent. have a distinct ethical significance.

Did he use EMP ?

The records of Methodism indicate clearly that instantaneous experience of ' salvation ' through religion is not peculiar to the period of adolescence, nor to neurotic or emotional types. The work of Starbuck, which was based upon a statistical inquiry,[2] and Dr. G. Stanley Hall's

---

[1] Sermon LXXXIII., *W.W.* vol. vi. p. 465. The italics are Wesley's.
[2] Starbuck, E. D., *The Psychology of Religion* (1899), chaps. xvi.-xxi.

valuable study of adolescence [1] have been largely responsible for the currency of the formula, ' Conversion is an adolescent phenomenon.' The similarity of the mental processes accounts for this identification. The autobiographies of Wesley's early preachers are filled with phrases which suggest the phenomena of adolescence : the sense of incompleteness and imperfection ; brooding, depression, morbid introspection, and sense of sin ; anxiety about the hereafter ; and distress concerning doubts. And the culmination of the process is the same, consisting as it does in a ' happy relief and objectivity, as the confidence in self gets greater through the adjustment of the faculties to the wider outlook.' [2] But neither in the Methodist documents nor in the wider history of religion, does this analogy cover the whole of the facts. John Wesley was converted at the age of thirty-five, and his brother Charles at the age of thirty-one. A number of the converts are described as middle-aged ; two only are called ' young persons ' ; some were parents whose children are referred to in the narrative ; [3] and several of those who became preachers and active workers were converted after the age of twenty-five,[4] which is the upward limit for normal adolescent development. The fact that a large number of the converts were of mature age might be anticipated when it is remembered that Wesley preached to new populations, who were beyond the range of the influence of the Church ; and that for this reason many of his hearers never had the opportunity in youth and adolescence to hear the message of the

[1] *Adolescence : its Psychology, Physiology, etc.*, 2 vols.

[2] James, *V.R.E.* p. 199.

[3] *E.g. J.W.J.* iii. 185-6 ; v. 19.

[4] *J.W.J.* vol. ii. 189, 199 ; iii. 23-4. John Murlin, *Wesley's Veterans*, vol. ii. p. 159.

Christian religion. These circumstances were paralleled in the first New England Revival, where the majority of the converts heard the Gospel for the first time, and the ages ranged from twenty-five to forty-five, some being still older.[1] This may only prove that there are exceptions to the rule formulated by Starbuck and Hall. But it is in harmony with the evidence of religious history. Dr. Thouless refers to St. Paul, St. Augustine, and Tolstoy as well-known examples of great religious leaders who were converted late in life.[2]

The evidence provided by the Methodist Revival experience does not support the conclusions of James [3] and Professor Coe,[4] whose investigations apparently proved that the subjects of instantaneous conversion were characterized by, first, pronounced emotional sensibility ; second, tendency to automatisms ; and third, suggestibility of the passive type. Nor are the examples of sudden conversion in Methodism traceable to overwrought nerves. Wesley noted in the cases which he investigated at Gateshead Fell, ' That all of them (I think, not one of them excepted) were persons in perfect health ; and had not been subject to fits of any kind, till they were thus affected.' [5] Dr. Caldecott, in his psychological study of Wesley's early preachers, says that, ' though these young men describe unusually intense emotionality, they were not of ill-balanced nervous systems ; they all lived vigorously, and most of them continued laborious pursuits until advanced old age ; they were not fretting under

[1] Steven, G., *The Psychology of the Christian Soul*, p. 174.

[2] Thouless, R. H., *I.P.R.* p. 187.   For evidence in favour of the older view, see Underwood, A. C., *Conversion*, chap. x.

[3] *V.R.E.* pp. 240-241.

[4] *The Spiritual Life* (New York, 1900), p. 112.

[5] *J.W.J.* vol. iii. p. 69.

disappointments, or depressed with the *ennui* of prematurely worn-out single emotions, the "sorrows of youth"; nor were they of melancholy temperament, apt to cherish sadness and gloom, averse to cheerfulness and joy; they struggled against the sadness they experienced in the first stage they describe, with an irresistible conviction that it need not be there if only joy could be obtained.'[1] A similar description is given by M. de Fursac of the converts in the Welsh Revival whom he interviewed. He writes, ' Tous les cinq (including ' un homme pieux ' who conducted them) sont des mineurs, dans la force de l'âge, de 35 à 50 ans, grands, bien développés, solides, les mains calleuses, rien du pseudo-mystique névrosé et débile, avide de sensations nouvelles, que nous présente de temps à autre notre vie moderne.'[2] Methodism has been peculiarly prolific of the type which combines healthy-mindedness with readiness for religious conversion. And with reference to the psychophysical effects, the general conclusion to be drawn from the story of the revival scenes is quite contrary to that of James, who inferred that, ' On the whole, unconsciousness, convulsions, visions, involuntary vocal utterances, and suffocation, must be simply ascribed to the subjects having a large subliminal region, involving nervous instability.'[3] These features of the conversion experience have been shown, where they occur, to be traceable to the stimulation of the primary instincts, and these native tendencies are not necessarily stronger in those whose nervous system is unstable.

The nature and significance of the conversion crisis in its relation to the organization of the religious sentiment

---

[1] *R.S.* pp. 8-9.   [2] De Fursac, *op. cit.* p. 61.
[3] James, *V.R.E.* p. 251.

in different individuals reveals considerable variation. In some cases, particularly in those of the adolescent type, the conversion marks the initiation of a process of integration in which there is still a period of storm and stress to be passed through. One convert wrote to Wesley, in a hitherto unpublished letter, ' When your Brother was preaching . . . I recieved the Remishon of my sins, tho I was not without Doughts and fears for 3 quaters of a Year, Yett the Lord was my keeper, though I was sometimes in heaviness through manifold temptations.'[1] In Dr. Caldecott's study of Wesley's veterans, he points out that, ' in two-thirds of the cases a series of vicissitudes after the first victory is recorded before a final harmony is won. . . . These vicissitudes continue for periods of all lengths : five, six, seven years ; one records a single lapse which lasted five years ; another, a Dorset soldier, one of twenty years.'[2] Parallel instances may be drawn from Hinduism, as for example in the case of Ramakrishna, the famous Bengalee saint and mystic and the founder of the religious order that bears his name. He passed through a period of mental conflict which lasted twelve years. Looking back on it, he says, ' a great religious tornado, as it were, raged within him during these years and made everything topsy-turvy.'[3] On the other hand, one-third of the cases examined by Dr. Caldecott record a prompt achievement of unity and mental harmony, and a clear current through the rest of life. ' The

[1] MS. Letter from Mary Bainton to John Wesley, dated Oct. 3, 1742. Copied by permission of Russell J. Colman, D.L., Norwich. The misspelt words are reproduced from the original letter.

[2] John Haime (1710-1784). See Caldecott, *R.S.* p. 21.

[3] Max Müller, *The Life and Sayings of Ramakrishna*, p. 41 ; quoted by Pratt, *R.C.* p. 132. Compare also the MSS. Letters from Susanna Designe to John Wesley, 1740-1741, quoted below, pp. 175-7. See Underwood, *op. cit.* pp. 65-6.

clearest case of this is a Cornish carpenter, but it is notable that the change in his case did not come till he was nearly thirty years old.' [1]   The conversion in these cases, of which there were twelve out of a total of thirty-four, marks the final stability of the religious sentiment.[2] Although the records are brief and incomplete, the average number of those whose conversion marks the completion, and not merely the initiation of harmonious life, would seem to be higher in the *Journal* than in the autobiographies of the veterans.   A typical piece of introspection from the conversion narratives in the *Journal* concludes, ' I had the witness in myself that He had made an end of sin and taken my whole heart for ever.   And from that moment I have never lost the witness nor felt anything in my heart but pure love.' [3]

[1] John Murlin (1722-99), *Lives of the Early Methodist Preachers*, vol. iii. pp. 293-306.   Caldecott, *R.S.* p. 22.

[2] But note also Mr. Shand's remarks on the flux and plasticity of the third and highest stage in the development of character, *F.C.* p. 173.

[3] M. B. ' who had long been a " mother in Israel," ' described her experience to John Wesley fifteen years after her conversion.   See *J.W.J.* vol. iv. p. 202.

IX

TYPES OF CONVERSION

An interesting variety of schemes has been produced by
the attempts that have been made to find a satisfactory
method of classifying cases of conversion. The principles
of division have too frequently been neither logical nor
psychological. Pratt distinguishes mainly emotional and
moral types.[1] Thouless discriminates between adult and
adolescent conversion, treating mystical experience with
adolescence, and subdividing ordinary adult conversion
into mainly moral, intellectual or social.[2] James describes
the gradual conversion type as ' healthy-minded,' and the
struggling and suddenly converted subject he calls ' the
sick soul.' [3] Höffding makes a similar distinction between
' expansive ' and ' discordant ' natures. A further distinction is made by Höffding, which finds frequent illustration in Methodism. ' Where development proceeds
by leaps, and where there is a tendency to emotional
states, we get a type which might be called *affective*. The
peculiarity of other natures causes their development to
proceed by small steps, and hence it presents the character
of continuity. . . . The *continuous* type (as we will call
this type) has a certain kinship with the expansive type.' [4]

[1] Pratt, *R.C.* p. 152.   [2] Thouless, *op. cit.* chaps. xiii. and xiv.
[3] James, *V.R.E.* chaps. iv.-viii.
[4] Höffding, *Philosophy of Religion*, pp. 284-288.

The relation of these classifications to the popular psycho-analytic distinctions of introversion and extroversion,[1] unstable-minded and stable-minded,[2] is manifest, and is typical of the way in which normal differences in human mentality are refined upon by specialized psychological vocabularies.

The inadequacy of these classifications is illustrated by the fact that the conversion of John Wesley may be so interpreted that it conforms to all the types described. His conversion was certainly an emotional crisis, yet he always claimed that it had a moral significance. The complete change of doctrine implicit in the whole experience is indicative of a definite intellectual content. Conflict with his social and family environment characterize it as a ' social ' conversion. Wesley's steady and lifelong pursuit of his vocation in active service for his fellows identifies him with the healthy-minded, expansive and continuous types. Yet his emotional discord and conflict, and the instantaneous conversion coincide with the experience of the ' sick soul,' the discordant, and the affective types. His immense activity marks him out as an extrovert, while his self-examination and ceaseless introspections give him a place among the introverts. In his conservatism, Wesley is ' stable-minded '; in his flexibility and adaptability he is ' unstable-minded.' On the whole, it is probable that Wesley's conversion is best described as of the intuitive or mystical type. The noetic quality which is the empirical basis of the doctrine of assurance—the experimental and unassailable certainty that a new and happy relation was established between

[1] Nicoll Maurice, *Dream Psychology*, chaps. xiv.-xv. ; Tansley, *op. cit.* pp. 101-102 ; based upon Jung, *Analytical Psychology*, chap. xi.

[2] Tansley, *N.P.* pp. 103-7 ; Trotter, *op. cit.* chap. ii.

him and the object of his religious sentiment—was the most marked and individual feature of his conversion.

An examination of the records of conversion contained in the *Journal* and in private MS. letters yields a three-fold classification only. A large class of cases must be described as instinctive and emotional ; a second group is of the intuitive or mystical type ; and a third is marked by practical or moral issues. It will be recognized that these classes have affinities with the old psychological analysis of mental activity into the ultimate factors of emotion, intellect and will. The principles of division may seem to be provisional and to some extent arbitrary, but their empirical justification is in the documents.

The crudest and most obvious examples of conversions that turn upon ' instinct experience ' are those in which the physical effects already analysed occur. And these, as Davenport discovered, are found most frequently among primitive and elemental types of humanity. The general features of the class are familiar, and they centre in the stimulation of powerful native propensities ; curiosity, fear, repulsion, and anger being commonly the most apparent. In its most elementary form, conversion of this kind involves violent terror and its expulsion by the more powerful sentiment of love. The more superficial aspects of the experience may be illustrated by one of the Irish cases. Wesley writes, ' She was crying, " I am dropping, dropping into hell ; its mouth is open, ready to swallow me up ! " I went to prayer again, and before we had done, God spoke peace to her soul. She was filled with joy unspeakable, and could but just say, " I am in a new world ! I am in a new world ! " ' [1]

[1] *J.W.J.* vol. iii. p. 423.

The conventionality of the phraseology here, and in the numerous cases of a similar type, cannot disguise the reality of the experience.

The violent stimulation of primitive instincts created a passional crisis which after the first elation and joy had faded, brought a dangerous reaction sometimes ending in moral collapse. This possibility, and other features of the emotional conversion type are illustrated by one of a series of letters written by his converts to John Wesley in the years 1739-1741.[1] On the letter of John Enser, dated July 24, 1740, Wesley had noted, with an exclamation mark, thus, ' in orca ! ' The letter runs thus :

' John Westly for I cannot use any apology neither rough nor smooth saving that for several reasons I choose to deliver my Horrid sentiments to you in writing. It is about 9 or 10 weeks ago since I received Justification or pardon applied to my Heart, the Lord being the Agent, your brother Charles the minister, att which time I was full of Love to God and man, full of Light in the Holy Scriptures, full of Joy in the Holy Ghost, full of Faith, full of Expectation of fresh Light, receiving many gracious promises, as, God careth for thee, whereby I was delivered from all my worldly cares, and walked on as though I had been walking in the air ; insomuch that I thought work was done. I told your brother God had got full possession

---

[1] All the sixteen letters, except one which is torn and incomplete, are indexed in John Wesley's handwriting, and the fact that they were preserved by Wesley is proof of the importance which he attached to them. The date of his reply is added, together with a cruciform mark, which is possibly a sign that he had prayed for the writer. The letters are in the Colman Collection, and form a packet of sixteen, labelled, ' Letters from female members of Mr. Wesley's Society,' in the Colman Collection of Wesley Relics ; Librarian, Mr. A. J. Quinton, 186 Thorpe Road, Norwich. They have been copied by permission of Russell J. Colman, D.L. The mis-spelt words and quaint use of capitals are reproduced from the MSS.

of my Heart. Tis true He gave me a caution not to be too sure. And now I have cause enough to remember, for now the scene is quite altered : things has now another face : now all things are past away, behold all things are become old. But not indeed properly, for I never before felt such a Hell as I now feel. I now am as very a devil as ever was or will be confined in the Everlasting Chains of darkness. I now hate God, hate my Brother, hate my Children, hate all that is good, and what adds much to my sorrow in it, I know God and the Father and our Lord Jesus Christ Loves me. I am as proud as Lucifer, as covetous as mamon, as hateful as Belzeebub, and as Lustful. As for my wife, I take no more notice of her,

> Than I do of the Spiders Webb
> Swept from the Wall by the Gidy Maid.

Dr Sir what shall I do in this condition ? I am just upon the point of breaking off from God, of declaring for the Devil. Therefore if you can help me by writing to me or talking with me you will ever be remembered by your poor & miserable & blind & naked felow creature.

JOHN ENSER.'

The description of the various feeling tones of expansion and elation which follow conversion is curiously complete. Emphasis is placed on all-embracing love, light, joy, expectation ; deliverance from anxiety.; a sense of security and completeness. The feeling that one is walking in the air is a sensation due largely to the vaso-motor relaxation which is brought about by mental exhilaration or religious concentration, as it is by the approach of sleep or anaesthesia.[1] The ecstasy of relief

[1] Horton, L. H., ' The Illusion of Levitation,' *Journal of Abnormal Psychology*, vol. xiii. pp. 42-5, 119-127 ; quoted by Pratt, *R.C.* p. 421.

and light-heartedness affects not only the senses of sight and hearing, but in some cases the more fundamental and less easily inhibited sensations of pressure and muscle and joint sensibility. The language of Enser may be figurative, but it is typical of a phenomenon which becomes more intense and realistic in the transports of the mystics. ' My body became so light during ravishment,' says St. Teresa, ' that it no longer had any weight, so that in fact sometimes I could not feel my feet touch the ground.' [1]

The phrase ' work was done ' is the clue to the darker aspects of the picture. Stress is placed all the time on the emotions experienced, never on any activity, purposive or altruistic. The work is of God, and it is complete in the inward raptures. A peculiarity of the letter is that it consists of one continuous sentence, without punctuation, and that the various forms of the first personal pronoun occur thirty-six times in what can only be analyzed into thirteen sentences. The whole drama is one of self-centred concentration on the affective or emotional experience ; no real change of character, no new devotion of self and its energies had been wrought. The room was empty, swept, and garnished, and waiting for the devil to return, bringing with him ' seven other spirits more wicked than himself,' to enter in and dwell there, that the last state of the man might be worse than the first.[2] Jesus knew what was in man, and the mental tragedy of the aimless, purposeless individual is nowhere better described. The touch of genuine tragedy is in

[1] St. Teresa, *Vie* (French translation by Bouix, Paris, Lecoffre, 1907), p. 200, and chap. xx. *passim* ; see Pratt, *op. cit.* p. 421. But note that St. Teresa regarded such experiences as abnormal. See Joly, *Psych. of Saints*, 94-99.

[2] St. Matthew xii. 44-5.

the passage, ' now all things are past away, behold all things have become old,' which tells of the complete antithesis to the normal conversion experience : ' if any man is in Christ, there is a new creation.' [1] The reaction from excessive emotional exaltation not only produces extreme depression, but it results in the weakening of moral control, with the tendency to the release of primitive passion, as evidenced in the list that Enser gives of his obsessing temptations. Indications that the inner discord is not resolved, and that interest in a complete moral victory is really dominant, are found in the prayer with which the letter concludes.

Further light is thrown upon the ' instinct experience ' in conversion by three letters written to Wesley by a school-mistress in Bristol. They illustrate the remark of Dr. G. Stanley Hall that ' True piety is earthly love transcendentalised, and the saint is the lover, purified, refined and perfected.' [2] Religion is not dishonoured by the discovery of its primitive psychological bases in potent tendencies, whether these be the fear or anger of the first stage, or the sex and parental love of the second stage in conversion. Susanna Designe writes, in her first letter, of her inability to declare to others what her Redeemer has done, and the ' unspeakable love ' that she experiences daily. ' O what a faint shadow is my stammering tongue able to represent. I am overcome with his love : Lost in wonder and amazement, and can only end in adoring silence, and pray to my Lord to reveal this mistery of his love to them by a glorious experience in their own souls. . . . I can say I am coming from the wilderness leaning upon my Beloved, and though some

[1] 2 Cor. v. 17.
[2] *Adolescence : its Psychology, etc.*, vol. ii. p. 294.

places of this wilderness is dark and gloomy, yet he is a guide to my feet and a lanthorn to my paths. . . . When I lift up my heart to the Lord, I find such a power drawing my soul into holy Breathings to Love the Lord with my whole heart, as I cannot express : such Longing Desires to be set free from myself. . . . When my soul is thus drawn out with these desires, I find my bodily strength fail me, and I am as weak as an infant. I feel such flames of love to my Dear Saviour and to all mankind as I cannot express.' [1]

Thirteen months later, in a much more pensive tone, she writes, ' I find great outward trials and inward fightings, but in ye strength of Jesus I still am conqueror over ye world, ye flesh, and ye Devil. Although I find all evil tempers in me, yet I do abhor them. My own heart is ye worst enemy I find to deal with. . . . I am such a mistery to myself as I cannot express, but I believe you will better understand me than I do myself. I have stronger convictions and self condemnation in my self than I had before I knew my sins forgiven, and although my words and actions as far as I know do agree with ye written Law of God, yet something within me condemns me in all I do and say.'

Four months later her confidence had gone, and she again wrote to Wesley : ' I am glad of this opportunity to let you know ye distress of my soul. I have been almost ever since you left Bristol in such hardness of Heart as I never felt before. I am worse than I was before I tasted ye Lord was gracious . . . ye tears that now flows from my eyes seemed to come from my Heart. I am ready to tell ye Stocks & Stones I am a Hippocrite . . . it is ye Hour & power of Darkness. I am miserable.

[1] Manuscript letter ; Colman Collection.

Sometime I would hope I am miserable because I find myself unholy, but I dare hardly harbour so good a thought of myself.   Yet I know ye Lord is with me & his power over me because I am kept from outward Sin, and what seemeth a mistery to me, when I am out among worldly people, I find a greater power to reprove gainsayers than ever I had, & cannot forbear where I see any marks of grace, admonishing them to believe in Christ, telling them of his great love and Readiness to save them. Though at ye same time I do not find any of ye love of God in my Heart. . . . .   I seem almost Stupid.   Sometimes I can hardly give a reasonable answer to any question that is ever so deliberately asked me.   Great peevishness attends me ; it is a burden to me.   But I find no way of escape. . . .   I grieve that I can grieve no more. . . .   Sometime a thought returneth backwards to think upon ye sweet communion I oft had with Jesus, but it brings no food for my soul.   I cannot dwell upon it scarce a moment. . . .   One thing I find very remarkable : in all my Darkness, when I meet my Bands, I neither want words to speak nor power to pray for them. Ye Lord for that time gives me Light and Decernment ; and afterwards I am shut up [in] the same Darkness, and when I come in secret to ye Lord, I am as a beast before him.   I am ready to hope my Lord is stripping me naked before him, that he may clothe me with himself.   O that he might empty me of everything and fill me with his love.'[1]

The lack of objectivity and the introversion here are emphasized by the comparative relief which was found in two different kinds of activity, when attention was directed to the admonition or edification of others.   Bad co-ordination was the result of excessive emotional stress,

[1] Manuscript letter ; Colman Collection.

and the inclination is not so much in the direction of moral collapse as towards mental disintegration. A misdirection of emotional life after conversion produced psycho-neurosis. There is no moral delinquency in question ; the writer is conducting her school, leading her ' Band,' exhorting gainsayers, and, as indicated by a postscript to her second letter, facing much opposition and persecution in the conduct of her school as a consequence of her association with the Methodists.

Irritability and intellectual inertness are referred to as causes for grief, but they are more probably the consequences of grief. Introversion when it becomes extreme is dangerously near to pathological conditions, and for this there is a biological reason. ' The process of extroversion is the primitive biological function of the mind. Biologically the mind and its powers only have significance so far as they can be *used* in life. They were developed in relation to the world in which the organism lived and their nature was determined, as we have seen, by the environment of the species, to which they were intimately adapted. The process of introversion is primarily a sign of lack of such adaptation.'[1] A danger of this kind is apparent throughout the history of the Revival, and is due to the excessive stimulation of primary impulses and emotions, and to the great importance that was attached to ' experience,' which frequently meant the concentration of attention upon religious feelings and affections.

The nature of the distress after conversion is very significant in this case. She was a mystery to herself. Her trouble could not be attributed to fear of the wrath of God, as she was not conscious of any such fear. The plaint is more akin to that of a lover separated from the

---

[1] Tansley, A. G., *N.P.* p. 102.

object of his love. She longs for ' ye sweet communion I oft had with Jesus.' The phrases in the earlier letters suggest the same type of religious attitude : ' leaning upon my Beloved ' ; ' a power drawing my soul into holy breathings to love the Lord ' ; ' such flames of love to my dear Saviour.' Apparently it is the transiency of these mystical ecstasies which is the cause of the grief expressed in the two later letters. The reality of the communion with the object of the religious sentiment was regarded as dependent upon the constancy of the emotional rapture. This confession, therefore, comes within the range of mystical experience, and forms a point of contact between the instinctive and emotional type and the intuitive or mystical type of conversion.

The fusion of instinctive and rational factors is illustrated by a few cases of what may be described as social conversion, in which the centre of the mental conflict is in the clash of individual with social impulses. An instinctive explanation is obviously inadequate for an experience of this kind, as the emotional elements in the situation are organized into the higher systems of the sentiments. Social conversion is exemplified in Methodism by the cases of Martin Madan,[1] a cousin of the poet Cowper, who was converted under Wesley's ministry, renounced his profession of barrister, and became an evangelical clergyman ; and the Countess of Huntingdon, who supported Whitefield and was instrumental in building Whitefield's Tabernacle, and many other chapels and preaching places.[2] In cases of this type and in that

[1] W.H.S. vol. v. pp. 142-5 ; Tyerman, L.T.W. vol. ii. p. 283 ; J.W.J. vol. iv. pp. 11-12, note.

[2] J.W.J. vols. i.-v. passim. See also N.H.M. vol. i. pp. 269-270 ; Tyerman, op. cit. passim.

of clergymen of the Church of England who openly avowed themselves converts to Methodism, there is in the conversion a struggle in which the contending interests are either individual conviction and social obligation, or the allegiance which is demanded by two mutually opposed communities. But although Methodism provides a few examples in which the conflicting claims of opposing loyalties intensify the critical nature of the mental revolution, there are none in which the breach with another religious or social system involved a complete and final breach in family and intimate personal relationships, as with St. Paul or the Sadhu Sundar Singh.[1] Consequently these conversion experiences have more affinity with the mystical than with the purely social or with the instinctive class of religious conversions. There is therefore no reason for constituting a distinct category for social conversions in the psychology of the Revival.

The general psychological features of intuitive or mystical conversion are set forth in the chapter dealing with John Wesley's religious sentiment. The distinctive mark of this class is the transition from an ordinary religious life to various stages of religious experience which can be described as mystical. ' By a mystic, we mean a person to whom the emotional religious experiences which occur at times to all religious persons have become stronger and more permanent. He has other experiences differing in many of their qualities from those of the ordinary religious person. The mystic is also much more liable to have experiences which would be considered pathological by the doctor—visions, voices, trances, etc. These marks are sufficient to indicate, for the present

[1] Streeter and Appasamy, *The Sadhu*; quoted Thouless, *op. cit.* pp. 201-2.

purpose, the kind of mentality covered by the word *mystic*. They are not intended to provide a definition of mysticism.'[1] As in the case of Wesley's awakening at the age of twenty-two and his conversion at thirty-five, mystical conversion is frequently preceded by an earlier conversion of the adolescent type. Pascal was first converted at the age of twenty-three, and his mystical conversion came eight years later.[2] Wesley's experience also illustrates the repression and inner conflict which precede intuitive conversion. Dr. Thouless describes the mystical change as 'the redirection of the whole of the *libido* into the religious sentiment,' or ' the religious sublimation of the entire instinctive nature.'[3] The emphasis in these definitions is placed on the ' energy of the mind,' and the instincts are regarded as the driving power. Very important aspects of Wesley's experience are comprehended in this psychological description, but no recognition is given to the noetic quality of the mystical communion. There is a positive intellectual content in Wesley's conversion ; and this element, based upon intuition, is one of the essential marks of mystical conversion.

Two examples of intuitive conversion are selected from the pages of John Wesley's *Journal*. Both the subjects were women already living in earnest devotion to the Christian faith ; and in one case visual, and in the other case auditory hallucinations occur.

' While one read the Passion Hymn,[4] on a sudden I saw

---

[1] Thouless, *I.P.R.* p. 205.

[2] *Vie de Blaise Pascal*, by Mme. Périer, his sister ; quoted by Thouless, *I.P.R.* pp. 206-8.

[3] Thouless, *I.P.R.* p. 213.

[4] ' Ye that pass by, behold the Man ' ; No. 24 in the 1808 edition of the hymns.

our Saviour on the cross, as plain as if it had been with my bodily eyes. . . . I could do nothing but weep and mourn, day and night (that is, from Friday to Monday). Then I saw, as it were, heaven opened, and God sitting upon His throne in the midst of ten thousand of His saints, and I saw a large book, in which all my sins were written ; and He blotted them out, and my heart was filled with peace and joy and love, which I have not lost to this hour.' [1]

The subject of the second example was in her own home on Sunday morning, and she described her experience thus : ' I was just going to open my Bible when a voice (whether inward or outward I cannot tell) seemed to say very loud, " God, for Christ's sake, hath forgiven thee." I started up, took the candle, and searched all about, to see if anyone was near ; but there was none. I then sat down, with such a peace and joy in my soul as cannot be described. While I was musing what it could mean, I heard it again, saying, " Go in peace, thy sins are forgiven thee." I trembled exceedingly, not with fear, but with such an emotion as I cannot express. Yet I got up a second time and opened the door to see if it was a human voice. Soon after it was repeated the third time, still louder ; which drove me on my knees to prayer, being overwhelmed with the love of God, and, for the time, utterly incapable of doubt or fear.' [2]

The conventionality and uniformity of these intro-spections is characteristic of the accounts of mystical conversion generally. A complete psychological explanation of these particular cases is impossible in the absence of fuller information as to the previous history of the subjects. Human love makes more insistent demands

[1] *J.W.J.* vol. iii. p. 374 ; cf. vol. iii. 156, 267.   [2] *Ibid.* p. 508.

[margin handwritten note:] And also render such accounts suspect. Such 'conventionality' makes one wonder just how often converts were describing their own actual experiences, and how often merely copying the style & content used by others.

upon mental energy than any other sentiment, and we know nothing of the love-interests in these cases. Nor is there detailed information concerning the subsequent life of the converts. But the main features provide material for a psychological description of mystical conversion. The sins referred to are probably superficial, as in the case of Bunyan [1] and Wesley, and would presumably refer to dancing, going to plays, reading trifling books,[2] or even laughing and jesting.[3] Consequently, from the point of view of social ethics, the moral significance of these conversions is negligible. The inner conflict and uneasiness due largely, as we have seen in Wesley's experience, to repression, are generalized as ' conviction of sin,' which has a specialized meaning, and refers to the *sense* of sin,[4] not to any recognition of definite acts or negligences. And this *sense of sin* was often fostered and ' hugged, exactly as the Catholic ascetic or Indian sadhu hugs physical sufferings.' [5] The moment when relief comes and mental harmony is attained is characterized by a sense of the inflooding of Divine grace, and it is always attributed to an external and supernatural power. ' God himself blotted out her sins ' ; the voice said, ' God hath forgiven thee.' It is the direct action of God upon the individual human life, and the mystical experience is characterized by the marks which James describes.[6] ' Such a peace and joy in my soul as cannot be described ' : ' such an emotion as I cannot express ' : it was ineffable.

[1] On the conversion of Bunyan, see especially Pratt, *R.C.* pp. 140-145.

[2] Cf. *J.W.J.* vol. iii. p. 220. [3] *Ibid.* p. 159.

[4] For a discussion of the Germanic tendency (as James says) to think of Sin in the singular and with a capital ' S,' see Ames, *Psychology of Religious Experience*, pp. 257-9 ; and Pratt, *op. cit.* pp. 111-115, 140-145, 152-155.

[5] Pratt, *op. cit.* pp. 146-7. [6] James, *V.R.E.* pp. 380-2.

The passivity of the subject is apparent in each case : ' While one read . . . I saw.' And the transiency of the ecstasy is also manifest in the phrase, ' for the time . . . incapable of doubt or fear.' The intuitive certainty of forgiveness through Christ in both cases is the intellectual content of the mystical conversion : the noetic quality of the moments when veritable communion with God is mystically realized.

The accompanying hallucinations are not necessary to mystical communion, and they are frequently found in the phenomena of conversion both volitional and emotional, as well as mystical. In these cases there is no strong excitement due to the revival atmosphere, and to the influence of crowd suggestion, as in the experiences described as collective hallucinations in an earlier chapter.[1] But the weeping and trembling indicate an affective state, and in each case the concentration of attention upon the desired religious experience creates a mental susceptibility to illusion. The content of the fallacious perception is obviously dependent upon memory and experience. In the first example the hearing of the words of the hymn would stimulate the sensory centres, and would also provide the material for the imagination. Thus in this case the hallucination would be peripherally initiated, while in the second case central initiation seems to be the only explanation, except that the Bible at hand would suggest the phraseology of the locutions.

The behaviour of the two women indicates a doubt as to the reality of an objective presence corresponding to the sensations. One writes, ' as if it had been with my bodily eyes ' ; and the other records a voice, ' whether inward or outward I cannot tell.' Dr. Thouless

---

[1] *Vide supra*, chap. vi. pp. 136-8.

would describe these as *imaginal* (a word used to indicate mental facts belonging to the same class as images) as distinct from *exterior* visions or locutions, in which the object seen or heard appears to the percipient to belong to the outside world ; and as distinct from *intellectual* visions and locutions, depending not upon anything seen or heard, but upon an inner recognition of a presence or communication. *Imaginal* experience is a term which more truly describes these phenomena for psychology than the term pseudo-hallucination.[1] ' The subject of a genuine hallucination may be aware that his own imagination has furnished the material for the vision. He is able to indicate the subjective character of the hallucination, but thinks it real, nevertheless, or at any rate, cannot escape it. . . . The presence of a certain feeling of subjectivity . . . ' does not ' disprove the sensory character of the experience. . . . The patient sees, hears, smells really, he does not merely imagine that he sees and hears.'[2] This general statement is borne out by the particular cases quoted : in the first instance by the weeping at the sight of the Cross, and in the second by the searching of the house for the speaker. The interpretation given by James and M. de Fursac, and already outlined above, applies equally to these experiences ; and the facts conform to the general law that the hallucinatory perceptions of healthy persons are subject to the same laws that govern all perception.[3]

Distinct from the conversions which turn upon instinc-

[1] Thouless, *op. cit.* pp. 73-6.

[2] Griesinger, *Die Pathol. u. Therapie d. psych.* (2nd ed. 1867), p. 86 ; Eng. Tr., *Mental Pathology and Therapeutics* (London, 1867) ; quoted by Parish, Edmund, *Hallucinations and Illusions : A Study of the Fallacies of Perception* (London, 1897).

[3] Parish, Edmund, *op. cit.* p. 341.

D.M.R. 2 A

tive fear or upon other primitive impulses, and from the experiences of the intuitive and mystical type, are the cases in which the struggle is mainly volitional or practical, and is concerned with what has been called ' a malady of attention.' [1] These involve a specific moral conflict, and are generally associated with the more flagrant types of vice, chiefly drunkenness [2] and ' immorality.' [3] The first conversion described in John Wesley's *Journal* illustrates the characteristic features of the class. One who had ' long used all the means of grace, had constantly gone to Church, and Sacrament, had read the Scripture, and used much private prayer,' was still ' enslaved to sin . . . especially to drunkenness . . . he had all the signs of settled despair, both in his countenance and behaviour. I desired we might join in prayer. After a short space, he rose, and his countenance was no longer sad. He said, " Now I know God loveth me, and has forgiven my sins ; and sin shall not have dominion over me : for Christ hath set me free." And according to his faith it was unto him.' [4]

Thirteen years later, Wesley was at Bolton, and he entered in his *Journal*, ' The barber who shaved me said, " Sir, I praise God on your behalf. When you was at Bolton last, I was one of the most eminent drunkards in all the town ; but I came to listen at the window, and God struck me to the heart. I then earnestly prayed for power against drinking ; and God gave me more than I asked ; for He took away the very desire of it. Yet I felt myself worse and worse, till on April 5th last, I felt

[1] Steven, G., *The Psychology of the Christian Soul*, chap. iv.

[2] See *J.W.J.* vol. ii. p. 80 ; iii. 521, 398 ; v. 20.

[3] See *J.W.J.* iii. 105.

[4] *J.W.J.* vol. ii. p. 80 ; see also private diary, in *J.W.J.* vol. ii. p. 84, note.

I could hold out no longer. I knew I must drop into hell that moment, unless God appeared to save me ; and He did appear : I knew He loved me, and felt sweet peace.   Yet I did not dare to say I had faith, till yesterday was twelvemonth God gave me faith, and his love has ever since filled my heart.' [1]

These narratives are typical of a very large number of revival conversions in which the will is prominent in its relation to moral conduct. The term ' enslaved ' to sin, used to describe the subject of the first record, is a common indication of the nature of the experience : it includes by implication the bondage of the will in vice ; the conscious revulsion from habitual drunkenness, and the strength of the *interest* in attaining freedom. The will, in the sense of the whole of the purposive activities of the self, is subordinated to the gratification of one overmastering passion. And the strength of this passion represses the aspirations and judgments of the higher nature, but even when it is unconscious, the discord is still there. Wesley's observation of the behaviour and the facial expression indicating despair is of importance in estimating the psychological factors involved ; and the same significance attaches to the standing erect and the change of countenance after prayer.

The case of the barber is peculiar, in that the realization of forgiveness was subsequent to the removal of the desire for drink.   His deepest craving was not for forgiveness, but for freedom.   The listening at the window was due to more than curiosity.   It was probably prompted by a repressed desire to escape from excessive drinking, and this unconscious *wish* accounts for the immediate result : ' God struck me to the heart.'   Forgiveness for the past was a mental necessity discovered after the moral discord had been resolved.

Conversion is an experience of normal human nature, and consequently the thoroughly typical Methodist conversion tends, as in the case of John Wesley, to merge the types which have been analyzed in a more comprehensive religious experience. The narrative of John Nelson's conversion is one in which instinct and emotion, intuition and will are combined. Nelson was a Birstall stone-mason, whose parents were godly people, and who had been subject to strong religious 'convictions' since he was ten years old. He was far from being an irreligious man, but he was the victim of violent passions, and at the age of thirty he was still continually struggling ineffectually against his besetting sin.[1] 'I was,' he writes, 'like a wandering bird, cast out of the nest, till Mr. John Wesley came to preach his first sermon in Moorfields. O, that was a blessed morning to my soul! As soon as he got upon the stand, he stroked back his hair, and turned his face towards where I stood, and I thought fixed his eyes upon me. His countenance struck such an awful dread upon me, before I heard him speak, that it made my heart beat like the pendulum of a clock; and, when he did speak, I thought his whole discourse was aimed at me. When he had done, I said, " This man can tell the secrets of my heart : he hath not left me there ; for he hath showed me the remedy, even the blood of Jesus." . . . Though it was a little after midsummer that I heard him, and it was three weeks after Michaelmas before I found the true peace of God, yet I continued to hear him as often as I could, without neglecting my

[1] ' John Nelson's Journal : Written by Himself,' in *Lives of the Early Methodist Preachers*, vol. i. p. 17.

work.' [1] After a period of struggle and defeat, Nelson writes, ' I then went into my chamber, shut the door, and fell down on my knees, crying, " Lord, save, or I perish." When I had prayed till I could pray no more, I got up and walked to and fro, being resolved I would neither eat nor drink till I had found the kingdom of God. I fell down to prayer again, but found no relief ; got up and walked again : then tears began to flow from my eyes, like great drops of rain, and I fell on my knees a third time ; but now I was as dumb as a beast, and could not put up one petition, if it would have saved my soul. I kneeled before the Lord some time, and saw myself a criminal before the Judge : then I said, " Lord, thy will be done ; damn or save ! " That moment Jesus Christ was as evidently set before the eye of my mind, as crucified for my sins, as if I had seen Him with my bodily eyes ; and in that instant my heart was set at liberty from guilt and tormenting fear, and filled with a calm and serene peace.' . . . ' My heart was filled with love to God and every soul of man : next to my wife and children, my mother, brethren, and sisters, my greatest enemies had an interest in my prayers ; and I cried, " O Lord, give me to see my desire on them : let them experience Thy redeeming love." ' [2]

The results of Nelson's conversion were seen in moral stability and increased personal efficiency. He was born in 1707, and he died in 1774 ; and after his conversion at the age of thirty, he was, for thirty-seven years, one of the noblest witnesses of the Methodist faith, and one of Wesley's most trusted companions. The similarity of his experience to that of Wesley will be noticed, in that after a period of disciplinary search he came under

---

[1] Nelson's Journal, p. 14.   [2] *Ibid.* p. 18.

the suggestive power of a profoundly spiritual personality. Under the sway of an emotional moment, repressions were released, the fear of the law of God was supplanted by overwhelming love to God and man. And a new intellectual content was given to religious experience in the conception of the protecting, redeeming love of God made manifest in Jesus Christ. As exhibited in the case of John Nelson, the outcropping of unconscious elements is not more characteristic of conversion than the rational and conative aspects of the emotional crisis. Religious conversion in Methodism is the harmonizing of the whole self in all its purposes and activities, through the dominant sentiment of love to God.

X

FACTORS INVOLVED IN CONVERSION

THE vital nature of the mental revolution at the moment of conversion is indicated by the fact that the whole of the self, both on its conscious and on its unconscious sides, is involved in the process. For purposes of analysis and psychological explanation, the factors into which conversion is resolvable may be conveniently divided into two classes : those which are concerned with the less conscious, and those that relate to the more conscious mental processes. The change in some cases is largely to be interpreted in terms of suggestibility, and there is marked evidence of the raising of repressions and the sudden culmination in consciousness of previously concealed mental processes. In other instances, the crisis is approached and passed with a conscious realization of nearly all the issues and factors involved. But no purpose would be served by distinguishing two classes of conversion experience based upon the preponderance of the conscious or unconscious factors. We have already considered specific conversion narratives, instinctive and emotional, intuitive or mystical, and moral or practical ; and certain elements are common to them all. Conscious and unconscious mental operations are inextricably mingled in conversion, as in all human activity.

Considerable attention has been given in recent years

to the conflict of impulses and systems in unconscious mental life, and light has been thrown upon the more obscure features of religious experience. Conversion in particular has been explained in terms of ' subliminal ' or ' subconscious ' or unconscious processes. Ample evidence of the value of this research is to be found in the Revival narratives, but it is all the more significant that one of the salient features of Methodist conversion is the conscious content, emotional, intellectual, and volitional. A psychological explanation is only possible when the experience is reviewed as a whole, from a biological and functional point of view. Progressive integration is the method of biological evolution, both of the individual and of the race. And in conversion, human nature advances a stage in that integration or unification which is a key process in mental development. The interpretation of that process must not be limited to any one aspect or element in it, least of all to those elements which do not emerge into consciousness.

The part played by the less conscious factors in conversion is still obscure. But the data provided by the Revival, and particularly by the detailed record of John Wesley's personal history, warrant the inference that suggestion and repression both enter into the experience. It is already sufficiently apparent that unconscious social *suggestion* created in a marked degree the sensitiveness, expectancy, and emotional excitability, and also provided, to a great extent, the religious ideas which determined the conscious interpretation of the crisis. A certain proportion of the converts would yield to the mass suggestion of the crowd, and others to the rhythm and passion of the hymn singing. Recognition must also

be given to the distinctive personality and gifts of the
preachers.   Many of them possessed something of Whitefield's oratorical powers.   The flame of passionate devotion
atoned for lack of gifts in others.   But the genius of the
movement was communicated largely through Wesley
himself.   Miss Wedgwood has referred to his peculiar
power of creating fear in the minds of his hearers.   Davenport says that ' in spite of the perfect outward calmness
and self-possession, Wesley was probably the most
terribly impressive preacher that England ever knew.
It would be hard to mention a man whose influence over
an audience can be so perfectly described by the term
" awful."   If it were not such a hateful word when
applied to so complex and so noble a personality, one
would say that it closely approached the hypnotic.' [1]
' His demand for instantaneous decision fell with terrific
force upon the plastic mental and nervous organization
of his hearers.' [2]   There is a definite hypnotic element
in the power of every orator and revival preacher, and
the general conditions of unconscious suggestibility in
the crowd combine with the spell of the preacher in
securing the desired response.

The evidence of unconscious conflict due to *repression*
is clear in some cases belonging to all three of the classes
which have been described.   Emotional conversion, particularly when it is of the adolescent type, turns upon an
exaggerated horror of sin which is due to a more or less
conscious struggle with the developing sex instinct.
Thus one of Wesley's preachers writes, some time before
his conversion, ' I thought no more about the girls whom

[1] Davenport, F. M., *op. cit.* p. 168.   *Cf.* John of Cronstadt and the
Russian peasants.
[2] *Ibid.* p. 170.

D.M.R.   2 B

I went to meet, and found I had work enough to take care of my own soul.' [1]   The human love interest was thrust out of consciousness as the result of a Methodist sermon against ' pleasure-takers.'   ' Immediately I found a kind of judgment-seat set up in my conscience, where I was tried, cast, and condemned ; for I knew I had been seeking happiness in the pleasures of the world and in the creature all my days, not in the Creator and Redeemer of my soul, the only central point of bliss.' [2]   The acute conflict had been ended by refusal of attention to the instinctive promptings, and a kind of chronic conflict resulted, manifesting itself in agonizing emotional tension which continued up to the moment of his conversion at the age of twenty-three.

It is not necessary to use the word *sublimation* to describe the release of this tension, and the restoration of inner harmony.   Sublimation seems to imply the assumption of a specific energy (the ' libido ' of the psycho-analysts) attached to specific instincts.   Apart from the fact that our records yield no justification for this assumption, the idea of sublimation seems to be mechanical and pathological, and it does not correspond to the experience as a whole.   The period of adolescence is best understood if it is regarded as a time of mental struggle when the wealth and power of developing human nature are drawn in the direction of the sex-instinct, and the genuine religious crisis serves the purpose of lifting the conflict out of the narrow issue, and directing the forces of character into broader and more consciously conceived activity.

What happens in adolescent conversion is equally

[1] George Shadford, *Wesley's Veterans*, vol. i. p. 176.
[2] *Ibid. op. cit.* p. 176.

characteristic of mystical conversion, with the difference that repressions have been operative in mature life, as in the case of Wesley, which have barred the activity of many normal human interests.   In these cases conversion marks the sudden release of unconscious repressions by means of an emotional experience, the result of which is seen in a literally more abundant life.

The third type of conversion in which the repressed system or complex manifests itself is that in which the issue is largely moral, involving a practical or volitional problem.   In the case of the drunkard, the question arises as to how the desire for drink was instantly taken away in the moment of conversion.   The psychological explanation would be that any habitual vice is abnormal, and necessitates the repression into silence and comparative unconsciousness of all the larger and nobler qualities of human character.   In the case of the Bolton barber, it is clear that a perverted appetite tendency dominated his life, but the stories of Wesley and his converts aroused the well-nigh unconscious higher nature, and after a short acute conflict, the emotional moment came in which, with almost explosive force, the powerful sentiment of love supplanted the lower and narrower instinct tendency for ever.   Other factors combined to constitute the experience as a whole, but this is one of the Methodist narratives in which the sudden emergence into consciousness of a previously buried ' complex ' is most clearly exhibited.

A satisfactory treatment of the psychological processes involved in conversion is impossible apart from a recognition of the fact that the new birth is a conscious experience and that the part played by unconscious factors is inseparable from the activity of the mind as a whole.

The crisis, while it may be predominantly emotional in tone, is unintelligible if it is isolated from the intellect and the will. All three of the ultimate factors of consciousness are potent in religious conversion, and although they may be treated separately for purposes of analysis, it must not be forgotten that they are inseparable in experience.

Determination and effort are a necessary part of the mental process of conversion ; and in all the narratives which give information of the experiences preceding conversion there is a period of ' seeking peace,' or ' seeking God.' ' I determined never to rest until I had a testimony in myself,' [1] ' earnestly resolving to sin no more,' [2] are typical of the attitude of many of the converts for some time before the actual moment of conversion. It might seem that the cases in which all effort is abandoned before peace can be obtained involve a negation of the part played by the will. But the contradiction is only superficial. Baudouin's explanation of the experience would refer it to the Law of Reversed Effort. ' When the will and the imagination are at war, the imagination *invariably* gains the day.' [3] Coué's formula is also expressed thus, ' In the conflict between the will and the imagination, the force of the imagination is *in direct ratio to the square of the will.*' [4] But the will is more than the momentary direction of energy to particular acts. And it is most peculiar to find one of the laws of auto-suggestion demanding that ' the will must not intervene,' while at the same time a parallel law invokes ' concentrated attention.' It must be remembered that

[1] Richard Whatcoat ; *Wesley's Veterans*, vol. ii. p. 220.
[2] John Haime ; *ibid.* vol. ii. p. 14.
[3] Baudouin, *op. cit.* p. 125.   [4] *Ibid.*

Meumann,[1] Wundt and James make attention the supreme characteristic of volitional action.[2]   And even if this be an exaggeration, there is no possibility of concentrated attention without purposive tendency.

The truth is that the ' surrender of the will ' in conversion is not the surrender of the will in any intelligible psychological sense.   When John Nelson cried, ' Lord, Thy will be done, damn or save,' he reached the point which is described as surrender ;   when striving ceases. And at that very moment, the joy of salvation flooded his being.   But all really vital processes are explained by the end and not by the beginning ;   and the end achieved was that which Nelson had been consciously seeking. The proposed change was definitely envisaged, and the will can only be understood as the total function of the personality exercised in the production of the desired experience.   The activity or behaviour revealing this purposive tendency is not so clearly exhibited in many of the converts as it is in the disciplinary search of John Wesley, yet the short conflict in which the will is exerted may represent, as in mystic experience, ' a deep rich age of growth, during some minutes of poor clock-time.' [3] In degrees varying with temperament and training, the ' will to believe ' is an essential factor in conversion, on the evidence offered by the Methodist records.   And the decision to commit the issue entirely to God, as in the case of John Nelson, frequently marks the moment when salvation is found.

The psychological processes involved in this achievement of unification and peace may be compared with the angels who bear the soul of Faust upwards, and

---

[1] *Intelligenz und Wille*, pp. 190-2.   [2] James, *P.P.* vol. i. p. 447.
[3] Von Hügel, *Mystical Element of Religion*, vol. i. pp. 107-8.

scatter roses on the defeated devils, singing as they mount to heaven :

> ' Freed is the noble scion of
> The Spirit-world from evil ;
> Him can we save that tireless strove,
> Ever to higher level.' [1]

The direct association of conation and knowledge is apparent in the definiteness of the idea of the end or goal of the process towards which the candidate for conversion is striving.   The idea is a concrete mental process ; and concrete thought not only involves but is a kind of conation.   Thinking is doing something to the elements that enter into experience.   All thought has reference to an end, and that end is the attainment of belief.   All doubt, denial and thinking lead up to an act, and the fundamental act of thought is judgment.   The ' Shall I, or shall I not seek salvation ? ' is not psychologically different from the ' Yes or No ' of purely intellectual decision.   And it can be maintained that the first step towards conversion is the consenting judgment.

A discussion of Methodist conversion is impossible without a recognition of the fact that it implied a metaphysical basis for morals.   The appeal to conscience and the moral law was an essential part of the preaching of Methodism.   When John Wesley preached a ' religion of love, and joy, and peace, having its seat in the inmost soul, but ever showing itself by its fruits, continually springing forth, not only in all innocence (for love worketh no ill to his neighbour), but likewise in every kind of beneficence, spreading virtue and happiness all around it,' and offered such faith in God as an instantaneous gift, he was appealing for decisions, but he was also

---

[1] Goethe, *Faust*, part ii. tr. Latham (Dent's ed.).

appealing for intellectual belief. The practical and the theoretical interests are parallel, and the judgment of value is inseparable from the judgment of fact.

This concrete mental process of judgment is the positive aspect of that element in the conversion experience which is described on the negative side as ' conviction of sin,' or ' sense of sin.' Wesley claimed to be a preacher to the conscience, and he defined conscience as ' a kind of silent reasoning of the mind, whereby those things which are judged to be right are approved with pleasure ; and those which are judged evil are disapproved with uneasiness.' [1] The definition might be commended for its freedom from the unscientific tendency to regard conscience as a peculiar innate faculty, or as a mental force ' in the same sense in which we speak of instincts as impulses.' [2] Wesley regarded conscience as having more than a verbal con- nection with consciousness. It was the judgment of the whole self, including rational and emotional elements. Wesley might have written, ' Conscience or (to speak more scientifically) the moral consciousness may be held to include not merely the capacity for pronouncing moral judgments, but the whole body of instincts, feelings, emotions, desires which are presupposed by and which influence those judgments, as well as those which prompt to the doing of the actions which they prescribe.' [3] But Wesley would continue, ' I doubt whether the very words, ' right and wrong," according to the Christian system, do not imply, in the very idea of them, agreement and disagreement to the will and word of God.' [4] In the

[1] Sermon, ' On Conscience,' *W.W.* vol. vii. p. 178.
[2] McKenzie, J. G., *Modern Psychology and the Achievement of Christian Personality*, p. 33.   Otherwise a useful work for Christian teachers.
[3] Rashdall, Hastings, *Theory of Good and Evil*, vol. i. 175.
[4] Sermon, ' On Conscience,' *W.W.* vol. vii. p. 181.

ethical judgment for which he appealed in his preaching,
the emergence of the whole self into view is conditioned
by a reference to the Infinite Perfection and Holiness
of God.

> ' The shame of self at thought of seeing Him
>   Will be thy veriest, sharpest Purgatory.' [1]

Wesley's religious or theological presuppositions led him
to the same conclusion which was reached along a very
different road by Kant, that the ' Idea ' of the Uncon-
ditioned is a fundamental condition, a chief producer,
of all experience properly human, rational and moral.[2]

In Wesley's *Journal*, in the manuscript letters, and in
the autobiographies which have been examined, the witness
is unvarying. ' Each seems to have set himself before
himself for judgment, asking, " What am I worth in
totality, integrally ? " and to have passed unreserved
judgment of worthlessness. In each of them this is done
by reference to the thought of an Omniscient Being before
whom he conceived himself as standing : that clear
reference to Infinity and Perfection, which most students
of the history of religion agree is its specific feature.
" Self-knowledge," Newman has said, " is the root of all
real religious knowledge " ; and the reference to the
Infinite is at the root of self-knowledge.' [3]   ' I heard a
voice,' says M. B., ' say, in my inmost soul, " Be ye holy
for I am holy." From that hour for a year and a quarter
. . . I did nothing but long and weep and pray for inward
holiness.' [4]   Another was ' cut to the heart, and felt the

---

[1] Newman, J. H., *The Dream of Gerontius.*

[2] *Critique of Pure Reason*, Müller's translation, pp. 546-553. See also
Kemp Smith's *Commentary*, and Von Hügel, ' Morals and Religion,' art
in *Hibbert Journal*, vol. xix. No. 4, July, 1921.

[3] Caldecott, A., *R.S.* p. 9.   [4] *J.W.J.* vol. iv. p. 202.

wrath of God abiding on him.' [1]   Matthias Joyce writes,
'The Holy Ghost showed me the spirituality of the law
in such a manner that I saw and felt my inward parts
were very wickedness.   I wondered that I was so great
a monster.   I groaned, being burdened with a deep
sense of the wrath of God.' [2]

The ' tension-relief ' situation thus created raises the
question as to the place of instinct in the experience of
conversion.   It is at once seen from our exploration of the
Methodist experience that the ' fear of God ' or the ' fear
of sin ' is not derived as a simple emotion from a primary
instinct or tendency.   The primitive and purely instinctive level of activity is very rare in human behaviour,
and the essential root of the emotional element in almost
all the cases under review is the fear of loss to the essential
self consequent upon a suddenly acquired sense of the
reality and holiness of God, and of the moral law by which
their lives were at once judged and condemned.[3]   In the
majority of the cases a complete identity is established
between the self-estimate and the consciousness of Divine
condemnation.   ' I wish I were dead ; if it pleases God to
save me, it is his infinite mercy ; if he damns my soul, be
it so, He is just and righteous.' [4]   The familiar formula,
' their sins were set in array against them,' and the phrases
' the wrath of God ' and ' the fear of hell ' must be con-
strued, not merely in the light of a modern psychology of
feeling and instinct, but in their relation to the will and

---

[1] *J.W.J.* vol. iv. p. 521.

[2] *Wesley's Early Preachers*, vol. iv. p. 241 ;   quoted by Caldecott,
op. cit. p. 9.

[3] On the biological basis of this fear, *vide supra*, p. 149.

[4] William Black (1760-1835) ;   *Wesley's Early Preachers*, vol. v. p. 243 ;
quoted Caldecott, *op. cit.* p. 11.

the consenting judgment, that is, in relation to the sentiments, ends, desires, ideals and purposes which were kindled by the Gospel message.

The fear which looms so large in the phenomena of the Revival is thus seen to be more than a single emotion ; it is an attitude or disposition which grows in complexity with the complex life of man. As Mr. Shand would say, it is a system. At the primitive impulsive level, fear is the great inhibitor of action, as the physical phenomena show. But at the higher levels, when it becomes a factor in a complex emotional situation, fear is a reinforcing, not an inhibiting agent. ' The individual, who is striving to gain a prize, redoubles his efforts, when he sees the danger of losing it.' [1] The prize envisaged by Wesley's hearers was a fuller and completer self-realization than they had ever dreamed of ; the life of those who had established a perfect correspondence with an ideal environment ; of those who were ' the children of God.' And with the perception or imagination of these new and immeasurable possibilities came the equally vivid consciousness of failure, and of inherent worthlessness and guilt.

The relief of the emotional tension was generally traceable to the sudden supplanting or inhibiting of the ' fear ' system by the dominating influence of a more powerful sentiment. As the fear of a mother will be supplanted completely by the parental instinct—' Nature's brightest and most beautiful invention ' [2]—and she will fight to the death in defence of her young, so fear, however powerfully excited, can be displaced by the absolute confidence of the young in the protecting care of the parent. The unassailable conviction of Wesley that God gave instantaneous forgiveness and peace of mind to

[1] Drever, J., *I.M.* p. 177.   [2] McDougall, W., *O.P.* p. 130.

those who were penitent, and that Christ died and rose again for this one end, overwhelmed his hearers with a sense of the magnitude of the love of God, and in the vast majority of cases produced the instantaneous release from otherwise intolerable mental agony.

> ' This I was worth to God,
>   Whose wheel the pitcher shaped.'

The emotional response to the new situation was that of boundless gratitude and unutterable joy and elation. One factor in the process is certainly the ' tender protective impulse evoked principally in the form of gratitude towards the protecting deities ' ; [1] or it might be described as the filio-parental aspect of the tender emotion.   There is a fine piece of psychological observation in the classic utterance of Saint John upon this subject : ' There is no fear in love ; but perfect love casteth out fear : because fear hath torment.   He that feareth is not made perfect in love.   We love him, because he first loved us.' [2]   ' The belief in such a love, however arrived at, does actually awaken in the converts a responsive love which explodes the emotional situation by its powerful energy, dispossessing, for the moment at least, all other emotions from their influence.' [3]   ' My heart was filled with peace and joy and love, which I have not lost to this hour,' [4] writes one.   Another speaks of being ' overwhelmed with the love of God, and, for the time, utterly incapable of doubt or fear.' [5]   ' I knew He loved me and felt sweet peace,' is the testimony of the Bolton barber.[6]   The Bristol

---

[1] McDougall, W., S.P., pp. 314-315.

[2] 1 John iv. 18-19.   But note that the sentiment of love includes fear as an essential element.   See Shand, F.C. p. 43.

[3] Caldecott, R.S. p. 12.   [4] J.W.J. vol. iii. p. 374.

[5] Ibid. vol. iii. p. 508.   [6] Ibid. vol. iii. p. 521.

schoolmistress writes of 'such flames of love to my dear Saviour and to all mankind as I cannot express.'[1]   'My heart, with a kind, sweet struggle melted into the hands of God,' says, not a mediaeval Spaniard, but a Yorkshire clothier of the eighteenth century.[2]

This 'sense of being loved by God, and the outgoing of responsive love to Him, is the central fibre, the unique and unanalyzable feature and factor'[3] in conversion. If it were simply a feeling-tone or single emotion, it would be subject to the law of decline.   But as a living experience, it tended to 'gather round it into a system the three great sentiments of Respect and Adoration for the Good, Respect for Truth, and Admiration for the Beautiful.' Or in other words, the whole personality was raised to a higher level of vitality and efficiency, through the organizing emotional experience of conversion.

The immediate and progressive result of the attainment of mental harmony was the integration and organization of all the constituent elements of character, and all the manifold activities of the mind.   The moral sentiment may be considered in relation to the practical and *volitional* side of human nature.   The reinforcing of the will was so marked that it gave the impression of the incoming of power from a supernatural source.   'It was a mighty rushing wind, coming into the soul, enabling me from that moment to be more than conqueror over those corruptions which before I was always a slave to.'[4]   The sense of adequacy for all the demands of life was due to the new co-ordination of all the mental resources, so that effort and volition provoked no conflict, but expressed the

[1] MS. Letter, *vide supra*, p. 176.   [2] Caldecott, *R.S.* p. 12.
[3] Caldecott, A., *Mystic Feeling and Emotional Life*, p. 9.
[4] *J.W.J.* vol. ii. p. 108.   *Cf.* James, *V.R.E.* p. 270, n. 2.

single aim to which the personality was directed, that of
doing good.   But ' morality is a continuing process, not
a fixed achievement,' [1] and conversion does not mark
the end of the process.   The essential thing in the
moral victory is the unification of character, and the
consciousness that the central self is identified, in spite
of upsurging impulses, with the pursuit of the Good,
or as Wesley would say, of Holiness and Christian
Perfection.[2]

Intellectual regeneration is also a result of conversion.
The quickening of the reasoning powers in Wesley's
converts was apparent in various ways.   Discussion of
doctrine, and the formulation of a Methodist theology
based upon their own experiences, were among the first
fruits of this mental vitality.   Wesley's correspondence,
even with illiterate people, is frequently upon points
of doctrine ; the question of ' election ' or predestination,
and the ' stillness ' of the Quietists were canvassed with
great animation.[3]   The production of a considerable body
of religious poetry must not be forgotten.[4]   But the
principal indication of a new intellectual alertness was
found in the concrete efficiency of the Methodist workman
and business man.   Not only were the converts founders
of private and profitable industrial concerns in many
cases, based, like those of the Quakers,[5] upon a new
commercial honesty, but they created the complex social
system of the Methodist Church, which is perhaps second
only to the Roman Catholic Church as a business organization in the religious world.   A value judgment upon this
achievement is not attempted here, but it is ample

---

[1] Dewey, John, *H.N.C.* p. 280.   [2] *Vide infra*, pp. 240-5.
[3] MSS. Letters, Colman Collection.   [4] *Vide infra*, p. 214.
[5] See Underwood, *op. cit.* pp. 224-5.

evidence of the organizing capacity and ability of the Methodist mind. And those who have made the most original contributions to Methodist thought and life have always traced their intellectual inspiration to the moment of their conversion.

The *emotional* elation is definitely related to admiration for the beautiful, and is characterized by a sense of newness and beauty in all nature and human nature. ' I am in a new world ' ; [1] ' As I walked home along the streets I seemed to be in Paradise. When I read my Bible it seemed an entirely new book. When I meditated . . . when I considered good or bad men, any or all the creatures which surrounded me on every side, everything appeared new, and stood in a new relation to me.' [2] The expansive tendency of joy is apparent in this, but the root of the experience is the love to God whose beauty and glory are conceived as being reflected in the whole of creation. And from this love to God arises a love for all mankind, which is the emotional source of all missionary activity. A new possibility of beauty is seen in all human nature.

> ' I did not think, I did not strive,
> The deep peace burnt my me alive ;
> The bolted door had broken in,
> I knew that I had done with sin.
> I knew that Christ had given me birth
> To brother all the souls on earth,
> And every bird and every beast
> Should share the crumbs broke at the feast.
>
> O glory of the lighted mind.
> How dead I'd been, how dumb, how blind.
> The station brook to my new eyes
> Was babbling out of Paradise ;

[1] *J.W.J.* vol. iii. p. 423.

[2] George Shadford, *Wesley's Veterans*, vol. ii. pp. 183-4.

> The waters rushing from the rain
> Were singing Christ has risen again.
> I thought all earthly creatures knelt
> From rapture of the joy I felt.' [1]

Thus in the language of a living poet is expressed the new splendour and meaning with which life is enriched immediately after conversion ; and the imagery and poetry find parallels in detail amid the wealth and wonder of the Methodist witness.   In all the history of psychological science there is no saying more profoundly significant than that of Jesus, ' Ye must be born again.'

[1] John Masefield, *The Everlasting Mercy*.

XI

THE GROUP SPIRIT

VITAL religion, by its very nature, must create and sustain a social relationship. The fact that Wesley's conversion took place in a Society is significant in two ways. It is *ipso facto* dissociated from the solitary ' illuminations ' of mysticism ; and the part played by the social group in his conversion is typical of the place occupied by communal organization in the history of Methodism.

Miss Wedgwood observed the distinctive social quality of the new movement, and explained the charge of Popery [1] which was often brought against the followers of Wesley on this ground. ' There were, however, some points of resemblance between the Romish Church and Methodism ; a strict religious body, meeting in private houses and enjoining confession and fasting, would often remind the superficial observer of the Romanists. But it was not so much this or that peculiarity which would have this effect ; it was the one fundamental fact of Methodism so often insisted on in these pages, that it was originally not a sect, but an order. Wesley had described the parochial organization of the Church of England as ' a rope of sand ' compared with his Society, and a Roman

[1] See *J.W.J.* He was accused of being a Papist ; vol. ii. pp. 262, 342 ; vol. iii. pp. 46, 110 ; vol. viii. p. 305.

Catholic priest might have done the same. They had
both a kind of organization which the Church had not,
and in the eyes of the world this was a striking resemblance.
And it was exactly this resemblance which revived the
popular hatred of Romanism. . . .   There was in that day
a hostility to this Church quite independent of religion. . .
The Roman Catholic is a foreigner on English soil, he
belongs not so much to those of his own race as those of
his own creed, and with whatever dislike to that creed we
regard him there mingles some patriotism, and a good
deal of inhospitality.' [1] In this comprehensive social
loyalty Methodism was true to its New Testament origin,
and in its spontaneous missionary activity is seen an
attempt to create a religious order or fellowship as wide
as humanity.

Nearly ten years before his conversion, early in 1729,
John Wesley had travelled many miles to ask the advice
of a ' serious man,' who had said to him, ' Sir, you wish
to serve God and go to heaven? Remember that you
cannot serve him alone. You must therefore find
companions or make them ; the Bible knows nothing
of solitary religion.' [2] Henry Moore traces the founding
of the Holy Club at Oxford to this advice. Apparently it
was the first suggestion of the idea of Christian fellowship
in the religious experience of Wesley.[3] The importance of collective sentiment and group loyalty was
realized the more quickly because of the opposition and
persecution with which the Oxford society was immediately faced. The devotional and ethical purpose which

[1] Wedgwood, Julia, *John Wedgwood and the Evangelical Reaction of
the Eighteenth Century*, pp. 283-4.

[2] Moore, Henry, *Life of Wesley*, vol. i. p. 162.

[3] *J.W.J.* vol. i. p. 469, note.

D.M.R.   2 D

had characterized the Holy Club was maintained in the meetings which Wesley organized in Savannah, and certain features of Oxford Methodism survived in the Societies of the Revival movement.

Antecedent to the Methodist Societies were the 'Religious Societies,' of which large numbers existed within the Church of England in the last years of the seventeenth century. But these societies collapsed early in the eighteenth century because they were confused in the popular mind with the Society for the Reformation of Manners [1] which excited much hostile criticism on account of a system of espionage which led to great abuses, corruption and private malice. Apparently the Aldersgate Street Society had come under Moravian influence, but it was a Church of England Society, and the association of the Wesley brothers indicates also an assimilation of the spirit and aims of the Oxford Methodists. But in the conversion of John Wesley the breach with the older societies became inevitable. 'In his case the birthday of a Christian was shifted from his baptism to his conversion, and in that change the partition line between two great systems was crossed.' [2]

The psychological factors involved in the growth of the Methodist Societies will be in some degree revealed by an examination of the first Rules of the United Societies.[3] These were published by John Wesley in 1743, and a later

[1] For Wesley's encouragement of this Society, see *J.W.J.* vol. v. pp. 4-5, note ; v. p. 101 ; vi. p. 223.

[2] Wedgwood, *op. cit.* p. 157 ; see also Simon, J. S., *John Wesley and the Religious Societies'* (1921), p. 27 ; for the Religious Societies, see Woodward, Dr., *The Rise and Progress of the Religious Societies*, and compare *J.W.J.* vol. ii. p. 71, note ; i. 447, 458, 475 ; ii. 70-6, 83.

[3] For a copy of these rules, see *N.H.M.* vol. ii. pp. 563-5.

edition in the same year was signed by both John and
Charles. The definition of a society in Rule 2 reads
thus : ' A company of men having the form and seeking
the power of godliness, united in order to pray together,
to receive the word of exhortation, and to watch over one
another in love, that they may help each other to work
out their salvation.' [1] The recognition and establishment
of this system marks the beginning of that group self-
consciousness which raised the collective life of Methodism
so far above the mass of the social life of the time. The
idea of the whole system with its complexity and unity
operated to create the group, and as the idea became more
concretely realized, it was more definitely formulated :
the collective sentiment grew up about it, and habit
and formal organization gave permanence and stability
to the group.

The full significance of this group formation cannot
be realized until we view it in contrast with the social
conditions of the time. Christian fellowship of the
Methodist type seems at the present time to be a very
elementary and familiar psychological phenomenon. But
the fact is that in Wesley's day, especially since the decay
of the ' Religious Societies,' such a fellowship was a
totally new and unique experience. Wesley regarded it
as supplying a manifest lack in the Church of England.
In the passage quoted by Miss Wedgwood, he says, ' Look
east, west, north, or south, name what parish you please,
is Christian fellowship there ? Rather, are not the bulk
of the parishioners a mere rope of sand ? What Christian
connexion is there between them ? What intercourse
in spiritual things ? What watching over each other's

---

[1] See *J.W.J.* vol. i. p. 51 ; vol. iii. p. 67, note ; vol. iii. pp. 68, 313 ;
vol. iv. p. 185.

souls ? ' [1]   But the absence of the social consciousness in
the Anglican Church was not the primary cause of the
success of the Methodist societies in Newcastle and Bristol
and in the new industrial as well as the mining areas.   The
shifting of the population and the creation of new populations, during the last forty years of Wesley's life, destroyed
the simpler conditions of group consciousness, which were
territorial and traditional ; even the kinship bond in many
cases being broken by the dispersion of families.   And the
old occupational associations were not yet replaced by
the later occupational and economic groups, Trades
Unions, Friendly Societies, Co-operative Societies and
Mechanics' Institutes.   The mobility of the population
created an opportunity for the rise and development of
a new group loyalty, and the provision of a basis for this
new social sentiment was one of the services rendered to
the national life by the Methodist societies.

The social implications of the experience of conversion,
with its sudden invasion of altruistic feeling,[2] its ' love
to all mankind,' found expression in the Methodist class
meetings, and ' bands ' and societies.   The individual
convert was less in danger of finding his vision fading
into the light of common day when he found himself in
a living association of kinsmen and comrades, who openly
testified of their ' experience,' and called upon him to
give his testimony in turn.   One of Wesley's early
correspondents writes, ' We find great power from the
Lord in our own private band, the Love of God shed
abroad in our hearts, our souls knit to one another, we
drink of one spirit and the Lord doth meet us, and that It

[1] See *N.H.M.* vol. i. p. 289 ; and for a similar account of the Church,
see *W.W.* vol. viii. p. 217.

[2] See Underwood, *op. cit.* pp. 230 ff. ;   Starbuck, p. 127 ;   James,
pp. 274, 278 ff., 369.

is no wonder we are Loth to part for we think four hours too little time for so heavenly a communion.' [1] 'Methodism presented the emotional experience as something within the range of all persons and in comparison with which all other attainments were insignificant. Learning, creeds, and doctrines ; social station, wealth, and achievement, counted for nothing against this immediate sense and evidence of the presence of God. Here was found a new social bond. All who possessed this experience understood each other and felt themselves the fortunate members of a mystic company.' [2]

In his discussion of the psychology of faith, Dean Inge writes : ' The faculties of our minds must be really unified before faith can fully come into its own. . . . The intellect is the latest born of our faculties, and the finest instrument we have. . . . But I have already shown that in the life of reason, thus conceived, the moral and the aesthetic consciousness find their full satisfaction, and are not relegated to a lower place.' [3] As we have seen the religious sentiment gathering into its system the three eternal ideas of Truth, Beauty, and Goodness, so we may observe the social sentiment in the Methodist community promoting a harmonious spiritual development, in which the thought, the will, and the emotional sides of mental life find their appropriate expression and activity.

The danger of unintelligent contentment with the sympathetic emotions of the little religious circle was not entirely avoided. But it must not be imagined that even in the early days of the Revival the intellectual possibilities

[1] Manuscript letter from Margaret Summirell to John Wesley July 23, 1740 ; Colman Collection.

[2] Ames, E. S., *op. cit.* p. 386.

[3] Inge, W. R., *Faith and its Psychology*, p. 233.

of group organization were quite neglected. There is
no justification for the statement that in the Methodist
fellowship the experience of the profounder human
qualities rendered ' doctrinal statements and theoretical
implications relatively formal and superfluous.' [1] Intellectual acuteness, like vivacity, is a social product ; and
the socialization of religious experience led to its more
exact definition and interpretation. The progressive
development of the group spirit raised the intellectual
level of the societies, because it led each member deliberately to subordinate his own judgment and opinion
to that of the whole fellowship. Methodist doctrine was
the direct result of collective deliberation, based upon
testimony and discussion in the societies, tested and
thought out by the leaders and by Wesley himself. It was
not the work of any one individual, but of an organized
group expressing itself in collective opinion. ' The life of
reason is the life of the " perfect man " grown out of the
dim mystical consciousness with which religion began;' [2]
and in the action and reaction of convert and class, of
individual and society, the vague undefined meaning
and values of religious experience took shape and were
expressed in concrete intellectual form, in the prose of
doctrinal teaching or in the poetry of Methodist song.
And the mind of the Methodist people matured in the
process, through the creative activity of its search for an
adequate interpretation of a living faith.

If the quest of Truth is evidenced by a body of ' sub-
stantial, practical, experimental divinity,' [3] the pursuit of
Goodness is manifest in the challenge of Methodism to the

---

[1] Ames, E. S., *op. cit.* p. 387. *Vide infra*, Chap. XII.

[2] Inge, W. R., *Faith and its Psychology*, p. 233.

[3] Wesley claimed this for his preachers, *W.W.* vol. viii. p. 213.

prevailing moral standards of the period.   The collective
volition and ethical value of the societies find expression
in the Rules already mentioned.   Rule 4 sets forth the
duty of ' avoiding evil in every kind ;   especially that
which is most generally practised.'   Profaning the Lord's
Day is specified, together with drunkenness, fighting,
' using many words in buying and selling,' [1] smuggling,
usury, uncharitable or unprofitable conversations, ' putting
on gold or costly apparel ' (in later editions this rule
specifically forbids ' particularly the wearing of Calashes,
High-heads, or enormous Bonnets '),[2] diversions which
cannot be used in the name of the Lord Jesus, songs or
books which ' do not tend to the Knowledge or love of
God ', ' softness, and needless self-indulgence ; laying up
treasures upon earth ;   borrowing without a probability
of paying ;   or taking up goods without a probability of
paying for them.' [3]   Rule 7 sums up the obligations of
members : ' These are the General Rules of our Societies ;
all which we are taught of God to observe, even in His
written word, the only rule, and the sufficient rule, both
of our faith and practice.   And all these, we know, His
Spirit writes on every truly awakened heart.   If there
be any among us who observe them not, who habitually
break any of them, let it be made known unto them who
watch over that soul as they that must give an account.
We will admonish him of the error of his ways ; we will
bear with him for a season ;   but then if he repent not, he
hath no more place among us.' [4]

[1] *Cf.* the Quakers' ' Yea ' and ' Nay,' and fixed prices.
[2] *W.W.* vol. viii. p. 295.   *Cf.* Green's *Bibliography*, p. 27.
[3] *W.W.* vol. viii. p. 260.   On the high moral tone of Wesley's preaching, see Abbey and Overton, *op. cit.* vol. i. p. 601.
[4] Rules, etc., Appendix D, *N.H.M.* vol. ii. p. 565 ; see also *e.g. J.W.J.*
vol. ii. p. 431, note ; ii. 517.

The purposive activity of the organized group thus embodied certain traditional sentiments, which were identified with the New Testament ethical ideal. But special emphasis was laid upon those moral qualities in which the general society of the time was conspicuously lacking : reverence, sobriety, peaceable tempers, honesty, particularly commercial honesty, self-control and self-denial, diligence and frugality, and loyalty to the group. These sentiments, permeating the whole Methodist Society, were impressed upon every member, especially new members, by way of mass suggestion and sympathetic contagion ; every new member found that his companions accepted without question these moral sentiments, and confidently expressed moral judgments upon conduct and character in accordance with them, and that they also displayed the corresponding emotional reactions towards acts ; that is to say, they expressed in verbal judgments and in emotional reactions their scorn for immorality, drunkenness, dishonesty and ungodliness, and their admiration for temperance, justice and godliness. The convert quickly came to share these ' moral emotions,' and soon found his judgment determined to accept these moral opinions, for they came to him with all the well-nigh irresistible force of opinion held by the group and expressed by its unanimous voice. And this ethical power of the Methodist societies was cumulative ; as the self-consciousness of the denomination developed, each member would acquire a more defined and powerful sense of community. ' And the more fully the consciousness of the whole group is present to the mind of each member, the more effectually will the whole impress its moral precepts upon each.' [1]

The organization of the United Societies into a

[1] McDougall, W., *G.M.* pt. i. ch. iv. p. 64.

Connexion,' with its system of official positions : leader, steward, lay preacher, itinerant preacher, circuit superintendent, made it possible for the leaders to influence and mould the form of these moral opinions and sentiments. Wesley never forgot that ' the startling effects of itinerant preaching are dearly purchased at the expense of regularity and Church order.' [1] As the supreme leader and founder of the group, with the rigid ethical standard of his High Anglican tradition, he maintained the discipline of the will among all his followers, and his prestige was both official and personal. This was true also in a less degree of all his army of preachers, officers and leaders. ' The organization of the whole group, with its hierarchy of offices which confer prestige gives those who hold these higher offices the opportunity to raise the moral level of all the members.' [2]

The aesthetic sentiment was weak in Methodism : the only beauty genuinely admired was the beauty of holiness, and this was generally conceived in terms of the Puritan austerity of John Wesley. Consequently the artistic impulse has only found expression in such forms as were consonant with the special aim of religious edification. Wesley's description of Cologne cathedral as ' mere heaps upon heaps ; a huge misshapen thing,' [3] is comparable with St. Paul's opinion of Athens and its Greek sculpture, which in his view was merely a ' city full of idols.' [4] This partial aesthetic blindness in the mind of early Methodism is reflected in the baldness of many Methodist buildings. On the other hand the dignity and poetry of the Bible found ample appreciation, as also did the vigour and

[1] Abbey and Overton, *op. cit.* vol. ii. p. 169.
[2] McDougall, *G.M.* p. 64.   [3] *J.W.J.* ii. p. 8.   [4] Acts xvii. 16.
D.M.R.   2 E

lyrical quality of the new hymnody. Biblical language
gave to the autobiographies of Wesley's preachers a touch
of style : occasionally one finds a noble nature, poetically
gifted, treating with simplicity or severity a serious
subject, and the result is plain thought, direct expression
nobleness and rapidity.[1] Frequently the preachers had
command of a clear nervous English ; their imagery and
symbolism were drawn largely from the Old Testament
and the Apocalypse of St. John. Their educational
attainments in many cases compared favourably with
those of the average clergy, and many of them ' became
really learned men.' [2] The hymns which were produced
and sung through the Methodist societies were many of
them of a very high order of religious poetry ; and the
editions of tune-books issued by the Wesley brothers
ultimately influenced the music of Christian worship
throughout the world.[3] Thus although it may be that
the Revival tended to produce a type of mind in which
the sense of beauty or the aesthetic judgment and emotion
were imperfectly developed, yet within the limits of the
well-defined purposes of the movement there were evi-
dences not only of artistic appreciation, but of artistic
production.

Early Methodism was prevented from developing a symbolic cultus or sacramental system by Wesley's lifelong

[1] *Cf.* Arnold, Matthew, *On Translating Homer*. *Cf. e.g.* John Nelson's
description of his experience when he first heard Wesley preach, *vide
supra*, pp. 188-9.

[2] See Bett, H., ' The Alleged Illiteracy of the Early Methodist
Preachers,' *W.H.S.* xv. 4. (Dec. 1925).

[3] Samuel Wesley (son of Charles), 1766-1837, composed tunes for all
Wesley's hymns. He also first introduced the works of Bach to
England. His son, Samuel Sebastian Wesley (1810-76), was organist
of Leeds Parish Church, 1842-8, and of Gloucester Cathedral, and he
inaugurated the modern phase of English Church music. See Naumann,
Emil, *History of Music*, vol. v. pp. 1289-93.

attachment to the Church of England. The members
of his Societies were instructed to attend Communion at
the established Church, and there were Methodist Societies
as late as 1870 in which no service was held during church
hours, and where the Sacraments were not administered.[1]
It was the urgent demand of the American Methodist
Societies which led Wesley to authorize his preachers to
administer the Sacraments. After the Revolutionary
War, the Episcopal clergy were so few that for hundreds
of miles the people were deprived of the Lord's Supper,
and there was no one to baptize the children.[2] Wesley's
action in this emergency was rapidly followed by the
development of a complete Church order within Methodism, and the two Sacraments of Baptism and the Lord's
Supper were regularly observed. Later Methodism has
evolved its own synthesis of the evangelical and sacramental principles, and regards them as equally rooted in
religious experience.

Early Methodism, however, developed its own symbolism, and the members discovered for themselves the
peculiar satisfactions which group self-consciousness
brings. In the first place, the consciousness of the society
and of oneself as a member of it brings a sense of power
and security, an assurance of sympathy and co-operation,
a moral and physical support without which man can
hardly face the world. The society is a source of settled
opinions and of definite guidance in conduct, ' which
obviates the most uncomfortable and difficult necessity
of exerting independent judgment and making up
one's own mind.'[3] Secondly, going back to a primary

---

[1] *N.H.M.* vol. i. p. 386, note.   [2] *Vide infra*, pp. 256-7.

[3] McDougall, *G.M.* p. 69; see also Wesley's arguments in favour of
joining a Methodist Society, *J.W.J.* vol. v. pp. 83-5.

instinctive tendency, the satisfaction of the gregarious
impulse is greater or more complete the more nearly alike
are the individuals congregated together. ' We find the
gregarious satisfaction in our own peculiar *set* only. . . ·
In savage life this shows itself in practices which accentuate
the likeness of members of a group and mark it off more
distinctly from other groups—for example, totems,
peculiarities of dress, ornaments, and ceremonies ; things
which are closely paralleled by the clubs, blazers, colours,
cries, and so forth of our undergraduate communities.' [1]

Robertson Smith in his *Religion of the Semites*, traces
to totemism the principle of the communion meal.[2] And
the whole of religion has been traced to group consciousness,[3] or to the ' herd instinct.' [4] These theories are not
an adequate explanation of the facts, and it is doubtful
if in human psychology the ' herd instinct ' is an instinct
at all. Dr. McDougall is very careful to distinguish the
gregarious instinct from various quite different social
instincts. But mingled with other elements of deeper
social and personal significance, the sources of group-
satisfaction which have been referred to are psychologically related to the Methodist stress on Communion, or
the Lord's Supper, the Methodist love-feast, with its
' specially made bread,' and tea or water—' the ordinary
beverage '—the class-meeting fellowship, the hymn-singing,
and the issue quarterly to every member of a ' class-ticket.'

The ticket of membership Wesley regarded as being
equivalent to the Pauline ' letters of commendation,' [5]
and he says they were of use, '(1) because, wherever those

---

[1] McDougall, *G.M.* p. 69.

[2] First ed. 1889 ; see Durkheim, Emile, *Les Formes Élémentaires de
la vie religieuse* (1912), pp. 126-7.

[3] Cornford, F. M., *From Religion to Philosophy*, p. 82 ; Pratt, 201.

[4] Trotter, *op. cit.* p. 113.   [5] 2 Cor. iii. 1.

who bore them came, they were acknowledged by their brethren, and received with all cheerfulness ; (2) when Societies had to meet apart, the tickets easily distinguished who were members and who were not ; (3) they supplied a quiet and inoffensive method of removing any disorderly member ; for, the tickets being changed once a quarter, and of course no new ticket being given to such a person, it was hereby immediately known that he was no longer a member of the community.'[1] The utility of these tickets, bearing the member's name and the signature of the leader or preacher, was immediately apparent. But the ticket came to possess a psychological significance and symbolism other than was intended by Wesley. Apart from the suggestion in the artistic and symbolic design of earlier issues, the ticket bearing the member's name acquired the character of a clan badge. ' Mais le totem n'est pas seulement un nom ; c'est un emblème, un véritable blason, dont les analogies avec le blason héraldique ont été remarquées.'[2] ' Le totem est, en fait, un dessin qui correspond aux emblèmes héraldiques des nations civilisées, et que chaque personne est authorisée à porter comme preuve de l'identité de la famille à laquelle elle appartient.'[3] A series of Methodist class tickets indicating years of unbroken communion with the group was very highly valued, and members occasionally have left instructions that their tickets should be buried with them.

Dr. McDougall's analysis of the tendencies of the group spirit, which are advantageous for the higher development of human life in general, is admirably illustrated by the

---

[1] Tyerman, *L.T.W.* vol. i. p. 354.   [2] Durkheim, *op. cit.* p. 158.
[3] Durkheim, E., *op. cit.* p. 159 ; quoted from Schoolcraft, *Indian Tribes*, vol. iii. p. 184.

Methodist Societies.   Beyond the comfort and satisfaction
of the individual members is the great socializing influence
of group self-consciousness. ' In the great majority of
cases it is the principal, if not the sole factor which raises
a man's conduct above the plane of pure egoism, and leads
him to think and care and work for others as well as for
himself.' [1]   ' The group spirit destroys the opposition
and the conflict between the crudely individualistic and
the primitive altruistic tendencies of our nature . . . the
individual identifies himself with the group . . . his self-
regarding sentiment becomes extended to the group
more or less completely, so that he is moved to desire and
to work for its welfare, its success, its honour and glory,
by the same motives which prompt him to desire and to
work for his own welfare and success and honour.' [2]   Thus
the altruistic emotion which is very marked as an immediate result of conversion is intensified and translated into
concrete activity by the spirit and the opportunities
provided by the social organization.

   The promoting of social life by the principle of multiple
group consciousness was manifest in the evolution of
Methodism in two ways.   In the first place, the social
spirit of the new religious order overflowed into occupational and economic groups.   The Methodists were in
many cases the original members of workmen's societies
which developed later into Trades Unions.   They were
accused of meeting in private houses, and forming plans
for advancing wages.[3]   Out of this activity arose the
common charge of sedition, and the names Brunswick

---

[1] McDougall, *G.M.* p. 78.   [2] *Ibid.* p. 79.

[3] Home Office Papers ; Letter from the Vicar of Sandal, near Wake
field.   See also Hammond, J. L. and B., *Town Labourer*, p. 277, for
this quotation, and evidence of a reversal of this attitude in Methodism
after Wesley's death.

and Hanover were given to many Methodist Chapels as a public proof of loyalty to the constitution. But ' when the industrial disturbances of later days reached a maximum of intensity and peril, the labour movement was to a marked extent leavened by the chapel and class meeting of Wesley's Societies. In them working-men had been trained not only in sympathy, but in organization, in financial administration, in methods of communication. The local preacher and the labour leader became for a long period almost synonymous terms. And it is impossible to doubt that at least one of the sources of the sanity and intelligence of the trades-union movement in Great Britain is the Wesleyan revival.' [1]

In the second place the multiple group consciousness [2] expressed itself in the formation of a hierarchy of group sentiments for a system of societies in which each larger community included the lesser ; each in turn being made the object of the extended self-regarding sentiment. The family, the village, the country as a whole, and later, the international system, as centres of social sentiment, found a parallel in the class-meeting, the society, the circuit, and later the district and the ' Connexion ' with its rapidly developing over-seas activity, as centres of a living social organism which has gathered around it a world-wide religious and social sentiment. ' It is due to Wesley's capacity for what has been happily called " the statesmanship of salvation," [3] that the movement which he inaugurated presents the aspect not of an injurious recoil, but rather of a great purifying social force working steadily for the evolution and regeneration of society.' [4]

[1] Davenport, F. M., *op. cit.* p. 177.   [2] McDougall, *G.M.* p. 80.
[3] Woodrow Wilson ; quoted by Davenport, *op. cit.*
[4] Davenport, *op. cit.* pp. 178-9.

XII

EXPERIENCE AND DOCTRINE

METHODIST doctrine affords a good illustration of the truth that man lives first and thinks afterwards. All the distinctive features of Methodist thought and teaching have their roots in a characteristic experience. Both in the theological writings of John Wesley, and in the hymns of Charles, there is emotion recollected in tranquillity. And some of the hymns possess the quality of incantation :[1] the almost magical power of the inspired phrase to reproduce in the reader the high moment experienced by the poet and reflected in the poem. That is one reason for the vitality of the Methodist evangel in its standard utterances : so closely does the poetic or imaginative form convey the vivid intensity of actual experience.

The psychological bases of Methodist doctrine will become apparent if we examine the philosophy and theology of the eighteenth century, with a view to the light they throw, by comparison and contrast, upon the evangelical witness.

In its relation to the philosophy of the age, Methodism is at once a reflection and a reaction. It reflects the individualism and reacts from the rationalism of the century. From the early days of the Revival to the present day, the individualism of contemporary moralists

[1] See Abercrombie, Lascelles, *The Idea of Great Poetry* (1925), p. 18.

has influenced the Methodist movement ; and, on the other hand, there was in evangelicalism a definite recoil from the worship of reason and from the formal intellectualism of the age.

The eighteenth century regarded religion as a purely individual experience. In an attempt to discover what was the essential nature of man, Hobbes [1] found it necessary to deny that man is naturally a social animal, and to assert the primacy of man's egoistic tendencies. ' This became the great point at issue between Hobbes and his critics, and led to the development in England and Scotland of a descriptive psychology of the active side of human nature.' [2] Although Shaftesbury,[3] ' the first moralist who distinctly takes psychological experience as the basis of ethics,' [4] Butler [5] and Hutcheson [6] set themselves to answer the psychological egoism of Hobbes, they were never free from the individualistic point of view, which indeed dominated both the English Empirical School and the Scottish Common Sense School of psychologists in the eighteenth century. The ' cardinal doctrine in moral psychology ' [7] which Hobbes reached as a result of his analysis of human nature was ' that all man's desires are essentially directed towards his own preservation and happiness, and what are apparently unselfish emotions are analysed and explained in terms of this self-regarding tendency.' [8]

[1] 1588-1679.   [2] Drever, J., *I.M.* p. 22.
[3] 1671-1713.
[4] Sidgwick, Henry, *History of Ethics*, p. 189.
[5] 1692-1752.   [6] 1694-1747.
[7] Sidgwick, *op. cit.* p. 163.
[8] Drever, *op. cit.* pp. 23-4.

D.M.R.   2 F

The concrete illustration of the influence of this philosophy on the mind of Wesley is in the distinct statement
which he made with regard to his main purpose at Oxford
and in the Georgia mission.   In a letter to his father, he
says, ' The question is not whether I could do more good
to others there or here ; but whether I could do more
good to myself : seeing wherever I can be most holy
myself, there I can most promote holiness in others.
But I can improve myself more at Oxford than at any
other place.' [1]   As to his aim in going to America, he
wrote, ' My chief motive is the hope of saving my own
soul.' [2]   And on the day when he embarked for the
voyage to Georgia, he entered in his *Journal*, ' Our end
in leaving our native country, was not to avoid want,
(God having given us plenty of temporal blessings,) nor
to gain the dung or dross of riches or honour ; but singly
this, to save our souls ; to live wholly to the glory of
God.' [3]   It may be pointed out that this attitude was
characteristic of Wesley only before his evangelical conversion, and that even at that time his activity belied
his philosophy.   But the emphasis, in early Methodism,
upon the purely individual idea of personal salvation is
largely a reflection of the mind of Wesley, and of the
eighteenth century individualism which dates back to
Hobbes.

The narrow conception of reason in the philosophy of the
eighteenth century was largely responsible for the divorce
of reason and revelation in the nineteenth century.   A
deep vein of transcendentalism and mysticism was
touched by Butler and Berkeley, but their approach to

[1] Tyerman, *L.T.W.* vol. i. pp. 96-7.   [2] *N.H.M.* vol. ii. p. 54.
[3] *J.W.J.* vol. i. pp. 109-110.

it was essentially intellectual. Dryden [1] was before his time when he wrote,

> ' Dim as the borrowed beams of moon and stars
> To lonely, weary, wandering travellers,
> Is Reason to the soul.' [2]

Instead of turning, like Dryden, from reason to Rome for his spiritual certainties, Wesley turned from the logical arguments of Butler to the experimental realities of passion and the human heart.

The spirit of early eighteenth century philosophy was most deeply influenced by Locke,[3] whose educational theory [4] and psychological essay [5] almost entirely ignore the emotional side of human nature. Wesley was probably unconscious of the extent to which he was influenced by the philosophic tendencies of the age, but his consistent appeal to experience is reminiscent of Locke's patient examination of particular facts. At the same time, Wesley's logical temper and training saved him from exalting experimental faith to the position of something independent of reason. ' I believe and reason too,' Wesley wrote, ' for I find no inconsistency between them. And I would as soon put out my eyes to secure my faith, as lay aside my reason.' [6]

The narrower rationalism of the age is also incidentally evidenced by the failure of psychology to become genetic, and by the analogous incapacity of the eighteenth century and of early Methodism to understand a child. Locke, who was a bachelor, would allow children to have only one

---

[1] 1631-1700.   [2] *Religio Laici* (1682).

[3] 1632-1704.   [4] *Thoughts Concerning Education* (1693).

[5] *Essay on the Human Understanding* (1690).

[6] ' Predestination Calmly Considered ' (1745), *W.W.* x. 267. See also ' The Case of Reason Impartially Considered,' *W.W.* vi. 331-341.

toy at once.[1] Wesley, who was childless, would never let children play at all.   He laid it down in the rules for his school at Kingswood that no time must be allowed on any day for play, on the ground that he who plays when he is a child will play when he becomes a man.[2] Innate tendencies, spontaneity, and ' enthusiasm ' were always under suspicion : common sense and probability were the guides of life. Religion was either a barren intellectualism or an equally fruitless respectability. The Revival under the Wesleys recovered living religion in England by delivering it from the impotence of ' reason ' and routine, and planting it deep in the instinctive and emotional life. In his personal life, Wesley's love for children discounted his theories, as in the work of the Revival his humanity transcended his philosophy.

The return of empiricism in recent philosophy gives an added significance to the appeal to experience, which is the generic idea of Methodism. ' The movement towards the method of Values went on all through the nineteenth century, and has become the first feature of the treatment of Theistic belief in the present generation.' [3] It is, of course, understood that experience must not ' be arbitrarily limited to the data of perception which intelligence works up into science ; that the appreciation of moral worth, or of value generally, is as true and immediate a part of our experience as the judgments of perception ; and that it, as well as they, forms a part of the data of

---

[1] *Thoughts Concerning Education,* xix. sec. 130.

[2] Rules of Kingswood School. See Tyerman, vol. ii. p. 10. Cf. Wesley's reports of conversions among children at Kingswood, *J.W.J.* vol. v. pp. 259-60 ; 388-92, 526. See also reports of the agony of children under Berridge's Revival, *J.W.J.* iv. 318, 518, 523.

[3] Caldecott, *The Modern Churchman,* Sept. 1925.

metaphysics,'[1] and of psychology. All the normal contents of consciousness, either our own in personal experience, or that which we infer to belong to the minds of others, in common experience, form the psychical facts upon which an empirical philosophy is based. And 'a philosophy which left one portion of human experience suspended without attachment to the world of truth is gravely open to suspicion ; and its failure to make the religious emotion speculatively intelligible betrays a speculative weakness.'[2] Our study of the working of the human mind as it is revealed in Methodist doctrine contributes data for a philosophy of values, because all the material provided in our documents must be ' regarded as having a place in, or as being a constituent of, some one's experience.'[3]

The historical origin of the appeal to experience need only be traced back to the Reformation. There is a direct relation between the Reformation of the sixteenth century and the individualism of Methodist doctrine. In mediaeval theory, Christendom was a single state under the secular headship of the emperor and the spiritual headship of the Pope.[4] They were the two vicegerents of the Deity. But in the sixteenth century the very conception of unity had been destroyed by the growth of coherent and powerful nations in France, Spain and England ; and the Reformation put an end to the ecclesiastical unity of Western Christendom. In politics and in religion was manifest the same vindication of the rights of the individual in face of the universal domination

---

[1] Sorley, *Moral Values and the Idea of God*, p. 7.

[2] Alexander, S., *Space, Time, and Deity*, vol. ii. p. 352.

[3] Ward, *Psychological Principles*, p. 27.

[4] For an ideal presentment of this theory see Dante, *De Monarchia*.

of Church and State.   In the Roman Church, the
individual was lost in the corporation which ensured his
salvation ;   he was saved through the prayers of the
saints, the grace of the sacraments, and the graduated
hierarchy of the Church by which he was linked to the
Supreme Head.   Against this excessive solidarity the
Reformation raised its protest.   ' Instead of a salvation
conditioned by corporate relations, we find the assertion
by Luther of the paramount importance of the inner life
of the individual.' [1]

The increase of religious liberty, which was the first
effect of the work of Luther, was coincident with a
dangerous exaltation of the authority of Scripture.
Liberation of conscience was not accompanied by a
commensurate intellectual emancipation, and the disintegration of the reforming groups created the opportunity
for the infallibilities of Calvin.

Among Protestants, however, one peculiarity of the
Methodist movement was its retention of and insistence
upon the objective authority of the Church conjoined
with the subjective reality and value of individual
experience.   Here again it is seen that the mind of
Methodism was the mind of Wesley.   He had a strong
Nonconformist ancestry on both sides, yet his parents
had returned to the Church of England.   Consequently
Methodism inherited from him the ' root idea of the
Independent joined to the root idea of the Anglican.' [2]
Wesley insisted throughout his life upon external authority
as well as upon inner illumination.   And though these
diverse principles are responsible for the struggles which
rent Methodism for some years after Wesley's death, yet

[1] Workman, H. B., in *N.H.M.* vol. i. p. 9.
[2] Workman, *op. cit.* p. 16.

hey have now been accommodated within the system
which gives to Methodism its distinctive place in the
history of the Catholic Church.[1]

The special form of the appeal to experience which is
he fundamental contribution of Methodism to the thought
f the Church is the doctrine of *Assurance*. The genuine-
ness of conversion, of reconciliation, of forgiveness and
f the soul's relation to God was determined by an appeal
o one's own consciousness. Wesley claimed the validity
f introspection as a ground for belief in objective reality.
Ie accepted the results of his own self-analysis as the
uthoritative decisions of God. Dr. H. B. Workman has
pointed out that ' never before in the history of the Church
ince the writings of St, Paul had the doctrines of Assurance
been so clearly enunciated.' [2]   The novelty of the doctrine
n the eighteenth century was the cause of great antipathy
nd even of persecution. A Methodist named Greenfield
aving been imprisoned, Wesley inquired the reason.
I asked a little gentleman at St. Just what objection
here was to Edward Greenfield. He said, " Why, the
man is well enough in other things ; but his impudence
he gentlemen cannot bear. Why, sir, he says he knows
is sins are forgiven ! " ' [3]   At a time when the majority
f thoughtful men, including representative writers of
he established Church, regarded all reference to the inner
ight of spiritual discernment with distrust and suspicion,
Wesley had, through a long and painful religious pilgrim-
ge, reached what was for him a ground of unshakeable
ertainty. He proclaimed that a man may know himself
orgiven, and that he has within himself, in his conscious-

---

[1] Workman, *op. cit.* p. 16.   [2] *Ibid.* vol. i. p. 21.
[3] *J.W.J.* June, 25, 1745, vol. iii. p. 186.

ness, the witness of his own relation to God. Man
strands of thought and experience went to the makin
of this empirical doctrine. But it is intellectually relate
to the appeal of philosophy to experience which originate
with Descartes.[1] Doubt can shake our dogmas an
opinions, but 'Cogito ergo sum': 'I am consciou
involves I am.' The reality of the thinker is not the sam
thing as the validity of the thought, but in method a
least we have in the doctrine of Descartes the philosophica
counterpart of the Methodist identification of consciousnes
and reality.

The psychological basis of the doctrine of Assuranc
was in the noetic quality of the conversion experience
As distinct from abstract reasoning towards a conclusio
in discursive thought, the knowledge claimed by th
convert is concrete, intuitive, and immediate. One i
what James called *knowledge-about*, and the other i
knowledge of acquaintance. 'Most languages expres
this distinction; thus, γνῶναι, εἰδέναι; *noscere, scire
kennen, wissen*; *connaître, savoir*.'[3] I know the colou
blue when I see it; I know an inch when I measure it
but *about* these things I know little. I cannot make
blind man feel what blue is like, nor tell a philosopher wh
distance is what it is. And so, as Newman would say
men discern the great fundamental truths of religion, no
step by step in logical process, but by an illative facult
which is nothing short of genius.[4]

With an intuitive certainty of this type, the Methodis
preachers called all men to partake of an immediat

---

[1] 1596-1650.   [2] *Vide supra*, pp. 87, 101-3.

[3] *P.P.* vol. i. p. 221. See also chap. xii. on 'Conception,' an
chap. xxii. on 'Reasoning.'

[4] *Grammar of Assent*, p. 326

experience, and ignorant, vicious and ungodly men were converted and sang,

> ' My God, I am Thine,
>   What a comfort divine,
> What a blessing to know that my Jesus is mine.' [1]

The Assurance, or Conscious Pardon, as it was called by John Nelson,[2] was immediate, but its ideational content was expanded by conceptual thought.   Truth is ' what man recognises as value when his life is fullest and his soul at its highest stretch.' [3]   And in the high moments of religious experience the philosophy of Methodism was developed, and found expression in verses such as these :

> ' We know by faith, we surely know,
>   The Son of God is come ;
> Is manifested here below,
>   And makes our hearts His home ;
> To us He hath, in special love,
>   An understanding given,
> To recognize Him from above,
>   The Lord of earth and heaven.' [4]

The spiritual experience thus described is native to the genius of Methodism, and if compared with the New Testament doctrine as interpreted by St. Paul,[5] it will be found that both are established upon the same psychological basis : an intuitive element in conversion, interpreted in the light of the Gospel of Jesus Christ.

Although conversion is an intimate, individual, and almost incommunicable experience, it was thus made a

---

[1] *A Collection of Hymns, etc.*, 21st ed. 1808, No. 205.

[2] Undated letter from John Nelson, quoted by Laycock, J. W., *Methodist Heroes in the Great Haworth Round*, 1734-1784, p. 10.

[3] Bosanquet, B., *Principle of Individuality and Value*, p. 3.

[4] *Methodist Hymn Book*, No. 120.   See *N.H.M.* vol. i. pp. 172.

[5] *Cf.* Rom. viii. 14-17 ; *cf.* 1 Cor. iii. 16 ; vi. 19.

foundation upon which is built a system of thought. The dangers involved in such a process are immediately apparent. An appeal to experience as the ground of reality may end in sheer individualism. And the logical end of the process which bases knowledge upon the feelings and ideas of individuals may easily become the nescience of Hume. From this danger, which beset the thinking of the English and Scottish philosophers in the eighteenth century, Methodism was saved by the development of the system of societies into a Connexion, with its constant appeal from individual experience to collective experience as the final court. And beyond the sane corrective of the corporate judgment within the Methodist organization, Wesley taught men who were individualists in the originating centre of their thinking, to look beyond their own faith and fear to the one great witness of the universal Church in all ages. 'Here properly comes in,' writes Wesley, ' to confirm this scriptural doctrine, the experience of the children of God ; the experience not of two or three, not a few, but of a great multitude which no man can number. It has been confirmed, both in this and in all ages, by a cloud of living and dying witnesses.' [1]

A serious danger in the early life of Methodism was the tendency of introspection to induce an unhealthy subjective habit of mind. The introvert becomes an egoist. Carlyle had some justification for regarding Methodism as ' a diseased self-introspection, an agonizing inquiry.' [2]

---

[1] *W.W.* vol. v. p. 119.

[2] Carlyle, *Past and Present*, p. 52. Chapman and Hall. Edinburgh Edition. *Cf.* p. 101, ' Methodism with its eye forever turned on its own navel ; asking itself with torturing anxiety of Hope and Fear, "Am I right ? Am I wrong ? Shall I be saved ? Shall I not be damned ? " —what is this, at bottom, but a new phasis of Egoism, stretched out into the Infinite ; not always the heavenlier for its infinitude ! '

In the earlier days the search for πληροφορία [1] or full assurance brought great distress to many earnest minds. But Carlyle was pleading for a happy objectivity which Methodism had already achieved for itself. ' Religion lies over them all like an all-embracing heavenly canopy, like an atmosphere and life-element, which is not spoken of, which in all things is presupposed without speech.' [2] Charles Wesley might easily have written that passage, but he would have wished to sing praise to a personal God.

> ' Thy goodness and Thy truth to me,
>   To every soul abound ;
> A vast, unfathomable sea,
>   Where all our thoughts are drowned.
>
> Throughout the universe it reigns ;
>   Unalterably sure :
> And while the Truth of God remains,
>   The goodness must endure.' [3]

Assurance, as it was understood by later Methodism, was saved from subjectivism by a larger conception of the grace whereby we are saved—' for if our heart condemn us, God is greater than our heart, and knoweth all things.' [4]

But egoism is a subtle foe, and afflicted the Revival leaders in a manner that is not confined to Methodism. A part of the pilgrimage of the Methodist Church is its progress from the intolerant spirit manifested in the dreary Calvinistic controversy between Whitefield and Wesley, to the larger inclusiveness which recognizes that the commonwealth of the Christian religion is catholic enough to include all the wealth of humanity in its widely varied types and temperaments.

[1] Col. ii. 2 ; Heb. vi. 11, x. 22.   [2] Carlyle, *Past and Present*, p. 52.
[3] *Wesley's Hymns*, 21st ed. 1808, pp. 241-2.
[4] 1 John iii. 20.   See Workman's valuable chapter on this subject, *N.H.M.* vol. i. pp. 28-31.

Although Wesley, by the nature of his own experience and work, was almost necessarily limited in his purview to a special type of conversion occurring in a moment of time, yet in his later years he wrote, on the subject of instantaneous conversion, ' Every man therefore may abound in his own sense, provided he will allow the same liberty to his neighbour ; provided he will not be angry at those who differ from his opinion, nor entertain hard thoughts concerning them. Permit me likewise to add one thing more : be the change instantaneous or gradual, see that you never rest till it is wrought in your own soul, if you desire to dwell with God in glory.' [1]   This fine candour and tolerance was a forecast of the temper and spirit of modern Methodism, which, while peculiarly true to its origin in its emphasis upon religious experience, and in its gospel of reconciliation and Assurance, insists no longer upon uniformity, and with Christian altruism respects the varied capacity for religious feeling which marks the men and women of real life. The mystical sense, the power of realizing the presence of God intensely and intimately, is not given to all men. And Christianity is not a religion for special types only, but for all humanity ; and in its name Methodism to-day addresses itself with an educational evangelism, to all nations and kindreds and peoples and tongues.

When it is considered with reference to the specifically religious conditions and to the theology of the eighteenth century, Methodism is seen to be at once a product and a factor. It was indebted to or moulded by the religious life of the period, and at the same time it developed on

[1] *W.W.* vol. vi. p. 464 ; *cf.* Tyerman, *L.T.W.* vol. i. p. 463 ; and Workman, *N.H.M.* vol. i. p. 33.

independent lines, and made an original contribution to the thought of the Church.

Methodism has been charged with intellectual poverty. Buckle, for example, wrote, ' they soon lost that intellectual vigour for which they were at first remarkable. Since the death of their great leaders, they have not produced one man of original genius ; and since the time of Adam Clarke, they have not had among them even a single scholar who has enjoyed an European reputation.' [1] But it must be remembered that the Methodist movement was not due to the discovery of an intellectual truth, but to the recovery of a life. The age needed to be recalled to the fact that religion is experience, to be enjoyed rather than to be contemplated, and with its home in man's emotional life. Schleiermacher [2] perhaps interpreted the religious philosophy of Methodism more truly than any contemporary writer. ' The true nature of religion is neither this idea nor any other, but immediate consciousness of the Deity as He is found in ourselves and in the world.' [3]

The religious attitude most characteristic of the eighteenth century is that described as Deism. Essentially rationalistic and anti-Christian, its distinguishing feature was antagonism to revealed religion. The general temper and spirit of the deists may be indicated by the titles of typical works. Toland's [4] *Christianity not Mysterious*, and Tindal's [5] *Christianity as Old as the Creation*, are

---

[1] Buckle, H. T., *History of Civilization in England*, vol. i. pp. 421-2. Note that this was written before the days of J. H. Moulton, Dr. A. S. Peake, and Dr. H. B. Workman, who, among other modern Methodist leaders, take rank as undifferentiated European and American scholars.

[2] 1768-1834.

[3] *Addresses on Religion* ; see Caldecott and Mackintosh, *Selections from the Literature of Theism*, p. 303.

[4] John Toland, 1669-1722.   [5] Matthew Tindal, 1657-1733.

sufficiently representative. Butler says in his preface to the *Analogy*, ' It is come . . . to be taken for granted, by many persons, that Christianity is not so much a subject of inquiry ; but that it is, now at length, discovered to be fictitious.' The idea prevailed among educated men that ' the supreme Being was fenced off from mankind by the laws of nature, and that human knowledge was bounded by the limits of sense-perception and logical reason. The Deity was treated as an absentee from his world ; and consequently men tended to become godless in practice as in thought.'[1] Wesley and the messengers of the Revival swept the country proclaiming an intimate communion with God as not only desirable but possible for every man. In the new religious movement God was realized as in living contact with His children. ' The sense of the divine was recovered ; the transcendent became again immanent to consciousness.' Methodists habitually described the Revival as ' the work of God ' ; and ' the life of God in the souls of men ' was Wesley's definition of religion. As contrasted with Deism the distinction of Methodism is that it discredited the cramped and narrow view of reason, expanded the theory of knowledge through the inclusion of a wealth of higher values, and taught its adherents that in the phenomena of the Revival they were to discern the very presence and power of God.

The recognition of Divine grace as operative within the human mind, giving mental and moral stability by means of religious assurance, explains the tendency of Methodism in the direction of religious determinism. The Calvinistic doctrines of the particular election of the redeemed, and

[1] Findlay, G. G., ' Methodist Doctrine,' *E.R.E.* viii. pp. 610-612.

the irresistible grace of God,[1] prevailed in Puritan theology,
and were accepted by Whitefield and his followers. They
sacrificed self-determination in their eagerness to ascribe
everything to God. But Wesley would have no tampering
with the will. He rejected Calvinism, as he rejected
pseudo-mysticism, because both lost sight of moral
personality in their vision of God. Calvinism, like Deism,
exalts the transcendence of God at the expense of His
immanence, and reduces finite will to an illusion, making
man, ' even in his acceptance of divine grace, the passive
creature instead of the consenting child of God.'[2] ' A
direct Divine compulsion would leave no more reality
to will than a direct material compulsion. To suppose
that will, directly controlled by God, effects anything, is
to suppose that the shadow moves the body. No one has
devoted more passion and subtlety to prove the opposite
than Calvin, and no one proves more clearly the utter
hopelessness of ascribing everything to God, either
directly or through the operation of the universe, and yet
of holding man responsible for his doings.'[3] Wesley
issued many manifestoes setting forth this issue with
unerring clearness. He argued that, ' God is willing that
all men should be saved, yet not willing to force them
thereto ; willing that men should be saved, yet not as
trees and stones, but as men, as reasonable creatures,
endued with understanding to discern what is good,
and liberty to accept or refuse it.'[4] Methodism was

[1] John Calvin, 1509-1564, *Institutes of the Christian Religion*, 1536.

[2] Findlay, *op. cit.*

[3] Oman, John, *Grace and Personality*, pp. 29-30.

[4] ' Predestination Calmly Considered,' *W.W.* vol. x. p. 224. *Cf.*
Sorley, W. R., ' The Spirit of God works in and through the spirit of
man, but in such a way as not to destroy human freedom. . . . Love
works through freedom ' (*Moral Values and the Idea of God.* p. 503).

based upon a relation between man and God which is personal and gracious, in which religious dependence upon God in no way minimizes the moral independence of man.

The vital nature of the experience of God compelled Methodism to reject the dogmatic infallibilities of Calvinism, in their limitation of the number of those who could be saved, and of the degree to which salvation was attainable. Although certain passages in the Bible reflect a determinism which colours all Eastern literature, the very nature of the Gospel as a whole excludes the Calvinistic inference. If an arbitrary decree of an omnipotent God predestined some of his creatures to damnation, the preachers of the Revival could not have announced that God ' willeth all men to be saved.' They proclaimed without any misgiving, ' Ye all may come, Whoever will.' But the psychological basis of the universalism of the Evangelical message was in vital religious experience.[1] It rested upon the empirical fact which was central in the individual and collective life of Methodism : the dominant sentiment of love, responding to the consciousness of reconciliation through the love and redeeming mercy of God. The noblest expression of this synthesis of the individual and the universal is in Charles Wesley's couplet :

> ' 'Tis mercy all, boundless and free,
> For, O my God, it found out me.' [2]

Here the sense of personal and individual values is enlarged to embrace the whole of human society.

The Methodist doctrine of *Christian Perfection* challenged both the moral standards and the current orthodoxy

---

[1] See Sermon on Free Grace, *W.W.* vii. pp. 356-69.
[2] See Wiseman, *N.H.M.* vol. i. p. 247.

of the eighteenth century. Amid indescribable corruption, the Revival preachers proclaimed an ideal of ethical value, not as a dream of heaven, but as a guide on earth. And again on the warrant of experience, they denied the tenet of Calvinism which maintained the necessary inherence of sin in the redeemed, and thus limited the degree of holiness attainable. One of the most courageous of the services rendered by Methodism to England was the launching of a campaign to spread ' real, essential holiness throughout the land.' And this attempt was distinguished by a firmly held and widely spread belief in the possibility and necessity of Christian Perfection. Redemption, Wesley argued, is intensive as well as extensive, saving the whole of man as well as all men.[1] He taught his people, on the basis of Scripture and experience, to seek and expect the power to become altogether holy and happy. And he quoted the Communion Prayer, ' that we may perfectly love Thee, and worthily magnify Thy Holy Name,' insisting that this is to ask from God no boon beyond His giving.[2] The class meeting, with this ideal, became a school of holiness. ' The glorious hope of perfect love proved an abiding spring of spiritual ardour and a powerful spur to moral endeavour.' [3]

Wesley rejected the Roman Catholic two-standard morality, which distinguishes the subordinate ' Christian ' perfection attainable by laymen from the supreme ' religious ' perfection of monastic and clerical life.[4] The

[1] See Wiseman, *N.H.M.* vol. i. p. 247.
[2] Findlay, *op. cit.* *Cf.* Platt, F., ' Christian Perfection,' *E.R.E.* ix.
[3] Findlay, *op. cit.*
[4] See Von Hügel, *Essays and Addresses on the Philosophy of Religion,* pp. 165-9. See Cadoux, C. J., ' Should we all be Perfect ? ' *Hibbert Journal,* Jan. 1923.

good sought was a positive good. And it was available for all men. Wesley taught that the ideal was not a negative and mischievous celibacy,[1] but a positive purity ; [2] not a lack of material things which may bring physical and spiritual disaster,[3] but a wise and benevolent use of them.[4] In this, of course, Methodism reflects the best Protestant tradition. Its heroes are not monks who escape the problems of social life, but men of affairs who face them, and amid them strive to realize the meaning and worth of the Christian ethic. Its saints are not ascetics, pursuing an exclusive holiness, but miners and weavers, business men and statesmen, whose hands are hard, or whose minds endure constant strain because of the daily struggle with ' worldly ' care.[5] Although the values of the contemplative life were not lost sight of by Wesley,[6] and its discipline is being recovered by many of his followers to-day, yet Methodism as a whole has never lost its conviction that the ideal of Perfection is found in the life lived by housewife and mother, by husband and father, and by all who in all ranks of society seek amid the ordinary duties of the common earthly life to fulfil the purpose of that life divine which is summed up in pure love of God and man.

The inconsistencies in Wesley's account of the doctrine of Perfection are due to the fact that he was more interested in the experience than in its psychology. His position was similar to that of St. Paul, who preached

[1] *W.W.* vol. x. p. 149. But note his exaltation of celibacy in *Thoughts on Marriage and a Single Life* (1743). *Cf. W.W.* xi 439-45.

[2] *W.W.* vol. vii. p. 284 ; v. 261 ; viii. 330.

[3] *W.W.* vol. vi. pp. 90-1.   [4] *W.W.* vol. vi. p. 222 ; vii. 274.

[5] On the Protestant moral ideal, see G. Cross, in *Journal of Religion,* March, 1922, p. 138. Quoted by Cadoux, *op. cit.* See also Platt, Frederic, ' Christian Perfection,' *E.R.E.* vol. ix.

[6] *Vide supra,* p. 86-7.

perfection as the normal Christian character,[1] but found himself faced with actual converts in all stages of frailty and immaturity.[2] Consequently Holiness is sometimes spoken of as a present attainment,[3] and sometimes as a future [4] and as yet unrealized ideal.   It is at once gradual [5] and instantaneous.[6] Entire Sanctification is not the same as sinlessness.[7] Undivided loyalty and love to God do not exempt a man from the possibility of mistakes, ignorance, infirmities, and temptations.[8]

The point at which Wesley distinguishes the beginning of Christian Perfection is that at which voluntary transgression ceases.   He hesitates to use the word ' sin ' for mistakes in judgment and practice that are consequent upon and inseparable from mortality.[9] Sometimes he seems to regard the physical body as responsible for human blunders,[10] but when faced with the issue, he will have nothing to do with the theory that the body is the seat of sin.[11]   There is a special value in his analysis of imperfections as moral or non-moral, according to the degree of deliberate choice or will they involve.[12]   Here he seems to arrive at a moral conception akin to the psychoanalytic doctrine which distinguishes between moral evil and moral disease ; though we should always remember his trenchant remarks on those who regarded their vices as infirmities.[13]

[1] 1 Cor. ii. 6 ; Phil. iii. 15 ; 1 Cor. xiv. 20 ; Col. iii. 14.

[2] 1 Cor. iii. 1, and *passim.*   [3] *W.W.* ii. 483, 502 ; xi. 392-3.

[4] *W.W.* vi. 5 ; xi. 372-3, 386.   *Cf.* Eph. iv. 13 ; Col. i. 28.

[5] *W.W.* xi. 372.   [6] *W.W.* viii. 316.

[7] *W.W.* xi. 380, 401.   [8] *W.W.* xi. 359, 402-3.

[9] *W.W.* xi. 383.   [10] *W.W.* xi. 383 ; vi. 451-2.

[11] *W.W.* vi. 395.

[12] *W.W.* vi. 394.   *Cf.* also Newman, J. H., *Evangelical Sanctity the Completion of Natural Virtue,* ' Oxford University Sermons,' p. 36.

[13] *W.W.* vol. vi. p. 4.

Morality is a continuous process, not a fixed achievement. It is related in some way to the capacity and situation of the individual.[1] Moreover, there is no end to the possibility of improvement, either here or hereafter.[2] But the progress is always conditional upon continued effort and striving.[3] 'What a grievous error,' says Wesley, 'to think that those who are saved from sin cannot lose what they have gained ! It is a miracle if they do not, seeing all earth and hell are so enraged against them ; while meanwhile, so very few, even of the children of God, skilfully endeavour to strengthen their hands.'[4]

It is seen that the contradictions inherent in the doctrine of Perfection as presented by Wesley are simply a reflection of the richness and breadth of the moral life, and of the gradualness of moral progress. But doctrines, like prophets, are known by their fruits, and amid the infinite variations of human character and circumstance, the ideal presented to the Methodist people produced a type of manhood and womanhood which reacted upon human society like a cleansing and refreshing stream.

When it is traced back to its origin, this ethical ideal is rooted in the organic principle of Methodism. The doctrine of Perfection is based psychologically upon experience. The possibility of 'perfecting holiness' is a necessary corollary of the gracious personal relationship with God which is established in conversion. Not only does that experience result in complete and permanent deliverance from every known sin,[5] but if the vital nature of the sonship achieved in conversion has any meaning,

---

[1] *W.W.* vi. 5-6. *Cf.* Luke xi. 47-8. See Jones, H., *A Faith that Enquires*, ch. x.

[2] *W.W.* xi. 386.   [3] *W.W.* xi. 386.   [4] *J.W.J.* vol. vi. pp. 32-3.

[5] For a wealth of evidence in proof of this statement, see Underwood, A. C., *Conversion*.

it must involve the possibility of ' perfect love without
a cloud between.'   ' All we have willed or hoped or
dreamed of good shall exist.'   Thus the Methodists sang,
in mystical ecstasy, but with experimental certainty :

> ' My God ! I know, I feel Thee mine,
>   And will not quit my claim,
> Till all I have is lost in Thine,
>   And all renewed I am.
>
> Refining fire, go through my heart,
>   Illuminate my soul ;
> Scatter Thy life through every part,
>   And sanctify the whole.
>
> My steadfast soul, from falling free,
>   Shall then no longer move ;
> But Christ be all the world to me,
>   And all my heart be love.'

XIII

HISTORICAL VALUES

So far, it is mainly the original issues of the evangelical movement that we have been tracing ; the development of an emotional revival as a result of the conviction which flashed upon the active mind of John Wesley at his conversion ; the stimulation of dormant instincts occasionally to the point of violence ; the power of religion to break the bonds of a narrow rationalism and to kindle in a neglected and debased population a new moral enthusiasm. We have seen that conversion opened the way to new intellectual insight, finely directed activity, and deeper emotional life. Within the circle of the movement, a new social order emerged, which created its own philosophy, interpreting religious experience in vital and imaginative form.

The mental and religious constitution thus revealed is the clue to the broader issues of evangelicalism, and it remains only to see how far we can find in the Revival an explanation of certain features in the history of the period which cannot be accounted for in other than psychological terms.

Before turning to the historical aspects of the problem, we may consider briefly the way in which the religious movement reacted on the literature of the immediately

succeeding age.   By facing a serious criticism directed
against both apostolic Christianity and Methodism, we
shall then be led to estimate the direct value of the Revival
for the social life of the period, and its indirect influence
on the history of modern England.   Finally we shall
return to the more purely psychological questions : What
are the mental factors which are fundamental in Methodism,
and has the essentially evangelical experience a permanent
place in human life and thought ?

In the world of literature, the evangelical movement
brings us to the threshold of the Romantic Revolt.   Perhaps the greatest contribution of Methodism to letters
was made indirectly by the creation of an atmosphere of
passion in which the new spirit of imagination and
reflection found its freedom.   ' With the middle of the
eighteenth century a great change began to make itself
felt in the thought and literature of Western Europe—a
change from the spirit of criticism to that of creation ;
from wit to humour and pathos ; from satire and didactic
verse to the poetry of passion and impassioned reflection ;
above all, a change from a narrow and cramping conception
of man's reason to one far wider and more adequate to
his powers.' [1]   A study of this Romantic Revolt reveals
the ' debt which English letters owes to the religious
revival, whether Evangelical or Methodist, of the
eighteenth century.   As to the ultimate effects of that
revival on the general life of the country, there have been
the inevitable differences of opinion.   But in literature,
and especially in poetry, it would seem to have worked
almost wholly for the good.   It disemprisoned a whole
world of thought and feeling which had been fast chained

[1] Vaughan, C. E., *The Romantic Revolt*, p. 3.

beneath the hide-bound formalism of the preceding era, and for want of which the land was perishing of inanition. The poetic revival began to make itself felt within a few years after the Wesleys' life-long mission was inaugurated. And, all things considered, it is difficult to resist the conclusion, not indeed that the religious movement was the cause of the literary movement, but that both sprang in the first instance from a common source ; and that, as years went on, the revival in literature was immeasurably quickened by finding an atmosphere charged with emotion and sympathy ready to receive it.' [1]

It may seem a far cry from romanticism in literature to humanitarianism in politics, but when we contrast Pope [2] with Wordsworth,[3] the differences that strike us are not unlike the difference between Walpole [4] and Wilberforce.[5] Parallel with the changes in literature, there are marked transformations in social organization and in political institutions. It is impossible to examine all or any of these here in detail. All that can be attempted is to indicate broadly some of the outstanding facts, and note the way in which these are the outcome of a change in mental and spiritual character. The nature of this change is the vital question for the psychology of the period.

We must first of all face the challenging judgment that the evangelical movement as a whole is not a rise ; it is a fall or failure of something : not a rise of religion, but a failure of nerve. This is the conclusion drawn after a comparison has been made between the eighteenth

---

[1] Vaughan, *op. cit.* p. 19.   [2] 1688-1744.   [3] 1770-1850.
[4] 1717-1797.   [5] 1759-1833.

century and the first. Methodism has frequently been described as a revival of apostolic Christianity,[1] but the implications of that claim have not always been realized. Professor Gilbert Murray writes, ' Anyone who turns from the great writers of classical Athens, say Sophocles or Aristotle, to those of the Christian era must be conscious of a great difference of tone. . . . It is hard to describe. It is a rise of asceticism, of mysticism, in a sense, of pessimism ; a loss of self-confidence, of hope in this life and of faith in normal human effort ; a despair of patient inquiry, a cry for infallible revelation ; an indifference to the welfare of the State, a conversion of the soul to God. It is an atmosphere in which the aim of the good man is not so much to live justly, to help the society to which he belongs and enjoy the esteem of his fellow-creatures ; but rather, by means of a burning faith, by contempt for the world and its standards, by ecstasy, suffering and martyrdom, to be granted pardon for his unspeakable unworthiness, his immeasurable sins. There is an intensifying of certain spiritual emotions, an increase of sensitiveness . . . a failure of nerve.' [2]

The accuracy of this interpretation of the Christian attitude in the first century may be questioned. Of its truth as applied to the Gnostics and Mithras-worshippers [3] I cannot judge. But the whole passage has been literally adopted as a description of the mind and temper of Methodism ; [4] and if we face the issues thus raised, in the light of Methodist history, we shall be better able to estimate the influence of the evangelical movement on the

---

[1] See *e.g.* T. Jackson, *Wesleyan Methodism a Revival of Apostolical Christianity*, 4th ed. 1839.

[2] Murray, Gilbert, *Four Stages of Greek Religion*, pp. 103-4.

[3] *Ibid.* p. 103.   [4] Hammond, J. L. and B., *Town Labourer*, p. 273.

general temper of the age, and its share in shaping the particular course taken by the current of modern history.

It is significant that when Professor Murray was studying the relations between Greek religion and the Christian era, his first impression was that the later phenomenon should be described as a rise of religion or mysticism. The suggestion that it was a failure of nerve was made by Professor J. B. Bury in private conversation,[1] and, accepting it as a correction, Professor Murray incorporated it in his argument, and entitled his chapter, ' The Failure of Nerve.' Dr. Bury, as the distinguished editor of Gibbon's *Decline and Fall of the Roman Empire*, evidently reflects Gibbon's estimate of Christianity, and the idea of a nervous breakdown is offered not as a private opinion, but as a mature judgment based upon a critical study of the history of the period as a whole. The attempt to value Methodism in the same way is based by Mr. and Mrs. Hammond upon a thorough piece of research into the social conditions affecting the town and country labourer, skilled and unskilled, in the period 1760-1832, and it must be treated with the respect due to a sincere and serious judgment.

Our study of eighteenth century England lends colour to the statement that the wealthy classes lived in the atmosphere of Sophocles, and the poor in that of Epictetus or St. Paul. Moreover, as Mr. and Mrs. Hammond justly point out, the new religion provided for the working classes what Greek and Roman literature gave to the ruling class : drawing aside the curtain from a remote but profoundly interesting world, in the pages of the Bible, and seeming thus to make their own world more intelligible. For the miner or weaver, the Chapel, with

---

[1] Murray, *op. cit.* p. 8.

its appeal to the emotions, and its preachers who drew on the resources of their Scriptures for their vivid and passionate pictures, perhaps, above all, with its hymns and congregational singing, took the place that theatres, literature, picture-galleries and operas took in the lives of others.[1]

In the early eighteenth century, the sense of strain or tension between man and his environment was markedly absent from the consciousness of the aristocracy, and in the main also from the mind of the intellectual and literary classes. For Dr. Johnson and his contemporaries, the world as they found it was good enough, and their aim was to preserve, not to enlarge or to improve it.[2] The middle classes cultivated a very individualistic form of Protestantism, based on Bible and sermon reading and private prayer, which they found quite compatible with the best sort of worldliness. Above them floated a sceptical aristocracy; and below lay a neglected heathendom.[3]

There is indeed a ' reverse to any pleasant picture of town life in the eighteenth century, and Hogarth painted it : behind his jolly *Beer Street* ran his foul *Gin Lane*. In every town, beside the prosperous masters, journeymen and apprentices, lived a mass of beings, physically and morally corrupt, for whose bodies no one, and for whose souls only the Methodists had a thought to spare.' [4] The conditions of existence among the neglected poor, in the eighteenth century as in the first, provided the

---

[1] See Hammond, J. L. and B., *Town Labourer*, pp. 272-3.

[2] Trevelyan, G. M., *British History in the Nineteenth Century* (1782-1901), p. 5.

[3] *Ibid.* p. 29.   [4] *Ibid.* p. 13.

environment wherein the transforming spiritual power of
the Gospel was amazingly manifest.

The upper classes, however, remained hostile to
Methodism, and ' the established Church thrust it out to
join its potent young force to that of the old Dissenting
bodies.   The ultimate consequence was that the Non-
conformists rose from about a twentieth of the church-goers
to something near a half,'[1] and the recruits to their ranks
became a kind of High Church of Dissent, infusing a
new spirit into English Nonconformity.   Social and moral
salvation came through Methodism to the class that was
most at war with its fate.   By the inherent vitality and
organizing power of the evangelical movement vast areas
of English life were saved from aridity or brutality.
Religious passion supplanted licentiousness, and revels
became revivals.   The dynamic of natural cravings and
instincts was redirected along lines of fruitful religious and
social activity.

The inertness of the Government, both in legislation and
in administration, during the beginnings of the Industrial
Revolution, involved the populations of the textile towns
and manufacturing areas in a prolonged physical and
moral calamity.   Democracy was blind and paralyzed,
unable either to see or to make use of its opportunities.
It has been said that the life and teaching and indeed the
whole spirit of Methodism were unfavourable to the
democratic movement and to the growth of the Trades
Unions.[2]   But in judging Wesley and his colleagues it is
well to remember the fact that ' Burke, for all his powers
of prophecy, Pitt for all his study of Adam Smith, Fox

[1] Trevelyan, *op. cit.* p. 25.
[2] Hammond, J. L. and B., *Town Labourer*, p. 282.

or all his welcome to the new democracy, no more understood the English economic revolution, and no more dreamt of controlling it for the common good, than George III himself.' [1]

Meanwhile a very real service was rendered to the factory worker by a religion which supplied nearly all that the industrial system, the State, and the Church denied him. He was invited to share in the management of the affairs of the religious society, to enter into a fellowship at the Chapel in which he was responsible for risks and adventures, and could take a pride in success and prosperity. ' As a mere exercise in self-government and social life, the Chapel occupied a central place in the affections and thoughts of people who had little to do with the government of anything else. The management of common enterprises, involving relations with others, . . friendships, quarrels, reconciliations, all the excitements that spring from the infinite surprises and subtleties of human character, brought too the exchange of ideas and prejudices, not only within a small circle, but outside : the diplomacy and agitation of controversy, the eager and combative discussion of rival doctrines. If there was too little vitality in the Church of the day, nobody could complain that the Chapels, contending for Wesley or Whitefield, were in any danger of falling asleep. . . . The men and women who were drawn into the brisk, alert, and ardent life of the new religion found plenty to occupy their minds and to stimulate faculties and interests that were otherwise left neglected.' [2] It may justly be claimed that a part of the function of Methodism in its relation to the new industrialist was that of education,

---

[1] Trevelyan, *op. cit.* p. xiv.
[2] Hammond, J. L. and B., *Town Labourer*, pp. 270-1.

since the aim of education is ' not to inspire blind con
fidence, but to fit men to deal with the situations of life.' [1]
We cannot discern here the note of pessimism, or despair
of normal human effort : on the contrary, there is a very
definite optimism and strenuous effort to help humanity
and promote social welfare.

It is not surprising to find that a recent inquiry into
the religious state of the people has suggested the con
clusion that the most vital forms of religion are found in
areas which have developed since the Industrial Revolu
tion, and represent rather a reawakening of spiritual
consciousness than a survival from the past. ' It was the
new scenes of missionary labour that profited most from
the growth of self-consciousness which underlay different
phases of the Evangelical movement, originating among
small groups of associates who met together for mutual
edification and the promotion of good works.' [2] A new
standard of individual and social values became possible
to the man who was taught to think of himself, not as a
tool of an industrial system, but as a child of God, whose
well-being and well-doing were the care of a special
Providence.

The relation of all this to the psychology of Methodism
is clear enough. It is a serious misreading of history to
identify asceticism, extreme mysticism, and indifference to
the welfare of the State with the religious movement
founded by John Wesley. The barrenness of the ancient
ascetic ideal and the dangers of mystical ecstasy were
both realized by Wesley, and though his followers were
bidden to fast, it was as a rational self-discipline, not a

[1] Rivers, W. H. R., *Psychology and Politics*, p. 105.
[2] Dobbs, A. E., *Education and Social Movements* (1919), p. 117.

a 'religious' mortification. He denounced the practices of those who neglected or macerated their bodies, for, he said, 'it cannot be pleasing to Him, nor become His followers, who came " not to destroy men's lives, but to save them." '[1]

The genius of evangelicalism is strangely complex, for while it included the incidental tendencies already examined in the direction of subjectivism and egoism, its essential nature was expressed in vigorous activity and a broad and beneficent altruism. Methodists were taught to look for confidence and hope and joy in this world, and to seek by normal human effort to promote the welfare of their neighbours. The ethical and social duties were never likely to be forgotten by those who came under the sway of Wesley's sanity and humour. ' In the nation at large, the Methodist Revival brought about a new moral enthusiasm which, rigid and pedantic as it often seemed, was healthy in its social tone, and whose power was seen in the decrease of the profligacy which had disgraced the upper classes, and the foulness which had infested literature ever since the Restoration. . . . A yet nobler result of the same movement was the revival of the spirit of mercy and kindness, and the new attempts to remedy the ignorance, the physical suffering, and the social degradation of the outcast and the poor. . . . A passionate impulse of human sympathy with the wronged and afflicted was the special glory of religion at the end of the eighteenth century, and it has a right to claim the honour of training and inspiring those uncanonized yet true saints—Wilberforce, Clarkson, and John Howard.' [2]

[1] Sermon on Fasting, *W.W.* vol. v. pp. 323-338. Cf. *J.W.J.* vol. ii. p. 257 ; iv. 243 ; vii. 51, note.

[2] H. D. Traill, *Social England,* vol. v. pp. 410-11.

The same impulse to serve humanity is manifest in the ceaseless missionary activities of all the branches of Methodism. A passion deeper than philanthropy sustained the early preachers ; Embury in New York ; Captain Webb in Long Island, New Jersey, Pennsylvania and Delaware ; and Asbury on his epic preaching tours from Maine to Virginia, through the Carolinas, over the Alleghanies into Ohio, Tennessee and the wilderness of Kentucky. Imagination is kindled by the records of their labours, and by the work of Nathan Bangs in Upper Canada, William Black in Nova Scotia, and Samuel Leigh in Australia and New Zealand,[1] and of many others who through faith subdued kingdoms, wrought righteousness, and obtained promises. The romance of missions is the heritage of Catholic Christianity, but no pages in the story are more inspired and inspiring than those which tell of the Methodist pioneers. The fruit of their labour is seen in the Canadian Methodist Church, the Australasian Methodist Church, the New Zealand Methodist Church and the Japan Methodist Church, each of which is a united and self-governing religious organization.[2] In the United States, the Revolution and Declaration of Independence which severed the American Colonies from the home country, led to the persecution of the Methodists, who were not unjustly suspected of royalist Toryism ;[3] but the effect of this was that the settlers were driven inland, where they occupied new country, and established new strongholds of Methodism.[4] Meanwhile many of the

[1] See *N.H.M.* vol. ii. chaps. iii-v.

[2] *Ibid.* But note that in 1925 the Canadian Methodist Church effected a Union with the Presbyterian and Congregational Churches to form the United Church of Canada.

[3] See Wesley's injudicious ' Calm Address to our American Colonies,' *W.W.* vol. xi. pp. 76-86.

[4] *Cf.* Acts ii. 19-21. See *N.H.M.* vol. ii. pp. 82-3.

Episcopal clergy had fled to England, and the complete
independence of the United States after the Treaties of
1782 accentuated the need for a new spiritual authority.
The constitutional development of the young democracies
provided a congenial ground for the growth of an independent and autonomous Church. Wesley consecrated
Dr. Coke and Francis Asbury as Presbyters, ' to be joint
superintendents over our brethren in North America ; ' [1]
and in 1784 the Methodist Episcopal Church in the United
States came into existence. Later developments led to
the formation of several branches of Methodism in the
States, with the result that the most representative and
powerful Protestant Church in America to-day is the
Methodist Church, with over thirty million members,
probationers and adherents in the United States and
Canada alone. It would be beside the mark to ask how
many of these have assimilated the spiritual ideals or
entered into the specific religious experience for which
Methodism stands. The reply would come back to us,
haunting and unforgettable, ' many are the wand-bearers,
few are the inspired.' [2] Yet our argument would stand.
The evangelistic zeal which set out to convert the world
cannot be the fruit of pessimism and loss of self-confidence :
it is the outcome of passionate confidence in personal and
religious values, and in the possibility of social and moral
redemption.

A further problem presented to the psychologist by the
Methodist movement lies in the fact that this period saw
the creation of modern England. How can we account

---

[1] Wesley's Circular Letter to the American Societies. See *Methodist
Magazine*, 1785, p. 602 ; *N.H.M.* vol. ii. pp. 85-6.

[2] Plato, *Phaedo*, xiii. 69, c.

D.M.R.   2 K

for the stability and greatness of England in the nineteenth
century ?   Why has modern England, of all the countries
of Europe, a history the least revolutionary, the most
exempt from violent crises, and sudden changes ?   This
is the question faced by a distinguished French historian,
who has given a lifetime to the study of nineteenth
century England, and he reaches a somewhat startling
conclusion.   Political institutions were of such a nature
that the social order might have degenerated into anarchy,
if there had been in England a bourgeoisie animated by
the revolutionary spirit.[1]   Capitalism is regarded by Marx
and his followers as the root of English history in this
period.   But the concentration of vast wealth in few hands
and the formation of huge armies of workers, suffering
poverty through the development of an unguided industrial system, provides an extremely unstable basis for
political and social life.   ' I was compelled,' says M.
Halévy, ' to examine the psychology, the mental and
religious constitution of the English people, in my search
for the basis of the stability of modern England.   And
it is to the great religious movement initiated by John
Wesley that we must turn.' [2]   He then proceeds to trace
in the history of Liberal and Tory policy up to 1840 the
supremacy of the political influence of evangelicalism.[3]
Events so diverse as the typically English achievement
of the electoral Reform Act of 1832, the early Acts for
the protection of factory workers, and the Act for the
Abolition of Slavery in the British Colonies, are shown

[1] Halévy, Elie, *Histoire du Peuple Anglais au XIX° siècle*, vol. i. (1912),
p. 401.

[2] *The Influence of the Evangelical Movement on the History of Modern
England*, Lecture in Leeds University, Oct. 22, 1925.

[3] See Abbey and Overton, *op. cit.* vol. ii. pp. 166 ff., for a discrimination of Methodism and evangelicalism.

to have been either the direct work of evangelical leaders,[1] or to have owed the support which placed them on the Statute Book to the unrecognized but dominating centre or evangelical party in politics.

During this period the Church made herself extremely unpopular, and the demand came very strongly for Disestablishment and Disendowment. It seemed at one time as though the Church was in danger of the treatment which had been meted out to her sister in France. But her enemies were too disparate: Bentham and his followers were anti-Christian; the Irish Catholics had their own interests to consider; and the Baptists and Congregationalists were mainly at that time political dissenters. Meanwhile the Methodist movement made itself felt. Wesley was not a willing Nonconformist. He liked bishops; he believed in organization and system; he liked the order of the Church. And when separation became inevitable, he left behind him within the Church of England a body of evangelicals, estimated in 1840 as including one-fifth of the Anglican clergy. No one, therefore, in the crisis thought of Methodism as against the Church. Consequently as a result of reforms on evangelical lines within its own borders, the Church of England emerged in 1840 stronger both in itself and in public opinion than ever.

Incidentally, we may refer to the benefit derived by the Tractarians and the Oxford movement as a whole from the Methodist revival of concern in religion. In some degree Wesley was the godfather of Newman and Manning; and the modern Anglo-Catholic movement

[1] Wilberforce was an independent Tory and an evangelical. Michael Thomas Sadler was a friend of Wilberforce, had known John Wesley, and was Superintendent of a Methodist Sunday School. Both Sadler and Shaftesbury were Tories, and both evangelicals.

derives a large proportion of its attractiveness and strength from its spiritual heritage of evangelical passion.

In the early days of the nineteenth century, however, the Methodist movement provided the necessary support for the Government in avoiding a revolution ; it secured the Church against the forces of anarchy ; and it enabled England to become the typical country in Europe for social order and political stability, and to stand out before the world as more than ever a Christian State.[1]

I have necessarily summarized M. Halévy's historical argument, and consequently it becomes somewhat crude and challenging ; but it is the result of a disinterested piece of conscientious and accurate scholarship, and, viewed in the light of the three volumes of his work already published,[2] it assumes the weight of an irresistible logical conclusion. We cannot, of course, take the wealth and confusion of modern English history and label it with a simple and unifying name : we should be generalizing and co-ordinating beyond the capacity of the facts. Yet, while differences of opinion will emerge as to M. Halévy's interpretation of history, there is in its favour a weight of evidence which compels us to seek an explanation of his inference in the psychology of the evangelical revival.

We now turn again to the mental factors which are more truly within our province, and we have to inquire how far they can be regarded as providing the historian with the solution of his problem. A further question will

---

[1] Apart from the incidental reference to the Oxford Movement, I have, in the preceding paragraphs, adhered as far as possible to M. Halévy's own words while summarizing his argument.

[2] Vol. i., vide supra, p. 258, note. Vol. ii. Du lendemain de Waterloo à la veille du Reform Bill (1815-1830) (1923). Vol. iii. De la crise du Reform Bill à l'avènement de Sir Robert Peel (1830-1841), (1923).

present itself when the social and historical values of the religious movement have been duly weighed, for our analysis of the facts will show that there are psychological meanings in the Revival of even deeper import than its influence upon modern history.

At the outset we must be on our guard against simple explanations of either historical facts or psychological processes. There are ragged edges and tangled ends in history which cannot be woven into an ordered symmetrical pattern, and clashing colours and incongruous forms in human life that will not be portrayed in any balanced and harmonious picture of the human mind. We can only hope that, by means of a review of the varied aspects of religious psychology considered in these pages, something of the spiritual element in history may emerge, together with a clearer conception of the universal nature of religion.

As an example of the tendency to simplify the problem, let us glance at the way in which the whole burden can be laid on the ' herd ' or the ' sex ' instinct. ' Religion,' writes Dr. Trotter, ' has always been to man an intensely serious matter, and when we realize its biological significance we can see that this is due to a deeply ingrained need of his mind. The individual of a gregarious species can never be truly independent and self-sufficient. Natural selection has ensured that as an individual he must always have an abiding sense of incompleteness, which, as thought develops in complexity, will come to be more and more abstractly expressed. This is the psychological germ which expresses itself in the religious feelings, in the desire for completion, for mystical union, for incorporation in the infinite, which are all provided for in Christianity and in all the successful sub-varieties of Christianity which modern times have seen develop.'[1] Similar unscientific dogmatisms are to be found in the writings of psychoanalysts.[2] 'All instincts go back to the sexual, so that *cherchez la femme* (under multitudinous symbolic disguises) is the last word of science with respect to the analysis of conduct. . . . It is surprising that men can engage in these enterprises without being reminded of their exact similarity to natural science before scientific method was discovered in the seventeenth century.'[3] Whatever unity there may be in life and religion, there is abundant evidence in the story of the Methodist Revival to justify our conclusion that religious experience cannot be traced to any single 'psychological germ' or mental root.

What, then, is the radical nature of the mental life that is credited with such widespread and varied activity? We come nearer to the heart of our subject when we turn to a scientific social psychology. Two phases of the community spirit have been examined in these pages: (*a*) the awakening of the mind of England through Colonial expansion and the Industrial Revolution, and its breaking away from the bonds of a narrow rationalism and a static society,[4] was followed by (*b*) the development of a religious order which has many of the marks of a social organism,[5] in its power of appropriating material from its environment, transforming itself and adapting itself to the changing conditions of English life in the

---

[1] Trotter, W., *Instincts of the Herd in Peace and War*, pp. 50-1.

[2] *Vide supra*, pp. 89-90 ; *cf.* Brill, A. A., *Fundamental Conceptions of Psychoanalysis*, chap. xii. pp. 320-1.

[3] Dewey, John, *H.N.C.* pp. 132-3 ; *vide supra*, pp. 6-8.

[4] *Vide supra*, chap. ii.   [5] *Vide supra*, chaps. v. and x.

eighteenth century. How far the group spirit, or national consciousness, can have contributed to the promotion of the religious revival, who shall say ? The social environment of Methodism moulded its structure, but had little to do with its character and spirit. And while the unity of the religious movement expressed itself in altruistic feeling, corporate judgment and common purpose, the essential nature of that mental unity has still to be discovered.

Community is a spiritual thing, and the human needs and purposes that created the Revival and the Methodist system have a vital bearing upon the psychological problem we are attempting to solve. There is a General Will which finds expression in the development of Methodism, and the clearest light upon the meaning of the movement in its social aspect comes from the conception of common purpose moving towards a common good. ' The General Will seems to be, in the last resort, the ineradicable impulse of an intelligent being to a good extending beyond itself, in as far as that good takes the form of a common good. Though this impulse may be mastered or cheated in a degree, yet if it were extinct human life would have ceased.' [1] Individuals can only realize such a good with fragmentary imperfection ; a community may realize it more completely in the sense that a ' plurality of human beings is necessary to enable society to cover the ground, as it were, which human nature is capable of covering.' [2] That is why we sing the song of England, and move towards a national good larger than that envisaged by our personal and private aims ; that is why we also have, beyond the vision of

[1] Bosanquet, B., *Philosophical Theory of the State*, p. 109.
[2] *Ibid*. p. 177.

England, a conception of a wider kingdom and a deeper, nobler good, in the League of Nations and the comity of all peoples. There is discernible in Methodism a purposive activity that goes beyond the limited and partial vision of its individuals, and indeed overleaps the bounds of the movement itself in its unmistakeable expression of some of the deepest cravings and aspirations of humanity, and in its spiritual identity with the holy Church throughout all the world.

Nowhere is this more clearly seen than in the doctrine of universal grace, in the moral ideal of Methodism, and in its humanitarian influence in history. In the action and reaction of evangelicalism upon human society we can trace a rational good [1] in which the whole body of impulses, feelings, and ideas is linked up into a harmonious system, guided and controlled by all-embracing purposes, consistently carried out in the world of mind and its experience. It is, however, to be regretted that the problem of the nature of social unity has not yet been approached more empirically and inductively.[2] All views which imply psychological unities transcending the individual mind ignore the distinction between content and process. Will and purpose cannot be predicated of society in the same sense as that in which we can predicate them of the individual. The unity of the individual mind is more than the unity of system ascribed to it by Dr. McDougall. What is needed is a psychological synthesis of the function of the self and the function of society, and such a synthesis is presented in the mental activity which it has been our task to study in these pages.

[1] See Hobhouse, L. T., *The Rational Good : A Study in the Logic of Practice*, 1921.

[2] See Ginsberg, Morris, *The Psychology of Society*, 1921.

On the side of history and social progress we have been considering mainly human well-being from the material and moral point of view ; the good envisaged has been largely a physical, social and political emancipation. Even from the highest moral standpoint, it is based upon a belief in the perfectibility of the human race by its own efforts.   But ' a revelation of spiritual meaning is another and a larger thing than an accumulation of advantages along the lines of humanism and philanthropy.' [1] What Methodism calls assurance of salvation is not accounted for by a social advance towards a human goal of perfection. Social security is not the surest foundation for stability of character.   And neither the all-embracing social purpose nor the moral ideal touches the real problem of the roots of evil in the human heart.   Society is nothing but individuals in relation, and ' the proposal to banish the thought of personal salvation in the name of advancing spirituality or social progress is strange folly.'

Philosophy and psychology alike are suffering from an over-emphasis upon social evolution.   It would be futile to say that the group mind or the common will would have recovered living religion in the eighteenth century without the work of John Wesley, or that the general effort of the community would have liberated the mind of Europe in the sixteenth century if the counsels of Erasmus had prevailed instead of the explosive methods of Luther History has its own logic, and there is a salt and salutary quality in the religious conviction which sustains Athanasius or Antigone against the world.   Moreover, spiritual illumination is individual, and while the matter

---

[1] Bosanquet, B., *The Meeting of Extremes in Contemporary Philosophy*, p. 207.

of Methodist history may be social and moral, its form is individual and religious.

The elusive quality of stability, manifest in the social organization and influence of Methodism, has its roots in the stability of individual character. In the psychological interpretation of that character we rely on the suggestions of life and experience already set forth in our earlier chapters. We are debtors to Greeks and barbarians ; to many conflicting psychological doctrines for the light they throw upon the various methods and operations of mental activity. The vitality of different schools of psychology is due to the fact that each has grasped a part of the truth about the mind. There are elements in personality that cannot be explained in physiological or mechanical terms, yet *Behaviourism* contributes a healthy objectivity to our understanding of character.[1] We have found reason to believe that *suggestion* has a place in religion as in all human life,[2] but it is a new name for an old influence ; and *autosuggestion* is a bad name for faith and prayer :[3] faith in the possibility of well-being and well-doing, and invocation of the order of the universe as our ally. *Psychoanalysis* goes deeper, and in its theory of systems of interest, or ' complexes,' arising from early constraints or repressions, throws light upon some of the mental processes in certain cases of sudden conversion.[4] To what extent the practice of analytical psychology, purely as a therapeutic method, is likely to issue in a religious attitude, will depend entirely upon the mind of the practitioner. The claim that an adequate account of psychoanalysis will be identical

[1] *Vide supra*, chap. iii. [2] *Vide supra*, pp. 91-3, 192-3.
[3] *Vide supra*, pp. 93-5. [4] *Vide supra*, pp. 95 ff. 193 ff.

with a philosophy of religion [1] cannot be substantiated. Purely as a means of adaptation to life, the treatment of the mind by analysis should have a more direct reference to one of the fundamental categories of psychology and ethics : that of purposive and rational control.

Animal psychology and the study of the *instincts* enable us to identify the part played in religion by impulse and native propensity,[2] and it is clearly evident that human action is, within certain limits, capable of explanation in terms of instinctive tendency. Yet when the whole range of religious experience comes under review, it is also apparent that while instinct and emotion are integral parts, they only attain their full value for psychology when they emerge into clear consciousness and are allied with reason.[3] The purely instinctive level of activity is very rare in human behaviour, and there is abundant evidence of devotion to high ends on account of their value, apart from any connection with primitive impulses or drives.

Closely related to the psychology of instinct is the mental activity peculiarly associated with *crowds*,[4] and with human responsiveness to *rhythm*.[5] In the work of the Revival, the effectiveness of these in the kindling of emotion has been fully recognized, yet neither the psychological crowd nor the varied range of appeal in hymn-singing provides a causal explanation of the facts. Both conditions have been operative many times in the history of religion without producing phenomena comparable with those witnessed in the evangelical revival.

[1] See Jung, C. G., *Psychological Types ; or the Psychology of Individuation*, tr. by H. G. Baynes.

[2] *Vide supra*, ch. iii. sec. 7 ; ch. vii. ; and pp. 201-2.

[3] *Vide supra*, pp. 179, 201-5.   [4] *Vide supra*, pp. 106-7, 116 ff., 125 ff.

[5] *Vide supra*, pp. 118-24.

They are valuable auxiliaries to religious emotion, but they are not creative agents.

It is the two categories of *function* and *sentiment* which provide the most satisfactory basis for a synoptic psychology. Mind is an active dynamic unity, the centre of the stability and indeed of the existence of the organism ; continuously at work, adapting the individual to his environment, and transforming the environment to the uses of the individual. And in the higher stages of this process, all the impulses, emotions, percepts, concepts and volitions are progressively unified under a dominant disposition or sentiment. The unity of character thus achieved is most clearly exhibited in the religious sentiment, and in Methodism this unification of the self is identified with conversion.

Our quest of the psychology of stability in national and personal life, in society and in the individual, has led us to the heart of evangelicalism, which is an immediate experience of God : for here are found at the same time adaptation to life without and harmony of life within. How can we describe the psychological process by which religion gives stability and unity to the individual life ? Any attempt in this direction will fail unless it takes account of the object of the religious sentiment, and of the social values of religious experience : ' peace with God ' is always identified with ' love to man.' Evangelicalism involves a definite attitude of the human mind towards God, the world and man.

The processes of individual conversion and of social organization in Methodism have been shown to involve increasing apprehension of the values of Truth, Goodness and Beauty. In what may be called the normal mysticism of the evangelical there is ' response to, and identification with, the pervading and abiding character of value and satisfactoriness in the universe which evokes from us the attitude of worship.' This attitude is ' really a universal characteristic of human nature, and makes us feel our self-transcendence and continuity with the greater world as an inevitable factor of our being.' [1] The validity of this objective reference derived from the sense of values is a question for the philosophy of religion, where it is now in the very forefront of interest ; and here is the point at which psychology may make a contribution to philosophy by providing the data from which the philosopher can draw his inference. Thus Dr. C. D. Broad writes, ' I think it more likely than not that in religious and mystical experience men come into contact with some Reality or some aspect of Reality which they do not come into contact with in any other way.' [2] The psychologist is entitled to ask one question at this point : in view of the experience upon which this conclusion is based, is it more scientific to use the word Reality as a verbal symbol for ultimate truth, goodness and beauty, or to use the word Father, a symbol much richer in its emotional connotation, and more consonant with the facts of religious experience ? The Real and the Apparent are no more strictly scientific terms than Father and Son. Alike they are imperfect figures of speech, and the whole truth is larger than either the philosophical or the personal terms.

So far as Methodism is concerned, belief in God was

[1] Bosanquet, B., *The Meeting of Extremes in Contemporary Philosophy*, 1921, p. 70.

[2] ' The Validity of Belief in a Personal God,' *Hibbert Journal*, Oct. 1925. See also *The Mind and its Place in Nature*, 1925.

based upon all the normal elements, traditional, natural, moral, emotional and rational.[1]   On the whole, however, it was in the emotional experience that faith found its surest foundation.   There is spiritual refreshing for the philosopher in the consideration of this fact, especially if he has been tempted to think that the human individual is so poor that he must rely on the one way of reflection and reason to attain the full consciousness of reality. ' The religious emotion is one part of experience, and an empirical philosophy must include in one form or another the whole of experience.' [2]   We are fully entitled to claim that emotion can make a definite contribution to our consciousness of reality, especially in view of the insepar-able union of mental and organic (or physical) energy in the state of emotion,[3] and in view of the range and importance of emotion in human life.   Science and philo-sophy can provide that consummate appreciation of the world's meaning which is found by others in poetry and music. ' Poetry is the breath and finer spirit of all knowledge.' [4]   Yet at the heart and core of all this emotional experience is a definite religious attitude. Religion is the region of the mental life where ' the human spirit lays aside the burdens of finite existence and attains the completest satisfaction and the largest sense of free-dom. . . .   For there its consciousness is absolutely free and is consciousness in truth because it is consciousness of absolute truth.   In terms of feeling its state is one of enjoyment, the joy of blessedness ; in terms of activity

---

[1] See Thouless, *I.P.R.* chaps. ii-vi.

[2] Alexander, S., *Space, Time and Deity*, 1920, vol. ii. p. 352.

[3] See a valuable discussion in Baillie, J. B., *Studies in Human Nature*, 1921, pp. 133-4, 223.

[4] Wordsworth, *Preface to the Lyrical Ballads.   Cf.* Aristotle, ' Poetry is a more philosophical and a higher thing than history ' (*Poetics*, ix. 3).

it spends itself in making manifest the honour of God and
showing forth His excellent glory.' [1]

The emotional centre of this individual communion with
God is in the Incarnation, for it is the Christian faith that
in the historical Jesus are gathered up all the values
which life holds. The truth that God is love, made flesh
in the life, and supremely revealed in the Cross of Jesus,
is the very life and spirit of Methodism. Here are focussed
and concentrated the law of gain through pain, of victory
through defeat,[2] and the reality of Truth, Goodness and
Beauty which satisfies the deepest cravings of the human
heart. The appeal of the Cross has never been equalled
in its power to stir the imagination and bring about that
subtle or convulsive change in mental life whereby all
things are made new.

The reconciliation achieved in conversion not only
brought apprehension of ultimate values as the source of
freedom and inner harmony ; ending mental conflict
and the consciousness of alienation from God ; but with
this inward peace came also a new sense of harmony
with the world of nature : an adjustment to the laws
and conditions of life as a whole—' a will identified with
the supreme good in a stable universe.' This experience
is founded upon a vital need of human nature. ' The
greatest minds of our race have found a peace almost
too deep for utterance in realizing and accepting the
inevitable order of the world. . . . Whether they achieve
it or not, there is an instinct for this peace in all human
beings.' [3]

[1] Hegel, *Philosophie d. Rel.*, quoted Baillie, *op. cit.* p. 223.

[2] See Inge, *Outspoken Essays* (Second Series), 1922.

[3] Denney, J., *Christian Doctrine of Reconciliation*, pp. 2-3. *Cf.*
Charles Wesley's hymn quoted above, p. 235.

' Felix qui potuit rerum cognoscere causas,
   Atque metus omnis et inexorabile fatum
   Subjecit pedibusque strepitumque Acherontis avari.' [1]

For the evangelical Christian, this reconciliation is interpreted in terms of forgiveness of sins, and the emphasis
is upon moral salvation through faith in Christ.   But it
may be claimed that the typical moment in the religious
experience of Methodism is also a true type of that
reconciliation between man and the necessity which en-
compasses him, between human nature and the universe,
which is at the heart of science and which is the theme of
the poet and the philosopher. [2]

Our sketch of the psychology of Methodism has gathered,
from the pages of a very human story, a wealth of religious
experience which centres in a definite attitude towards
ultimate reality and towards the universe.   It remains
only to speak of the social implications of the evangelical
experience—those revolutionary principles which sent
the stirrings of a new life wherever the English language
was spoken and from end to end of the whole commonwealth of men.   Service for humanity, unwearied and
undiscouraged, finds its unfailing inspiration in a religious
experience that centres in the Cross.   ' As our faith . . .
receives increase, if not its very being, from this grand
event, . . . so does the love of our neighbour also, our
benevolence to all mankind, which cannot but increase
in the same proportion with our faith and love of God.
For who does not apprehend the force of that inference
drawn by the loving Apostle : " Beloved, if God so loved
us, we ought also to love one another." ' [3]   That is

[1] Virgil, *Georgicon*, ii. lines 490-2.
[2] On the whole subject of reconciliation, see Denney, *op. cit.* chap. i.
[3] *W.W.* vol. vi. p. 220.

Wesley's direct way of expressing what we prefer to describe as a synthesis of self and society, of the individual and the universal, based upon the intuition attained in evangelical conversion. History has proved that this large inclusiveness of religious altruism is not based upon a single emotion or simple feeling-tone which would be subject to the law of decline, but upon a living experience which gathers round it all the great sentiments, and persists in personal and social life as a vital and creative spirit.

APPENDIX I

IMPORTANT DATES

June 17, 1703.   John Wesley born.

December 18, 1707.   Charles Wesley born.

February, 1708.   Epworth Parsonage destroyed by fire.

1714.   George Whitefield born.

September, 1725.   John Wesley ordained.

December, 1725.   Christmas at Buckland and Stanton.

March 17, 1726.   John Wesley Fellow of Lincoln College, Oxford.

October 14, 1735.   John and Charles Wesley, Benjamin Ingham and Charles Delamotte set sail for Georgia.

February 1, 1738.   John Wesley lands in England from Georgia.

May 24, 1738.   John Wesley's conversion.

January 1, 1739.   The Fetter Lane Love Feast.

February 17, 1739.   Whitefield's first field preaching.

1739.   Methodist Societies founded in London and Bristol.

1742.   Wesley in Newcastle-on-Tyne.

1743.   Rules of the United Societies published.

July 4, 1776.   American Declaration of Independence.

1784. Wesley consecrated 'Superintendents' for America.

1784.   Methodist Episcopal Church in the United States founded.

March 2, 1791.   John Wesley died.

c. 1760-1830.   The Industrial Revolution.

c. 1778-1805.   The Romantic Revolt in European Literature.

1789-1815.   The Revolutionary and Napoleonic Era.

APPENDIX II

PARALLEL TABLE REFERRED TO IN CHAP. VII

SYMPTOMS RECORDED IN WESLEY'S *Journal*	SYMPTOMS OF INSTINCTS
	(1) CURIOSITY
Gaping and staring (*Journal*, iii. 14, 483).	Eyes and mouth widely opened (Darwin, *Origin of Emotions*, quoted James, ii. p. 479).
Crowding around (*Journal passim*).	Flock draws nearer (McDougall, *S.P.* p. 58).
	(2) FEAR
Run out in all haste (ii. 204).	Escape by rapid movement (Shand, p. 200).
Sweat and 'Bones shook' (ii. 186, 415).	Cold perspiration (Darwin, pp. 290-2).
Strong trembling (ii. 228; iii. 111).	Trembling of muscles (Darwin).
'He did shiver every bone of him' (ii. 299).	Superficial muscles shiver (Darwin).
'Stand motionless as a statue' (iii. 299).	Stands motionless (Darwin).
Could not breathe (iii. 69).	Breathless (Darwin).
Pulse hardly discernible (ii. 332).	Sudden stopping of heart-beat and respiration (McDougall, *S.P.* 53).
Heart failing (ii. 279).	Sudden stopping of heart-beat and respiration (McDougall, *S.P.* 53).
Could not breathe (iii. 69).	Sudden stopping of heart-beat and respiration (McDougall, *S.P.* 53).
Breast heaving (ii. 191).	Breathing laboured (Darwin).
Pale face (ii. 298).	Skin becomes pale (Darwin).
Quite choked (iii. 69).	Gasping and convulsive motion of lips (Darwin).
Almost strangled (ii. 347).	Gulping and catching at throat (Darwin).

SYMPTOMS RECORDED	SYMPTOMS OF INSTINCTS
Tongue hanging out (iii. 63).	Mouth dry (Darwin).
Voice lost (iii. 52).	Silence (Shand, 200).
Heart swelled ready to burst (iii. 69).	Heart beats wildly (Darwin).
Stony eyes (ii. 298).	Protruding eyeballs (Darwin).
Convulsive tearings (29 cases).	Convulsive movements (Darwin).
Dropped as dead (56 cases and *passim*).	General convulsions and even death (McDougall, p. 50).
Use of all limbs quite taken away (ii. 390).	Paralysis of movement (McDougall, p. 53). (Cf Instinctive concealment.)
Stamped and struggled (ii. 347).	Frantic bodily efforts (McDougall, p. 53). (Cf. Instinctive flight.)
Souls and bodies well-nigh torn asunder (ii. 247).	Frantic bodily efforts (McDougall, 53). (Cf. Instinctive flight.)
Request to a friend, 'Stand by me; don't stir from me' (iii. 94).	Clinging to someone or something for protection (Shand, 201).
Strong or bitter cries (*passim*).	Cry for help or protection (Shand, 202).

The relation of fear to anger accounts for the way in which the symptoms combine in some of the cases in the following table:

SYMPTOMS RECORDED	SYMPTOMS OF INSTINCTS (3) ANGER
Face distorted into most terrible form (iii. 63-4).	Face red, swollen, eyes protuberant (Lange, quoted by James, ii. 460).
Hearts swelled ready to burst (iii. 69).	Heart beats violently (Lange).
Furiously gnashing teeth (ii. 299 and *passim*).	Clenching of teeth (James, ii. 452).
Gnashing teeth, biting lips (ii. 187).	Open mouth to bite (McDougall, p. 61).
Roaring as out of the belly of hell (ii. 180, 298, 299, 376).	Loud roars and bellowings to frighten opponen (McDougall, p. 61).
Roared aloud (iii. 52, 344).	
Raged beyond measure (ii. 415).	

SYMPTOMS RECORDED	SYMPTOMS OF INSTINCTS
Knitting brows (ii. 187).	Contracted brows (Darwin).
Stamped and struggled (ii. 347 and *passim*).	Vague kicking and struggling, and movements which antagonize each other (Stout, *Manual of Psychology*, p. 319).
Convulsive motion in every part of the body (ii. 189, 221).	Impulse to vigorous action (James, ii. 452).
Breast heaving (ii. 191).	Ebullition of chest (James, ii. 452).
'I could have killed him'[1] (MS. letter). 'I could have torn him in pieces' (MS. letter).	Impulse to kill (James, ii. 409 ff. ; McDougall, 59-61 ; and Drever, 178 ff.).

(4) REPULSION

Spitting, and all expressions of strong aversion (ii. 300).	Reject from the mouth ... substances noxious or evil-tasting (McDougall, *S.P.* pp. 55-6 ; *O.P.* 147 ff.).
'I found such a rising against him' (MS. letter, Colman Collection).	Shrinking with a creepy shudder (McDougall, *S.P.* 56).

[1] Letter from Elizabeth Spring to John Wesley. Refers to the teaching of Charles Wesley. The second quotation is from a letter from Mary Purnell to J. W. and refers to the preaching of Hall. Both letters are in the Colman Collection.

APPENDIX III

BIBLIOGRAPHY

List of works and editions which have been used, or to which reference has been made.

I. PHILOSOPHY.

ARISTOTLE, Metaphysics, Bk. I. tr. A. E. Taylor. 1907.
,, Poetics, ed. Butcher, S. H. 1907.
BACON, FRANCIS, Novum Organum. 1620.
BALDWIN, J. M., Dictionary of Philosophy. 2 vols. N.Y. 1901.
BOSANQUET, BERNARD, Principle of Individuality and Value. 1912.
,, ,, The Meeting of Extremes in Contemporary Philosophy. 1921.
,, ,, Philosophical Theory of the State. 1899.
BUTLER, JOSEPH, Analogy of Religion, ed. Gladstone. 1907.
,, ,, Analogy and Sermons, ed. Angus. N.D.
CALDECOTT, ALFRED, Philosophy of Religion. 1901.
,, ,, and MACKINTOSH, Readings in the Literature of Theism. 1904.
DESCARTES, Philosophical Works, ed. Haldane and Ross. 2 vols. 1912.
DEWEY, JOHN, Human Nature and Conduct. 1922.
,, ,, Reconstruction in Philosophy. 1921.
EDWARD, KENNETH, Religious Experience: its Nature and Truth. 1926.
FARNELL, L. R., The Evolution of Religion. 1905.

GALLOWAY, GEORGE, The Philosophy of Religion. 1920 ed.
GREEN, T. H., Prolegomena to Ethics, ed. Bradley. 5th ed.
1906.
HOBBES, THOMAS, Leviathan. 1651. (Routledge's ed.)
HOERNLÉ, R. F. A., Matter, Life, Mind, and God. 1923.
HUME, DAVID, A Treatise of Human Nature (1739), ed.
L. A. Selby-Bigge, Oxford, 1896.
HUTCHESON, F., Nature and Conduct of the Passions. 1728.
KANT, IMMANUEL, Critique of Pure Reason, tr. Max Müller.
2nd ed. 1920.
„   „   Prolegomena to any Future Metaphysic,
tr. Mahaffy and Bernard, vol. ii. 1889.
LAING, B. M., A Study in Moral Problems. 1922.
LOCKE, JOHN, Essay on the Human Understanding. Bohn's ed.
„   „   Thoughts Concerning Education, ed. Daniel.
MURRAY, GILBERT, Four Stages of Greek Religion. 1912.
OMAN, JOHN, Vision and Authority. 1902.
„   „   Grace and Personality. 1917.
OTTO, RUDOLF, The Idea of the Holy. Oxford Press, 1925.
RASHDALL, HASTINGS, Theory of Good and Evil. 1907.
„   „   Philosophy and Religion. 1909.
ROYCE, JOSIAH, The World and the Individual. 2 vols. 1901.
SABATIER, AUGUSTE, Esquisse d'une philosophie de la religion.
SHAFTESBURY, ANTHONY, EARL OF, Characteristics of Men,
Manners, etc. 3 vols. 1732.
SIDGWICK, HENRY, Outlines of the History of Ethics. 2nd ed.
1888.
SMITH, JOHN, Select Discourses. (1660.) 1859.
SORLEY, W. R., Moral Values and the Idea of God. 1916.
SPENCER, HERBERT, Principles of Psychology. 1873. 2 vols.
SPINOZA, BENEDICT, Ethics. Everyman ed.
TAYLOR, A. E., Elements of Metaphysics. 1903.
VAUGHAN, C. E., The Romantic Revolt. 1907.
WALLACE, E., Outlines of the Philosophy of Aristotle. 1887.
WATERHOUSE, ERIC S., The Philosophy of Religious Experi-
ence. 1923.

II. PSYCHOLOGY.

1. GENERAL.

ARISTOTLE, De Anima, ed. Wallace, Text and tr. 1882.

HALL, GRANVILLE STANLEY, Adolescence : its Psychology and its Relations to Physiology, Sociology, Sex, Crime and Religion. 2 vols. 1904.

HOBHOUSE, L. T., Morals in Evolution. 2 vols. 1906.
,,　　,,　　Mind in Evolution. 2nd ed. 1915.
,,　　,,　　Development and Purpose. 1913.
,,　　,,　　The Rational Good : a Study in the Logic of Practice. 1921.

JAMES, WILLIAM, Principles of Psychology. 1890.

McDOUGALL, WILLIAM, An Outline of Psychology. 1923.

MEUMANN, E. Intelligenz und Wille. Leipzig. 1908.

STOUT, G. F., Analytic Psychology. 2 vols. 1896.
,,　　,,　Manual of Psychology. 2nd ed. 1901.

WARD, JAMES, Psychology, art. in Enc. Brit. 9th ed.
,,　　,,　Psychological Principles. 2nd ed. 1920.

WUNDT, W., Lectures on Human and Animal Psychology. 2nd ed. Leipzic, 1892, tr. Titchener and Creighton.
,,　　,,　Physiological Psychology. Vol. I., tr. Titchener. 1904.
,,　　,,　Elements of Folk Psychology, tr. Schaub. 1921.

2. SOCIAL.

GINSBERG, MORRIS, The Psychology of Society. 1921

LE BON, GUSTAVE, Psychologie des Foules. 28th ed. 1921.

MACIVER, R. M., Community ; a Sociological Study. 1917.

McDOUGALL, W., Social Psychology. 18th ed. 1922.
,,　　,,　The Group Mind. 1921.

ROSS, E. A., Social Psychology.

TROTTER, W., Instincts of the Herd in Peace and War. 1916.

WALLAS, GRAHAM, Human Nature in Politics. 1908.
,,　　,,　The Great Society. 1914.

3. INSTINCT, EMOTION AND BEHAVIOUR.

DARWIN, CHARLES, The Expression of the Emotions in Man and Animals. 1872.

DEWEY, JOHN, Human Nature and Conduct. 1922.

DREVER, JAMES, Instinct in Man. 2nd ed. 1921.

HOLT, E. B., The Freudian Wish.

McDOUGALL, W., Body and Mind. 1913.

,,   ,,   Psychology the Study of Behaviour. 1914.

,,   ,,   Primer of Physiological Psychology.

RIBOT, THEODULE ARNAUD, The Psychology of the Emotions. London, 1897.

SHAND, ALEXANDER F., The Foundations of Character. 2nd ed. 1920.

WATSON, J. B., Psychology from the Standpoint of a Behaviourist. 1922.

,,   ,,   Is Thinking merely the Action of Language Mechanisms ? Brit. Jour. Psych. XI. i. 87-104.

,,   ,,   Behaviourism. 1925.

4. THE UNCONSCIOUS AND THERAPEUTICS.

BAUDOUIN, CHARLES, Suggestion and Autosuggestion, tr. E. and C. Paul. 1921.

BINET, ALFRED, and FÉRÉ, CHARLES, Animal Magnetism. 1887.

BRILL, A. A., Fundamental Conceptions of Psychoanalysis. 1922.

FLÜGEL, J. C., The Psychoanalytic Study of the Family.

FREUD, SIGMUND, Die Traumdeutung. 1909.

,,   ,,   Wit and its Relation to the Unconscious, tr. Brill. 1916.

,,   ,,   Introductory Lectures on Psychoanalysis. 1923.

HART, BERNARD, Psychology of Insanity. 1912.

HARTMANN, EDWARD VON, The Philosophy of the Unconscious.

JUNG, C. G., The Psychology of the Unconscious. 1916.

,,   ,,   Psychological Types; or the Psychology of Individuation, tr. Baynes, H. G. 1924.

MYERS, C. S., Introduction to Experimental Psychology. Cambridge, 1911.

,,   ,,   Present Day Applications of Psychology. 1918.

NICOLL, MAURICE, Dream Psychology. 1917.
PRINCE, MORTON, The Unconscious. N.Y. 1914.
RIVERS, W. H. R., Instinct and the Unconscious. 1920.
  ,, ,, Conflict and Dream. 1923.
  ,, ,, Psychology and Politics. 1923.
  ,, ,, The Relations of Complex and Sentiment,
      in Brit. Jour. Psych. vol. xiii. pt. 2.
TANSLEY, A. G., The New Psychology. 1922 ed.
  ,, ,, The Relations of Complex and Sentiment, in
      Brit. Jour. Psych. vol. xiii. pt. 2.

5. PSYCHOLOGY OF RELIGION.

AMES, EDWARD SCRIBNER, The Psychology of Religious
 Experience. London, 1910.
BARRY, F. R., Christianity and Psychology. 1923.
CALDECOTT, ALFRED, Psychology and Religion. 1907.
  ,, ,, The Religious Sentiment. 1909.
  ,, ,, Mystic Feeling and the Emotional Life.
      The Quest, vol. xii. No. 3. April, 1921.
COE, G. A., The Psychology of Religion. Chicago, 1916.
  ,, The Religion of a Mature Mind. 1903.
CUTTEN, The Psychological Phenomena of Christianity. N.Y.
 1908.
DAVENPORT, F. M., Primitive Traits in Religious Revivals.
 N.Y. 1905.
DE FURSAC, J. ROGUES, Une mouvement mystique contem-
 porain. Alcan, 1907.
DELACROIX, Etudes d'histoire et de psychologie du mysti-
 cisme. Paris, 1908.
DURKHEIM, EMILE, De la definition des phénomènes religieux.
      L'année sociologique. II.
  ,, ,, Les formes élémentaires de la vie reli-
      gieuse. Alcan, 1912.
EDWARDS, JONATHAN, Thoughts on the Revival of Religion
 in New England.
HASTINGS, JAMES, ed. Encyclopaedia of Religion and Ethics.
 Various articles.

HÜGEL, BARON FRIEDRICH VON, The Mystical Element of Religion. 2 vols. 1909.

INGE, WILLIAM RALPH, Christian Mysticism. 1899.
,,   ,,   Faith and its Psychology. 1909.
,,   ,,   Outspoken Essays. (2nd Series.) 1922.

JAMES, WILLIAM, The Will to Believe. 1897.
,,   ,,   The Varieties of Religious Experience. 1903.
,,   ,,   Pragmatism. 1907.

JOLY, H., Psychology of the Saints. 1898.

LEUBA, J. H., The Psychology of Religious Mysticism. 1925.
,,   ,,   A Psychological Study of Religion. 1912.

MARK, H. THISELTON, The Unfolding of Personality. 1910.

McKENZIE, J. G., Modern Psychology and the Achievement of Christian Personality. 1923.

PRATT, JAMES BISSETT, The Religious Consciousness. 1921.

PYM, T. W., Psychology and the Christian Life. 1921.

ROBINSON, H. WHEELER, The Christian Doctrine of Man. 2nd ed. 1913.

ROUSE, RUTH, and MILLER, H. CRICHTON, Christian Experience and Psychological Processes. 1920.

SARKAR, JADUNATH, Chaitanya's Pilgrimages and Teachings. Calcutta, 1913.

STARBUCK, EDWIN DILLER, The Psychology of Religion. 1899.

STEVEN, GEORGE, The Psychology of the Christian Soul.

STRATTON, G. M., Psychology of the Religious Life. 1911.

STREETER, BURNETT H. (Ed.), The Spirit : God and His Relations to Man. 1919.

THOULESS, ROBERT H., An Introduction to the Psychology of Religion. Cambridge, 1923.

UNDERHILL, EVELYN (Mrs. Stuart Moore), Mysticism : a Study in the Nature and Development of Man's Spiritual Consciousness. 4th ed. London, 1912.
,,   ,,   The Mystic Way : A Psychological Study of Christian Origins. 1913.
,,   ,,   The Life of the Spirit and the Life of To-day. 3rd ed. 1923.

UNDERWOOD, A. C., Conversion, Christian and Non-Christian. 1925.

WATERHOUSE, ERIC S., The Psychology of the Christian Life. London, 1913.

WEBB, CLEMENT C. J., Group Theories of Religion and the Individual. 1916.

III. HISTORICAL BACKGROUND.

ADAMS, GEORGE BURTON, European History. N.Y. 1906.

BOSWELL, JAMES. Life of Samuel Johnson. Oxford Edition. 1904.

BUCKLE, HENRY THOMAS, History of Civilization in England. Longmans. 1902 ed.

BURNET, BISHOP GILBERT (1643-1715), History of My Own Times (1st vol. 1723 ; 2nd vol. 1734). 6 vol. ed. by Dr. Routh. Oxford, 1823.

CAMBRIDGE MODERN HISTORY, Vol. VI. (especially chap. ii. pp. 77-89).

DOBBS, A. E., Education and Social Movements : 1700-1850. 1st ed. 1919.

DOYLE, J. A., The English in America. 3 vols. 1882-7.
　　,,　　,,　　The Middle Colonies. 1907.
　　,,　　,,　　The Colonies under the House of Hanover. 1907.

GENTLEMEN'S MAGAZINE. 1739.

GIBBON, EDWARD, Autobiography (1827). World's Classics. 1907.

GODLEY, A. D., Oxford in the Eighteenth Century. 1908.

GRANT, A. J., Outlines of European History. 1907.

GREEN, JOHN RICHARD, Short History of the English People. ed. in 3 parts. 1907.

HAMMOND, J. L., and BARBARA, The Town Labourer 1760-1832. 1st ed. 1917. New impression 1920.
　　,,　　,,　　,,　　The Village Labourer 1760-1832. 1st ed. 1911. New impression 1920.

HERVEY, LORD JOHN, Memoirs of the Reign of George the Second. 3 vols. ed. Croker. 1884.

LECKY, W. E. H., A History of England in the Eighteenth Century. 1878-90. 7 vol. ed. 1913.

MACAULAY, T. B., LORD, The History of England. 1848-55 Chap. III. ed. Notcutt.

MAHAN, A. T., The Influence of Sea Power upon History; (1660-1783). 1889.

MYERS, PHILIP VAN NESS, General History. 1906. Ginn & Co.

OVERTON, J. H., Life in the English Church, 1660-1714.

   ,,   ,,   William Law : Non-Juror and Mystic. 1881.

ROBINSON, JAMES HARVEY, Readings in European History. 2 vols. 1904. Ginn & Co.

STEPHEN, LESLIE, English Literature and Society in the Eighteenth Century. 1910.

   ,,   ,,   History of English Thought in the Eighteenth Century. 1876-81.

TOYNBEE, ARNOLD, The Industrial Revolution of the Eighteenth Century in England. New ed. 1908.

TRAILL, H. D., Social England. Vol. V. 1896.

TREVELYAN, GEORGE MACAULAY, British History in the Nineteenth Century (1782-1901). 1919.

WALPOLE, HORACE, Letters. ed. Cunningham. 9 vols. 1857-1891.

   ,,   ,,   Memoirs of the Reign of King George the Second, ed. Lord Holland. 2nd ed. 1847. 3 vols.

   ,,   ,,   Memoirs of George III. ed. Barker. 4 vols. 1894.

IV. METHODISM.

ABBEY, C. J., and OVERTON, J. H., The English Church in the Eighteenth Century. 2 vols. 1896.

BRADBURN, SAMUEL, Select Letters of John Wesley. 1837.

BRASH, BARDSLEY, Wesley, E.R.E. vol. xii. pp. 724-7.

CLARK, A., Memoirs of the Wesley Family. 1822, 1836.

EAYRS, GEORGE, Letters of John Wesley. 1915.

FINDLAY, G. G., Methodist Doctrine, art. in E.R.E., vol. viii.

FITCHETT, W. H., Wesley and his Century. 1906.

GLEDSTONE, J. P., The Life and Travels of Whitefield. 1871.

GREEN, RICHARD, Bibliography of the Works of John and Charles Wesley. 2nd ed. 1906.

    ,,   ,, The Mission of Methodism. 1890.

HAMPSON, JOHN, Life of Wesley. 3 vols. 1791.

HUMPHRIES, A. LEWIS, The Holy Spirit in Faith and Experience. 1911.

JACKSON, THOMAS, ed. Lives of the Early Methodist Preachers, chiefly written by themselves. 4th ed. 6 vols. 1871.

JONES, D. M., Charles Wesley : A Study. N.D. London.

LAYCOCK, J. W., Methodist Heroes in the Great Haworth Round : 1734-1784.

LEGER, J. AUGUSTIN, John Wesley's Last Love. Paris, 1862.

LELIÈVRE, MATTHEW, John Wesley : His Life and Work, tr. A. J. French. 1871.

METHODIST MAGAZINE.

MORAVIAN MESSENGER. 1877.

OVERTON, J. H., The Evangelical Revival in the Eighteenth Century. 1886.

    ,,   ,, John Wesley. 1891.

    ,,   ,, and F. RELTON, The Church of England from 1714 to 1800. 1906.

PLATT, FREDERIC, Christian Perfection, art. in E.R.E.

RIGG, J. H., The Living Wesley. 1891.

RODRIGUEZ, ALPHONSUS, The Practice of Christian Perfection (Seville, 1614). Eng. tr.

SIMON, J. S., The Revival of Religion in the Eighteenth Century. 1907.

    ,,   ,, John Wesley and the Religious Societies. 1921.

    ,,   ,, John Wesley and the Methodist Societies. 1923.

SOUTHEY, ROBERT, The Life of John Wesley (1820). Oxford Edition, with Coleridge's Notes. 1925.

SPOONER, W. A., Bishop Butler. 1901.

STEVENSON, G. J., The Methodist Hymn-Book and its Associations. 1870.

TAYLOR, JEREMY, The Rules and Exercises of Holy Living and . . . Holy Dying (1650-51). 1817 ed.

TELFORD, JOHN, The Life of John Wesley. 1886.

,, ,, The Methodist Hymn-Book. 1907.

TYERMAN, LUKE, The Oxford Methodists. 1873.

,, ,, Wesley's Designated Successor : John William Fletcher. 1882.

,, ,, The Life and Times of John Wesley. 6th ed. 3 vols. 1890.

Unpublished Manuscript Letters and Note-Books in the Colman Collection at Norwich. Consulted by permission of Russell J. Colman, D.L., J.P.

WEDGWOOD, JULIA, John Wesley and the Evangelical Reaction of the Eighteenth Century. 1870.

WESLEY, CHARLES, Journals. 2 vols. 1849.

WESLEY HISTORICAL SOCIETY : Proceedings.

WESLEY, JOHN, Journal. Standard Edition. Curnock. 8 vols. 1909-1916.

,, ,, Works. 14 vols. ed. 1840-42.

,, ,, A Collection of Hymns for the Use of the People called Methodists. 1769. 1808 ed.

WHITEFIELD, GEORGE, Journals. 1738, 1741, 1744.

WORKMAN, H. B., TOWNSEND, W. J., and EAYRS, G., New History of Methodism. 2 vols. 1909.

WORKMAN, H. B., Methodism. Cambridge, 1912.

INDEX

INDEX

Canada, 20, 256, 257.
Carolina, 21, 22, 256.
Cartesianism, 232.
Celibacy, 242.
Christian Library, Wesley's, 87.
Church of England, 22, 39, 40, 211, 259.
Class-meeting, 110-11, 212.
Class-tickets, 220-1.
Coe, G. A., 165.
Coleridge, S. T., 24, 92 n., 117 n.
Collective consciousness, 19, 211.
Colman Collection of Wesley Relics, 47, 101, 151, 167, 172 n., 176.
Colonies, British, 20-23, 256-7, 262.
Common sense, 25, 225, 228.
Communion, 219, 220.
Community, 263 ff.
Complex, 68, 74-5, 95, 96 ff., 152, 195, 266.
Complex emotions, 149, 150, 155, 202.
Conation, 198.
Conceptual thought, 233.
Congregationalists, 23, 259.
Connecticut, 21.
Conscience, 55, 199-201.
Contagion, 9, 117, 138, 216.
Conversion, 158-207, 233, 268-73. Wesley's, 73 ff.
Co-operative Societies, 38, 212.
Coué, 8, 92, 94, 196.
Courtship tendency, 62, 64.
Credulity, 117.
Cross, G., 242 n.
Crowd-psychology, 9-10, 106-7, 116-18, 125-39, 267.
Curiosity, 25, 38, 117, 143, 144-6.
Curnock, 16-17, 43 n., and *passim*.

Danger, 146-9.
Darwin, Charles, 13 n., 143.
Davenport, F. M., 118, 142, 171, 193, 223.
Defoe, Daniel, 33, 37.
De Fursac, J. R., 18 n., 123 n., 137, 166.
Deism, 31, 114, 237-8.
Delaware, 22, 256.
Denney, J., 271-2.

Descartes, 232.
Designe, Susannah, 175-9, 203-4.
Determinism, 7, 238 ff., 240.
Dewey, J., 11, 24, 27, 65 n., 132 n., 205, 262.
Disgust, 150.
Dissociation, 70, 97.
Dobbs, A. E., 254 n.
Dobson, Austin, 33 n., 34 n.
Doctrine, Methodist, 32, 122, 214, 224-45.
Domination, 9, 132-3.
Doyle, J. A., 20, 22 n., 23 n., 108 n.
Drever, J., 52 ff., 55, 64, 75, 144-5, 146, 155 n., 156 n.
Durkheim, E., 19, 220, 221.
Dryden, J., 227.
Dynamogenesis, 133.

Eayrs, G., 70 n., 113 n.
Education, 121, 122, 253.
Edward, Kenneth, 15 n.
Edwards, Jonathan, 130.
Egoistic tendencies, 222, 235, 255.
Elation, 98, 206.
Eliot, George, 39.
Embury, Philip, 256.
Emotion, 11, 12, 75, 79, 118-24, 143, 201, 206, 247-8, 270-1. characteristics of, 52 ff., 143-57. James-Lange theory of, 12 n., 156.
Emotional tendencies, 74, 270.
Empiricism, 7, 228-9.
Enclosures Acts, 36.
Endowment, congenital, 7.
England, modern, 257 ff.
English empiricists, 225.
Enser, John, 172-5.
Enthusiasm, 85, 142, 228.
Environment, 8, 11, 77.
Epistemology, 10.
Erasmus, 265.
Ethical values, 135, 150, 163, 199, 215-7, 240-5.
Evangelicalism, 219, 246 ff., 255, 258 ff., 268.
Evolution, mental, 5, 37.
Expansion of England, 20-3.
Experience, 1, 13-4, 224-45, 268.
Experimental psychology, 10.

Wesley, Samuel, Jr., 51,
  Samuel, Sr., 53-5, 59.
  Samuel, son of Charles, 218 n.
  Samuel Sebastian, 218 n.
  Susannah, 53 ff.
Wilberforce, 248, 255, 259 n.
Will, 11, 93-4, 162, 186-8, 204-5,
  214-7, 239.
Wiseman, F. L., 240 n., 241 n.
Witness of the spirit, 91.

Whatcoat, R., 196.
Whitefield, G., 69 n., 106-11, 126,
  179, 193.
Wonder, 38, 119, 141.
Wordsworth, 248, 270.
Workman, H. B., 20 n., 85, 87,
  230-1, 236, 237 n.
Wundt, Wilhelm, 9, 197.

Young, Arthur, 36, 37 n.